W9-AOK-619

Property of
EAMILY OF FAITH
LIBRARY

REFERENCE MATERIAL
Do not Remove
from the Library

MODERN CRITICISM AND THE
PREACHING OF THE OLD TESTAMENT

By GEORGE ADAM SMITH

D.D., LL.D.

The Book of Isaiah. 2 vols.

Vol. I., Chapters I.-XXXIX. Vol. II., Chapters XL.-LXVI. Per volume, $1.50.

The Book of the Twelve Prophets Commonly Called The Minor.

Vol. I., Amos, Hosea, and Micah. Vol. II., Zephaniah, Nahum, Habakkuk, Obadiah, Haggai, Zechariah I.-VIII., Malachi, Joel, Zechariah IX.-XIV., and Jonah. Per volume, $1.50.

The above four volumes are contained in the "Expositor's Bible."

The Historical Geography of the Holy Land.

Especially in relation to the History of Israel and of the Early Church. With Scripture index and 6 colored maps, *specially prepared*. Octavo, cloth, 720 pages, $4.50.

_____

A. C. ARMSTRONG & SON

NEW YORK

MODERN CRITICISM

AND THE PREACHING OF

THE OLD TESTAMENT

*Eight Lectures on the Lyman Beecher
Foundation, Yale University*

BY

GEORGE ADAM SMITH, D.D., LL.D.

PROFESSOR OF OLD TESTAMENT LANGUAGE AND LITERATURE
UNITED FREE CHURCH OF SCOTLAND GLASGOW COLLEGE

Property of
FAMILY OF FAITH
LIBRARY

SECOND EDITION

NEW YORK

A. C. ARMSTRONG AND SON

3 & 5 WEST 18th STREET, NEAR 5th AVENUE

MCMI

21698

Copyright, 1901, by
A. C. ARMSTRONG & SON

SEM
221.6
S648 m 2

UNIVERSITY PRESS . JOHN WILSON
AND SON · CAMBRIDGE, U. S. A.

Family of Faith Library

TO

THE REV. TIMOTHY DWIGHT, D.D.

PRESIDENT OF YALE UNIVERSITY, 1886-1899

THE REV. GEORGE P. FISHER, D.D.

DEAN OF THE DIVINITY SCHOOL, 1895-1901

AND

THE REV. CHARLES RAY PALMER, D.D.

ONE OF THE FELLOWS OF THE UNIVERSITY

THIS VOLUME OF LECTURES

DELIVERED WHILE THEY WERE IN OFFICE

IS GRATEFULLY DEDICATED

Family of Faith Library

PREFACE

THE Eight Lectures in this volume — or at
least as much of each as it was possible
to read within the time allotted — were
delivered before Yale University in 1899.
I have thought it best to leave them as
Lectures: that is, in the style of spoken
discourse. With one exception they are
printed as they were prepared for delivery.
but I have worked into four of them — II.,
III., IV. and VI. — some materials from books
which have appeared since they were spoken:
Canon Driver's Essay on Hebrew Authority
in *Authority and Archæology, Sacred and
Profane*, edited by Mr. Hogarth; Professor
Budde's Lectures on the Religion of Israel
before the Exile; and Professor Charles'
Jowett Lectures, entitled *A Critical History
of the Doctrine of a Future Life*. Lecture
VII. on the Preaching of the Prophets to

their own Times has been wholly rewritten
in order to introduce a detailed account
(of which only a brief summary could be
spoken) of the Influence of the Prophets
upon the Social Ethics of Christendom.
In the Introduction and in Lectures I.,
III., IV. and VII. there are some paragraphs
from an address on *The Preaching of the
Old Testament to the Age*, delivered in
1892, and now out of print.

The objects of the Lectures are, in the
main, three: a statement of the Christian
right of criticism; an account of the modern
critical movement so far as the Old Testament is concerned; and an appreciation of
its effects upon the Old Testament as
history and as the record of a Divine
Revelation. Obviously eight Lectures cannot provide an exhaustive treatment of these
themes; but the Lectures contain, I trust,
enough to serve their purely practical aim,
and to exhibit to students and preachers
the religious effects of the critical interpretation of the larger half of the Scriptures

of the Church. In the Fourth Lecture the line of argument is intended for believers in the Christian doctrine of Revelation. I have always felt that for those who believe in the Incarnation the fact of a Divine Revelation through the religion of early Israel, as critically interpreted, ought not to be unintelligible. If we recognise that God was in Christ revealing Himself to men and accomplishing their redemption, it cannot be difficult for us to understand how at first, under the form of a tribal deity — the only conception of the Divine nature of which at the time the Semitic mind was capable — He gradually made known His true character and saving grace.

In connection with the subject of Lecture v., 'The Spirit of Christ in the Old Testament,' I desire to acknowledge my indebtedness to the late Principal Patrick Fairbairn's *The Typology of Scripture* (2 vols., 6th edition, Edinburgh 1876). It is a work distinguished not less by sagacious criticism

b

of the older theories of typology than by original insight into the ethical virtue of the institutions of Israel. Although constructed upon lines not followed by the critical interpretation of the Old Testament, it not seldom anticipates methods and ideas which have only recently passed into acceptance.

GEORGE ADAM SMITH.

CONTENTS

LECTURE V

LECTURE VI

LECTURE VII

LECTURE VIII

INTRODUCTION

To follow the long succession of men who have filled this lectureship, and to attempt — in response to your call — some addition to their numerous illustrations of the genius and office of the preacher, involves an adventure which can be justified only by one or other of the following considerations.

First, that of so wide a field as that of the Christian pulpit, there is some portion which, though not altogether neglected by my predecessors, has received from none of them a particular or exclusive treatment. Or secondly, that, in some department of the subject the materials have passed through those furnaces of criticism which our generation has so zealously fired, and have there undergone changes that render imperative some new appreciation of them for the purposes of practical religion.

I believe that for the subject I have chosen, not only one but both of these reasons are urgent. None of my predecessors has attempted a full exposition of the material which the Old Testament offers to the Christian preacher.

A

This fact alone might have determined the subject of the following course; but at the same time, as every one is aware, there is no part of the preacher's field or material which has been the object of more industrious research or of more unsparing criticism than the several Books of the Old Testament, and the national history of which they form the record. For over a century every relevant science, every temper of faith, and, one might add, almost every school of philosophy, have shot across this narrow field their opposing lights : under which there has been an expenditure of individual labour and ingenuity greater than has been devoted to any other literature of the ancient world, or to any other period in the history of religion. No memory or institution of Israel, no chapter or verse of her sacred texts has escaped this strenuous revision: nor, with the exception of the New Testament, is there any field on which such revision could have raised questions of more moment for the practical religion with which the duty of the preacher is identified. Beyond the problems of integrity and authenticity, in the narrower sense of these terms; beyond the greater question how much actual history has been left to us in the Old Testament by the processes of criticism, there remains the most important interest of all: Can we still receive the Old Testament as the record of a genuine revelation from God? But indeed your own experience more than any words of mine will have convinced you of the practical value, at this time, of some attempt to appreciate the effects of criticism upon the inspiration and material for preaching which the Christian Church has always drawn from the larger half of her canonical Scriptures.

Before we begin, it is well that we should impress ourselves with the sacredness of the task which we propose. This is no common ground we are to be treading. It is not some outlying province of the Kingdom of God, some questionable frontier of our fatherland, which we are called to debate; but (if I may continue the figure) it is that country of which our Redeemer was Himself a native; whose character He defined in absolute contrast to the rest of the world; whose history He interpreted as the Divine preparation for His own Advent; whose laws He fulfilled as the expression of the everlasting righteousness of God; and much of whose language He perpetuated in the wider Kingdom He came to found.

In short, it is with Christ's Bible we have to do; the larger part of the Scriptures bequeathed to His Church; and we have to do with this not simply in its historical interest but in its religious value for living men.

The Old Testament, one cannot too often remember, lies not *under* but *behind* the New. It is not the quarry of the excavator or archæologist —a mere foundation packed away out of sight beneath the more glorious structure which has been reared upon it. Far rather — if I may borrow a metaphor from the political geography of the day — far rather is the Old Testament the 'Hinterland' of the New : part of the same continent of truth, without whose ampler areas and wider watersheds the rivers which grew to their fulness in the new dispensation could never have gained one-tenth of their volume or their influence. And upon that vast Hinterland the Gentile Church of Christ, passing to it across the New Testament, has settled and been at home for centuries ; has found in it her school and her sanctuary ; has met with her God, has breathed the air of His righteousness and heard His words, as powerful as when they were first uttered, to move men to repentance and faith in God and the hope of an endless life.

It is upon all this — Christ's Bible and the Church's Bible, Christ's Fatherland and the Church's Fatherland — that we are called to estimate the effect of one of the most thorough intellectual processes of our time.

LECTURE I

THE LIBERTY AND DUTY OF OLD TESTAMENT CRITICISM AS PROVED FROM THE NEW TESTAMENT

FEW realise that the Church of Christ possesses a higher warrant for her Canon of the Old Testament than she does for her Canon of the New.

The New Testament Scriptures were selected and defined, no man exactly knows how, except that it was the Church herself which did the work. The formal decrees of Councils[1] appear to have been only confirmatory of the common use and practice of the Church under the guidance of her Lord's Spirit. This practice had risen gradually and with differences in different parts of Christendom. The Church was the recipient of a number of writings, some anonymous, but the most bearing the name of an apostle or of a disciple of the apostles. From these a selection was slowly effected, partly by the spiritual taste and insight of the various

[1] The Canon was discussed and defined by the great Councils of the fourth century. The Third Council of Carthage, 397 A.D., recognised our present New Testament.

congregations, partly on the strength of tradition, and partly by the opinions and discussions of the doctors of the Church.[1] That is to say, the New Testament Canon was a result of criticism in the widest sense of the word.

But what the Church thus once achieved, the Church may at any time revise. As a matter of fact she has never renounced her liberty to do so, and it has not been heretics alone who have disputed the rights of certain books to belong to the New Testament. To mention but a few instances, Gregory and Zwingli both rejected the Apocalypse, and Luther the Epistle of St. James. Augustine testifies that all the authorities of his time were not agreed as to the Canon,[2] and even Calvin appears to leave the question still open.[3]

These are enough to recall to us, that what was the decision of the Church's criticism at the beginning is not beyond the Church's criticism now, unless indeed we have ceased to believe in that education of the Spirit which Christ promised to His people, and refuse to employ the finer

[1] The most summary evidence of the gradual criticism and selection which led to the formation of the New Testament Canon is found in Eusebius, *Hist. Eccl.* (325 A.D.), bk. iii. 25: where the undisputed books are distinguished from the disputed and the spurious. Among the still disputed books, Eusebius places James, Jude, 2nd Peter, 2nd and 3rd John, Hebrews, and the Apocalypse. He himself appears to question the Apocalypse.

[2] *De Doctrina Christiana.*

[3] *Antidote to the Council of Trent:* 4th Session. Cf. *Institut.* iv. 9, § 14.

instruments of criticism which God's providence has put into their hands to-day.

So it was with the growth of the Canon of the New Testament, and what I wish to emphasise is that — with one important exception — the Canon of the Old Testament came to us in no other way. We are ignorant of vast stretches of its history; but we know enough to be sure that the theory of its origin which lately prevailed among Protestants, and which ascribed the Canon of the Old Testament to a single decision of the Jewish Church in the days of her inspiration, is not a theory supported by facts. The growth of the Old Testament as a Canon was very gradual.[1]

Virtually it began in the reign of King Josiah in 621 B.C., with the acceptance by all Judah of the Book of Deuteronomy as the divine law of their life, and its first stage was completed by the similar adoption of the whole Law, or first five Books of the Old Testament, under Nehemiah in 445 B.C. When the other two divisions were added is somewhat uncertain: the Prophets[2] probably before 200 B.C., and the Hagiographa[3] from

[1] The text-book in English on the subject is that by Professor Ryle of Queen's College, Cambridge, *The Canon of the Old Testament*. See also the article by Professor Budde in *The Encyclopædia Biblica*, vol. i.

[2] That is, according to the division of the Hebrew Bible, Joshua, Judges, Books of Samuel and Kings; Isaiah, Jeremiah, Ezekiel, and the Book of the Twelve Prophets.

[3] The Psalms, Proverbs, Job, Canticles, Ruth, Lamentations, Ecclesiastes, Esther, Daniel, Ezra, Nehemiah, and Chronicles.

a century to two centuries later. The strict
definition of the third division was not complete
by the time of Christ, nor was the selection of
the whole twenty-two (or twenty-four) Books
effected either before or after that time by a
miraculous decree from Heaven, or by any
decision of a Jewish Council. The only decision
of the kind which is known to history is that
said to have been made by a Synod of Jamnia
in 90 A.D., and this Synod appears to have
provided merely a few puerile reasons for con-
firming the canonicity of certain Books, which
had already for nearly two centuries enjoyed
the reverence of the people. In contrast to this
tardy and partial influence of a Council, it is
very probable that what secured to the Prophets
and the Hagiographa their canonical rank, was
their inherent worth and vitality as tested by
popular use. True, it may have been necessary
that, before the authority of some of these Books
was recognised, they should be proved to be
ancient, and should wear, like the Law, the
name of some great Prophet in Israel; and it
is also true that this notion may have led to
errors about their date and authorship, which we
are only now able to correct. But it was not
the famous names they wore which buoyed these
Books upon the reverence of the Church; for
other writings, which we know, wear the same
names, but have not therefore been lifted into

the Canon. Nor was the alleged antiquity of the Books indispensable or conclusive. The early collections of Israel's songs have not survived; while the Maccabean Psalms must have been received into the Canon at a date at which their recent origin was still remembered. But the Maccabean Psalms were associated with a great deliverance of His people by God; and all the rest of the literature, which was really ancient, had won the proof of its divinity either by the vindication of its predictions by history, or by the power it evinced of living and giving life from age to age. Without such effects and testimonies in the experience of the nation, no name, whether it really belonged to a book or had been thrust upon it, no ascription of antiquity and no official decree could have availed to bestow canonical rank. Not learned discussion by scribes and doctors, whose reasons, so far as they have come down to us, are all afterthoughts and mostly foolish ones, but proof beneath the strain of time, persecution, and the needs of each new age — these were what proved the truth of a Book, enforced its indispensableness to the spiritual life of God's people, or to their national discipline, and declared the will of Providence regarding it. In short, we see the same processes at work for the formation of the Canon of the Old Testament as we do for that of the New.

Yet, as I have said, the Old Testament Canon

is accredited in addition by an authority, of
which the New Testament is devoid. This is the
authority of Jesus Christ Himself. In the days
of our Lord, the Scriptures of the Jewish Church
were practically the same which form our Old
Testament, arranged as they still are in the
Jewish Bible in the three divisions of Law,
Prophets, and Hagiographa, beginning with
Genesis and ending with Chronicles. The New
Testament writers take for granted that there is
a well-known and definite body of Scriptures,
which is quoted by Christ Himself as the Law,
the Prophets, and the Psalms.[1] We do not indeed
know the exact contents of that third division,
to which Christ gave the name of its most conspicuous member. On the one hand, the Book
of Daniel — with the exception of certain Psalms,
the latest Book of all — is frequently acknowledged by New Testament writers; and Christ
Himself seems to testify to the limits of the
Hebrew Canon, exactly as they now lie in Genesis
and Chronicles.[2] But, on the other hand, neither
our Lord nor the Apostles make any quotation
from Ezra, Nehemiah, Esther, Canticles or
Ecclesiastes, the three last of which Books were
not yet recognised by all the Jewish schools.

This possible deduction, however, is insignificant, and we do not exaggerate if we say that the

[1] Luke xxiv. 44.
[2] Matt. xxiii. 35, compared with Gen. iv. and 2 Chron. xxiv. 21.

Bible of the Jews in our Lord's time was practically our old Testament. For us its supreme sanction is that which it received from Christ Himself. It was the Bible of His education and the Bible of His ministry. He took for granted its fundamental doctrines about creation, about man and about righteousness; about God's Providence of the world and His purposes of grace through Israel. He accepted its history as the preparation for Himself, and taught His disciples to find Him in it. He used it to justify His mission and to illuminate the mystery of His Cross. He drew from it many of the examples and most of the categories of His gospel. He re-enforced the essence of its law and restored many of its ideals. But above all, He fed His own soul with its contents, and in the great crises of His life sustained Himself upon it as upon the living and sovereign Word of God. These are the highest external proofs — if indeed we can call them external — for the abiding validity of the Old Testament in the life and doctrine of Christ's Church. What was indispensable to the Redeemer must always be indispensable to the redeemed.

But while we look to Christ as the chief Authority for our Old Testament, we must never forget that He was also its first Critic. He came to a people, who lived under a strict and literal enforcement of the Law; and whose religious leaders at the time aggravated the strictness and complexity of the Law by a mass of traditional precepts. Not only did Jesus reject these traditions. He equally rejected some parts of the Law itself, and directed His own conduct in sovereign indifference to many other parts. This statement is not contradicted by the well-known verses : *Think not that I came to destroy the Law or the Prophets ; I came not to destroy but to fulfil. For verily I say unto you, Till Heaven and earth pass away, one jot or one tittle shall in no wise pass from the Law till all be accomplished.*[1] If, as most critics allow, the second of these verses be a genuine utterance of our Lord, its words must be interpreted by His own definition of what the Law was. Christ effected that definition in various ways. Upon more than one occasion He extracted the ideal or essential part of the Law and defined it as the whole : *Whatsoever ye wish that men should do to you, so also do ye to them, for this is the Law and the Prophets ;*[2] and again : *Thou shalt love the Lord thy God with all thy heart, and thy soul, and thy mind, and thy neighbour as thyself. On these two commandments hangeth all the law.*[3] Sometimes He took special precepts of the Law, like the sixth and seventh Commandments, and enforced a fulfilment of them far beyond their

[1] Matt. v. 17, 18.   [2] Matt. vii. 12.
[3] Matt. xxii. 40.

literal meaning.[1]   Or He took the rigorous
precept, *an eye for an eye, and a tooth for a tooth*,
or the statement which is not found in the Old
Testament in so many words, but which expresses the temper of much of the Law: *Thou
shalt love thy neighbour and hate thine enemy*,[2]
and He reversed them.   Or He took the law of
divorce and declared it to have been temporary,
granted to a rude age of the nation's development and now to be abrogated.[3]   Or He ascribed
the character of transitoriness to the whole of
the Old Testament: *the law and the prophets were
till John; from that time the kingdom of heaven is
preached*.[4]   That is to say, a new dispensation
had opened, in which the older revelation enjoyed
no longer the same rank or significance.

Jesus, it is true, rendered obedience to many
of the formal statutes.   He paid the Temple-
tax,[5] and commanded the Leper whom He cured
to *show himself to the priest and offer the gift
which Moses commanded*.[6]   But these and other
details He enforced on the ground not of principle
but of expediency, and in order to prevent
needless scandals in the way of others.[7]   The
expediency was due to the circumstances of
His own time, and with these would pass away.

---

[1] Matt. v. 21 ff. anger; 27 ff. lust.   [2] Matt. v. 38 ff., 43 ff.

[3] Matt. v. 31 ff., and elsewhere.

[4] Matt. xi. 12 ff. ; Luke xvi. 16.

[5] Matt. xvii. 24–27.   [6] Matt. viii. 1–4.

[7] Matt. xvii. 27.

To many other observances of the Law, Christ
showed, by His neglect of them, or by His
positive transgression, a high superiority. He
touched the Leper and did not feel Himself
unclean; [1] He reckoned all foods as lawful; [2]
He broke away from the literal observance of
the Sabbath Law.[3] He left no commands about
sacrifice, the temple-worship, or circumcision, but
on the contrary, by the institution of the New
Covenant, He abrogated for ever these sacraments
of the Old.

Thus, as Professor Denney remarks,[4] Christ
'presents a positive new standard of life, from
which legalism has disappeared, a standard of
love exhibited either in His own example or in
that of His heavenly Father by which all men
are to be judged. . . . All these modes of con-
ceiving the standard of disciple-life, though not
annulling the Law but fulfilling it, are nevertheless indifferent to it, either as a historic document
or as a national institution.' [5]

Let us now pass to the Apostles. From the
first the Apostles employed the Old Testament
in all their preaching, whether apologetic or
practical. Even those of them who emphasise

[1] Matt. viii. 1–4.   [2] Mark vii. 15; Luke xi. 37; cf. x. 7.

[3] Matt. xii. 1–12; Luke xiii. 10–17; xiv. 1–6; John v. 1–17.

[4] Messrs. Clark's *Bible Dictionary*, art. 'Law in the New
Testament.'

[5] On the whole subject see especially Robert Mackintosh,
Christ and the Jewish Law. London, 1886.

the exhaustion of the old dispensation are ready, like the author of the Epistle to the Hebrews, to draw from its Scriptures declarations of the character and will of God, examples of faith, and directions both for conduct and worship. Paul affirms that, while the Gentile has not been left without a revelation of God, it has been the glory of the Jew to possess a definite and authoritative expression of God's will in the Scriptures. To the Jew have been intrusted the oracles of God ; [1] which reveal His character,[2] and the purposes of His Providence both with regard to Israel [3] and other nations, as well as His statutes for man's daily life. Paul even includes the ceremonial Law [4] within this divine endowment of his people. Moreover, the Scriptures of the Jews are prophetic, the history and the institutions recorded in them are typical, of the new dispensation itself.[5] In every way the Old Testament is of significance to the Church of Christ. *Whatsoever things were written aforetime, were written for our learning, that we through patience and comfort of the Scriptures might have hope.*[6] *Now all these things happened unto Israel by way of figure; and they*

---

[1] Rom. iii. 2.

[2] Rom. iii. 4 (Ps. li. 4) ; Rom. ix. 15, 17, 20 (Exod. xxxiii. 19; Isa. xlv. 9, 10) ; Rom. xi. 34 (Isa. xl. 13) ; 1 Cor. ii. 16, etc.

[3] Rom. iv. 3 (Gen. xv. 6), 17 (Gen. xvii. 5) ; ix.-xi., etc.

[4] Λατρεία, Rom. ix. 4.   [5] 1 Cor. x. 1 ff., etc.

[6] Rom. xv. 4.

*are written for our admonition, upon whom the
ends of the world are come.*[1]

But we must go further and notice that these
opinions of the abiding validity of the Old Testament were held by the Apostles along with a very
strict belief in the inspiration of its text.[2] In the
inspiration of the letter of the Old Testament
the Apostles sometimes appear to have as explicit a confidence as the Jewish doctors of their
time.   Not only is it God's Spirit who, according
to them, speaks by the mouths of prophets and
psalmists, but every word which they quote —
however detached from its context and however
much in their application of it they may change
its meaning from that which it plainly bears in
the original — is in their belief a word of God.

At first sight this apostolic testimony seems
to exclude modern criticism from every right or
claim to apply its methods to the Old Testament.
A little observation, however, will show us that
the very opposite is the case; and that the treatment of the Old Testament by the Apostles, so far
from silencing critical questions, raises these in a
somewhat more aggravated form than the Old
Testament by itself does.   For, in the first place,
let me remind you, the apostolic writings nowhere
define the limits of the Old Testament Canon.

[1] 1 Cor. x. 11.
[2] Compare Reuss, *History of the Canon of the Holy Scriptures*,
trans. by Hunter, pp. 12 ff.

On the contrary, their employment of what the
Church now regards as extra-canonical writings,[1]
and their appeal to questionable traditions as if
these were of equal validity with writings which
we regard as canonical, seems to indicate that
the Apostles fixed no such hard lines round the
Scriptures as the Jewish, and some parts of the
Christian, Church afterwards fixed. Again, let
us take a still more significant fact. For the
most part the writers of the New Testament,
whether in the Gospels or the discourses of the
Book of Acts or the Epistles, draw their Old
Testament citations from the Greek version or
'Septuagint.' Not only does that version contain
a number of Books which the Hebrew Canon
excludes;[2] but in the Books which it has in
common with the latter we can see that the
Hebrew text, from which the translation was
made, sometimes varied substantially from the
canonical Hebrew text; and even where the text
has been the same, the Greek version often gives
a different meaning from that of the original.
And although in some of these differences
between the Hebrew and the Greek, the latter

[1] 1 Cor. ii. 9; Heb. xi. 37; Jude 9, 14 f., where the Book of
Enoch is directly quoted. For other New Testament passages
which it has influenced, see *Encyc. Biblica*, i. p. 225, § 32.

[2] Which fact, taken along with the Apostles' use of apocryphal writings as 'Scripture' or as true history, seems to imply
that the Apostles accepted the wider Canon of the Hellenist
Jews rather than the Hebrew one. But this is not certain.

has the sounder reading and enables us to correct the former, yet in other cases it is clear either that the translators' reading of the text was wrong or that they were mistaken in their rendering of it into Greek. Of these discrepancies between the Greek and the Hebrew there are instances among the citations made from the Old Testament by New Testament writers. Paul himself, while proving his acquaintance with the Hebrew original,[1] quotes from the Greek even where this differs from the Hebrew. In one passage the Greek enables him to quote some words of Hosea in an opposite sense from that in which the Prophet employed them.[2] And in general, indifference is shown about the exact words of the citations. They are quoted loosely, as if from memory; different passages are mingled and even at one point,[3] under the Scriptural formula, *as it is written*, an apocryphal writing is fused with one from the Book of Isaiah.

Nor is that all, for when we pass from the quotation of the Old Testament text by the Apostles to their interpretation of it, we find much more that raises questions. In his exegesis of the Old Testament, Paul, upon several occasions, follows the allegorising methods of the Jewish

[1] *E.g.* 1 Cor. xv. 54, quoting from Isa. xxv. 8 : the LXX. in which passage makes Death triumph. Paul follows the Hebrew sense, while adopting a slightly different reading.

[2] 1 Cor. xv. 55.

[3] 1 Cor. ii. 9.

schools of his time;[1] in one instance he calls the literal meaning of an Old Testament passage impossible and substitutes for it a metaphorical application of his own, although there can be no doubt that the literal meaning was that of the original author.[2]

We have now before us the essential facts in the use of the Old Testament by Christ and His Apostles. What conclusions may we draw from them?

The first is that of the abiding value of the Old Testament for the life and doctrine of the Christian Church. That which was used by the Redeemer Himself for the sustenance of His own soul can never pass out of the use of His redeemed. That from which He proved the divinity of His mission, and the age-long preparation for His coming, must always have a principal place in His Church's argument for Him. Not less than His Apostles will His Church see revealed in the Old Testament the character of God; while some of His attributes —

[1] 2 Cor. iii. 13 ff.; Gal. iv. 22 ff.

[2] Deut. xxv. 4 forbids the muzzling of the ox which treads out the corn. In 1 Cor. ix. 9 Paul denies that this can be the intention of the Holy Spirit. '*Doth God*,' he says, '*take care for oxen? Or doth He say it altogether for our sakes?*' The latter, he asserts, in spite of the fact that one of the most beautiful traits of the Book of Deuteronomy is the tenderness with which it makes provision for animals. Professor Findlay's attempt to prove that Paul is merely extracting the moral essence of the Deuteronomic injunction, fails to explain the very definite language of the verse (*Expositor's Greek Testament*, ii. p. 848).

such as His Creative Power and His Providence—
are there illustrated to an extent for which the
brief space of the New Testament leaves no room.
Not less than the Apostles will the Church continue to find faith and every virtue exemplified
in the heroes of Israel.

But along with this warrant of the permanent
religious value of the Old Testament, Christ and
His Apostles have nowhere bound the Church
either to obedience to all its laws, or to belief
in all its teaching. On the contrary, our Lord
Himself has set us the example of a great Discrimination. He came not only to do the Law,
but to judge the Law, and while there are parts
of it which He renounced by simply leaving them
silently behind Him, there are other parts upon
which He turned with spoken condemnation.
He did not allegorise or spiritualise them as has
always been the manner of some of His followers,
bound to the letter of Scripture and seeking to
escape the consequences of their bondage by
thus compromising with the truth ; but He strictly
condemned them. And this Discrimination of
our Lord between what was binding in the Law
and what was not, has for us consequences not
merely moral but intellectual as well. For the
judgement, which both He and His Apostles often
emphasised, that in Old Testament laws and
institutions, ideals and tempers, there is very
much which was rudimentary and therefore of

transient worth and obligation, opens up the whole question of the development of revelation and justifies what is so large a part of modern criticism, — the effort, namely, to fix the historical order of the Old Testament writings and to define the stages by which the primitive reve- lation of God to men was carried onward and upward to its summit in Christ Himself. Besides, Christ's attitude to the Law reminds us that similar opposition exists within the Old Testament itself, between the ethical teach- ing of the Prophets and the priestly concep- tions of religion. The determination of these two conflicting tendencies in the development of Israel's faith is another of the offices of Criticism.

But the Apostles go further. Although unable to free themselves from the strict views of inspira- tion which the Jewish schools enforced and which seem to preclude all liberty of criticism, their practical use of the Old Testament only serves to suggest how clamant the need of criticism is — and that in every department of criticism which the modern Church has developed. Is it the question of the Canon? The New Testament writers bequeath that question to the Church; making it by their quotations from extra-canon- ical writings a more difficult one than it is with the Jewish doctors themselves. Is it the question of the Text? Their use of the Septuagint raises

that question in every possible detail. Is it the
question of the interpretation of the Text?
Some of their interpretations, as we have seen,
are a direct challenge to our sense of truth to
discover what the Old Testament writers actually
intended, apart from the meanings, which temporary and often false fashions of exegesis put
upon their words.

In short, the New Testament treatment of the
Old not only bequeaths to the Church the liberty
of Criticism, but along many lines the need and
obligation of Criticism: not only delivers us
once for all from bondage to the doctrine of
the literal inspiration and equal divinity of all
parts of the Old Testament, but prompts every
line of research and discussion along which the
modern criticism of the Old Testament has been
conducted. The task, therefore, of the following
Lectures is a double one: to inquire, first, whether
this criticism has been true to the liberty which
the New Testament sanctions, and serviceable in
solving the problems which the New Testament
raises; and second, whether, in this loyalty and
in this service, modern criticism has conserved or
has imperilled that permanent religious value of
the Old Testament which Christ and His Apostles
so fully enforced. In other words, we have to
examine how far the freedom and thoroughness
of Criticism during this century have affected our
belief in the Old Testament as the revelation of

God, the prophecy of Jesus Christ, and the example and proof of faith.

Before we begin this inquiry some preliminary recollections are necessary. The Christian Church has twice over forgotten the liberty wherewith Christ has made her free; and in two directions has attempted to enforce the literal acceptance of the Old Testament, with results, in both cases, disastrous to the interests of religion.

We are all aware that at various periods in the history of Christendom a spirit arose amongst its leaders not very different from that which moved so large a party in the primitive Church, and even some of the Apostles themselves, to insist upon the letter of the Law of Moses as binding upon all Christians. In later ages the representatives of this spirit did not propose, as those Jewish Christians did, to enforce circumcision, sacrifice and other items of the Mosaic ritual; but in the same temper of literal obedience to the Old Testament they effected what was even worse. They revived many of the rigours of the Law, and quoted the most cruel tempers of the old dispensation, as the sanction of their own bigotries and persecutions. No branch of the Church has been innocent of this disloyalty to her Lord. If the tyrants and inquisitors of the Roman Church, in the days of its imperial power, have claimed the relentlessness of the old law as authority for their unspeakable cruelties to those whom they deemed heretics, our own Puritan fathers, on both sides of the Atlantic, have not hesitated to defend their intolerance of opinions which differed from their own, their purchase and holding of slaves, their harshness to criminals, and their torture and murder of witches by an appeal to the laws and customs of Israel.   One is not sure whether the evil is even yet dead.   A mitigated but very pregnant expression of it has just been uncovered in a letter by John Henry Newman of date 1875.   Speaking of the cruelties of the Inquisition he says :

'As to Dr. Ward in the *Dublin Review*, his point (I think) was not the question of cruelty, but whether persecution, such as in Spain, was *unjust ;* and with the capital punishment prescribed in the Mosaic Law for idolatry, blasphemy, and witchcraft and St. Paul's transferring of the sword to Christian magistrates, it seems difficult to call persecution (so-called) *unjust.* I suppose in like manner he would not deny, but condemn the *craft* and *cruelty* and the wholesale character of St. Bartholomew's massacre ; but still would argue in the abstract in defence of the magistrate's bearing of the sword and of the Church's sanctioning of its use in the aspect of justice, as Moses, Joshua, and Samuel might use it against heretics, rebels, and cruel and crafty enemies.' [1]

---

[1] *Contemporary Review*, Sept. 1899, p. 362: A letter from John Henry Newman to J. R. Mozley, of date April 4, 1875.

The spirit, then, lives, though the flesh be weak! Taking this remarkable document along with the utterances of Protestant divines of forty years ago in the Southern States in defence of slavery, we may partly understand why — not the Old Testament, as Professor Goldwin Smith has ignorantly judged but — the literal enforcement of the Old Testament, in disloyalty to Christ, should be called 'a millstone about the neck of Christianity.' From the first generation of the Church to the last but one, the theory of the equal and lasting divinity of the Jewish Scriptures has been fertile in casuistry, bigotry and cruel oppression of every kind.

But while all that is now mainly a matter of historical interest, we have suffered in our own generation, and to a high degree still suffer, from the enforcement of the same spirit, operating in another direction. The advocates and agents of Biblical Criticism have often been charged with the creation of sceptics, and we may fully admit that where criticism has been conducted in a purely empirical spirit and without loyalty to Christ, it has shaken the belief of some in the fundamentals of religion, distracted others from the zealous service of God, and benumbed the preaching of Christ's gospel. Yet any one who has had practical dealings with the doubt and religious bewilderment of his day can testify that those who have been

led into unbelief by modern criticism are not
for one moment to be compared in number
with those who have fallen from faith over the
edge of the opposite extreme. The dogma of
a verbal inspiration, the dogma of the equal
divinity of all parts of Scripture, the refusal to
see any development either from the ethnic
religions to the religion of Israel, or any development within the religion of Israel itself — all these
have had a disastrous influence upon the religious
thought and action of our time. They have not
only produced confusion in some of the holiest
minds among us. They have not only paralysed
the intellects of those who have adopted them,
as every mechanical conception of the truth must
do. But they have been the provocation to
immense numbers of honest hearts to cast off religion altogether. Men have been trained in the
belief that the holiest elements of our creed, nay
the assurance of the existence and love of God
Himself, are bound up with the literal acceptance
of the whole Bible, of which the Old Testament
forms by much the greater part; so that whenever their minds awoke to the irreconcileable
discrepancies of the Old Testament text, or their
consciences to the narrow and violent temper
of its customs, and they could no longer believe
in it, as the equal and consistent message of God
to men, their whole faith in Him, suspended
from their earliest years upon this impossible

view of it, was in danger of failing them, and in innumerable cases did fail them for the rest of their lives.

Like every man who has read a little and thought a little, I was aware of this great and tragic commonplace of our day. But during the last year I have come across so many instances of it — each the story of a human soul — that it has become vivid and burning in my mind. It has been my privilege to go carefully through the correspondence of one, who probably more than any of our contemporaries, was consulted by persons of the religious experience which I have described. Many address him from the silence and loneliness of those far margins of our world where men have not yet largely settled, and the few who come have leisure and detachment enough to think freshly upon the old ways in which they have been trained ; but others are residents of the centres of civilisation, and their words are heavy with what I feel to be the greatest pathos of our life — the hunger of souls starving unconsciously within reach of the food they need. One and all tell how the literal acceptance of the Bible — the faith which finds in it nothing erroneous, nothing defective, and (outside of the sacrifices and Temple) nothing temporary — is what has driven them from religion. Henry Drummond was not a Biblical scholar ; he was not an authority on the Old Testament. But the large trust which his personality and his writings so magically produced, moved men and women to address to him all kinds of questions. It is astonishing how many of these had to do with the Old Testament : with its discrepancies, its rigorous laws, its pitiless tempers, its open treatment of sexual questions, the atrocities which are narrated by its histories and sanctioned by its laws. Unable upon the lines of the teaching of their youth to reconcile these with a belief in the goodness of God, the writers had abandoned, or were about to abandon, the latter ; yet they eagerly sought an explanation which would save them from such a disaster.

I know no sadder tragedy than this innumerably repeated one, nor any service which it were better worth doing than the attempt to help men out of its perplexities. I firmly believe that such an attempt must lie along the lines indicated by Christ and His Apostles, and followed by the textual and historical criticism which takes its charter from Christ Himself. And if I am right, then we shall find in the task on which we have entered with this lecture, interests and responsibilities which are not merely scholastic or historical, but thoroughly evangelical —concerned with faith, and the assistance of souls in darkness, and the equipment of the Church of Christ for her ministry of God's Word.

LECTURE II

THE COURSE AND CHARACTER OF MODERN
CRITICISM

WE have seen that the treatment of the Old
Testament by the New leaves us with a double
result. In the first place, our Lord and His
Apostles use the Hebrew Scriptures, and commit
them to us as the living Word of God: the
Revelation of His Nature and Providence, including in the latter His choice of Israel to be
His 'Servant' to the world, His preparation for
the advent of Christ, and His purposes of grace
to all mankind. But in the second place, our
Lord makes a great discrimination in His judgement of the Law and its ethical tempers, and
teaches us to read the Old Testament as the
record of a progressive revelation; while the
Apostles bequeath to the Church unsolved all
other problems of criticism, whether textual or
historical. We must clearly recognise that our
Lord did not count the whole of the Old Testament as equally Divine; that He set us an
example of liberty in judging the facts which

it presents to us; and that the Criticism with which we have to deal — whether it be the Lower Criticism or the Higher — is not the product of the modern mind, looking at the Old Testament alone, but that some of the problems arise in Christ's own treatment of the Hebrew Scriptures, and that others leave the hands of His Apostles in an even more acute form than that in which they issue from the Old Testament itself.

Starting, then, from these our chief authorities, the task of the following lectures is a double one. We have to inquire: *first*, how far Modern Criticism, in the use of the liberty which Christ exemplified, has succeeded in solving the problems bequeathed to the Church; and *second*, whether in solving them Modern Criticism tends to impair or to fortify our belief that the Old Testament contains a real revelation of God. For us preachers the latter is the cardinal question; but the former is preliminary and indispensable to it. In this lecture I propose to give an account of the general course of Biblical Criticism during the last century. The best way of doing this will be by the examination of certain charges which have recently been made against the general methods of Criticism. In discussing these, I fear that I must describe a number of things which have been often described, and are well known to many of you; but the ignorance of them, which is still shown in some quarters, makes their repetition, however trite, an inevitable duty.

The charges made against modern criticism may be summed up under three heads.

First, that the modern criticism of the Old Testament is a movement of recent growth, and that its results are, therefore, precarious.

Second, that Old Testament criticism proceeds only on linguistic and literary evidence, which, being estimated by modern tastes and standards, must be largely subjective and uncertain.

Third, that critics ignore the evidence of archæology, geography and the allied sciences ; and that this is hostile to their conclusions.

I. *The General Course of Modern Criticism.*

Many of the opponents of Old Testament criticism have represented the movement as if it were but the growth of yesterday, with results so hastily and arbitrarily reached that they are certain to be reversed by the discoveries and debates of to-morrow — like Jonah's gourd, the son of a night, in a night they shall perish ! If this were so we might at once abandon the task we have set ourselves. It would not be worth our attention to examine the effect of a movement so sudden and precarious upon the Church's age-long attitude to the greater part of her sacred writings. But the science of Old Testament

criticism is not the thing of yesterday which
its assailants pretend. Even within its modern
development — which is all we have got to do
with just now — it covers a period of more than
two hundred years. It has achieved a career,
that is to say, as long as those of many of the
historical and physical sciences. Nor, within
the last century at least, has it been served by a
less constant succession of able experts; while
its methods have been equally without dogmatic
bias, and so far as their materials go, as trustworthy and exact. Consequently the progress
of the science has resembled that of every other
intellectual movement of our time which has
issued in generally accepted results. It has been
slow, gradual and severely contested. It has
suffered from digressions, pedantries, extrava-
gancies. It has been forced to abandon some
positions which it had previously occupied with
confidence: and upon innumerable details it
still exhibits among its supporters difference of
opinion. But with few or no preconceptions, it
has started from facts easily ascertained within
the sacred text itself; each step forward which it
has taken has been planted on other facts in the
same field or upon reasonable inferences from
these. It has suffered from, and has benefited
by, the personal jealousies and ambitions of its
agents, who have left few fresh proposals or discoveries undisputed: and it has issued in a large

and increasing agreement upon certain main lines of conclusion.

Let us look for a little at the details.[1] The modern criticism of the Old Testament may be said to have begun in 1680. In that year a French priest called Simon drew attention to the fact that within the Book of Genesis the same event is often described in different words. He emphasised especially the two accounts of the Creation, which lie side by side in the opening chapters, and the two accounts of the Flood which are fused together in chapters vi–ix. For these Simon suggested different authors, whose writings Moses had put together. Such was the beginning of the criticism of the Pentateuch. You will observe not only how simple it is and how easily verified, but that also, so far from its motive being a prejudice against the Mosaic authorship of the first Book of the Bible, it took this for granted. Notice particularly that it starts from *the fact of two accounts of the same events*. It is on the presence of many such 'doublets' in the Hexateuch and historical books that the modern criticism of the Old Testament is based.

Seventy years after Simon another Frenchman,

---

[1] The English reader will find full accounts of these in Cheyne's *Founders of Old Testament Criticism*, or in a more summary form so far as Hexateuchal criticism is concerned in the introductions to Addis's *Documents of the Hexateuch*: Nutt, London, vol. i. 1892, vol. ii. 1898.

Astruc, published his *Conjectures on the Original Memoirs of which it appears Moses made use in composing the Book of Genesis*.[1] That is the full title of his work, and it also proves how independent was the literary criticism of Genesis of any desire to deny the Mosaic, or ancient origin of the Book. After dividing the two narratives of the Creation as Simon had done, Astruc pointed out that each of them had a distinguishing mark. The first, Genesis i.–ii. 4*a* always speaks of the Creator as Elohim, the Hebrew term for God; the second, Genesis ii. 4*b*–iii. calls Him Jahweh or Jahweh-Elohim, the name of Israel's national deity. Again we have a simple fact which any reader can test for himself.

Had this difference between the Divine Names stood by itself, its discovery would have led to nothing but confusion; because the texts have often been copied, and, as any one may see from a comparison of the most ancient versions with the Hebrew, the copying scribes sometimes substituted the one Divine Name for the other. Besides, there were occasions in the course of the narrative, which usually employs the national name Jahweh, to substitute for this the more general title Elohim, as for instance when the writer is treating of the essential character of God or is introducing the statements of persons

[1] Brussels, 1753: x. and 525 pages 12mo.

who were not Israelites and who did not know
God as Jahweh. The distinction, therefore, between the Divine Names is too precarious to
determine a distinction of authorship. But
shortly before 1780 Eichhorn, a German Hebraist,
who had arrived independently at Astruc's conclusion, confirmed and corrected its results by
another discovery. He showed that the difference
in the name of the Deity was accompanied by
several other linguistic variations. The passages
which use Elohim speak of Him as *creating* the
world, and talk of *the beasts of the earth;* the
passages which usually employ the name Jahweh
speak of Him as *making* or *forming* the world,
and talk of *the beasts of the field.* These are but
two instances out of many : Eichhorn had struck
a line of differences too numerous and too distinctive to prove fallacious. This, however, was
not final : a few years later, in 1798, Ilgen, another German, observed that within those parts
of Genesis in which Elohim was used there are
also double accounts of the same event, which can
be distinguished from each other by differences
of style and vocabulary. Ilgen is therefore called
the discoverer of the Second Elohist.

Now it was natural that since the main distinction among these documents lay in the name
of the Deity used by each, that distinction should
not at first have been explored beyond the sixth
chapter of Exodus where God reveals Himself

under the name Jahweh, for up to this point there
is an obvious reason why the Elohist documents
should refrain from using the name Jahweh. But
another and independent line of criticism had
already been started which was carrying the discrimination of the documents farther on. One
of the representatives of this — perhaps the
originator — was a Roman Catholic priest, a
Scotsman, called Geddes.[1] That remarkable
man did not work on the lines laid down by
the critics I have mentioned. Where they,
struck by the different names for Deity, distinguished two or three documents, Geddes,
confused by the presence of a large variety of
differences and discrepancies, which he did not
stop to classify, rushed to the conclusion that
these were proofs of a great number of independent sources. This Fragmentary Hypothesis, as it was called, was taken up in
Germany by Vater. So far as it affirmed the
presence of many documents it did not at the
time contribute to the progress of criticism in
that direction,[2] but because the boldness of its
authors did not confine it to Genesis and the
first six chapters of Exodus it opened the way

[1] See his *Life*, etc., by John Mason Good; London, 1863. His
O. T. work is entitled *The Holy Bible . . . faithfully translated
from corrected texts of the originals, with various Readings, Notes,
and Critical Remarks ;* two vols., London, 1792–97. *Critical Remarks on the Hebrew Scriptures :* vol. i., *Pentateuch,* 1800.

[2] Yet the justness of much of the reasoning connected with this
hypothesis has been proved by more recent scholars; see below.

to the analysis of the rest of the Pentateuch and even of Joshua.[1]

From 1805 onwards De Wette demonstrated the singularity of Deuteronomy both as regards its doctrine and its style; a singularity so conspicuous even to the tyro in Hebrew that the absence of an earlier discovery of it now seems astonishing. Not only the favourite phrases and formulas, the favourite interests and ideals, of this Book, but its treatment of the same events, and its laws for the same matters are so different from those of preceding parts of the Pentateuch,[2] as to prove beyond all doubt difference of authorship and date. Here, then, is a fourth document. Next, Bleek, who had been partly anticipated by Geddes, proved that the Book of Joshua forms an indispensable supplement to the Pentateuch by carrying on the history and enforcing the legislation of the latter — not on one line but to different degrees on all the lines, sometimes conflicting, of the four documents. Then from the beginning of Genesis to the end of Joshua the attempt was made to disentangle these documents by Ewald. And ultimately — to pass over several intermediate confirmations of the main

[1] For Geddes's share in extending the process to Joshua, see article 'Joshua' by the present writer in Hastings's *Bible Dictionary*.

[2] For details I must refer the reader to the introduction to Driver's *Commentary*; Moore's article in the *Encyclopædia Biblica*; and Ryle's in Hastings's *Bible Dictionary*.

lines of analysis — Hupfeld [1] arrived independently
at Ilgen's conclusions about the two Elohists,
and established them upon a sounder basis. He
took, for instance, the well-known double accounts
of the origin of the names Bethel and Israel.
One of these (Gen. xxxv. 9–15) relates that
Elohim appeared to Jacob as he came out of
Padan-aram, and that, therefore, Jacob called the
name of the place Beth-el or *house of God;* but
the other (Gen. xxviii. 10–22) relates that God
appeared to Jacob at the same place on his
departure for Padan-aram, and that it was at
this earlier time that the place was named
Bethel: in conformity with which God, when He
appears to Jacob in Padan-aram, calls Himself
the God of Bethel (Gen. xxxi. 13). Again, according to Genesis xxxii. 23–33, the name Israel
was first given to Jacob when he wrestled with
the Unknown on the banks of Jabbok; and it
was then said: *thou shalt no more be called Jacob.* [2]
But in Genesis xxxv. 9–15 the origin of the name
Israel is dated at Bethel on Jacob's return from
Padan-aram.   These are only two of several
variations, not only of style but of substance,
which prove the presence in the story of Jacob

[1] In *The Sources of Genesis* (*Die Quellen d. Genesis*), 1850.

[2] It is not quite certain whether this narrative is from the
Elohist or the Jahwist. The divine name is Elohim, but there
are other parts in the style which lead many to attribute it to the
Jahwist. See below on the acknowledged impossibility of always
discriminating between the Jahwist and Elohist.

of two documents both using the name Elohim.
Hupfeld made an even more important observation. He remarked that these two Elohist documents are not so closely related to each other as
one of them is to the Jahwist. This one, which
he calls the Second Elohist, differs from the
Jahwist generally only in details — though also in
certain conceptions of the Deity — and is so interwoven with the latter that the two are often
indistinguishable and were evidently combined
before being attached either to the First Elohist
or to the Deuteronomic writer. The First
Elohist, on the other hand, has a character all
its own. Of the bulk of the Hexateuch it supplies
by far the greater part; of the plan which runs
through the Hexateuch [1] it is the upholding
frame. Hence it has been called the Grundschrift
or Basal Document; but because it contains the
larger part of the legislation, and that part is
distinguished from the rest by an elaboration of
laws concerning the priesthood and ritual, it is
now more usually called the Priestly, while the
name Elohist is reserved for Hupfeld's Second
Elohist.

Before the middle of the century, then, the
main lines of the analysis of the Hexateuch were
laid down, and all the effect of subsequent criticism has been to confirm and develop them.
The evidence that there are four main documents

[1] This is more true of Genesis to Deuteronomy than of Joshua.

has been revised and the conclusion corroborated by a large number of independent scholars in several countries and schools of Christendom. Kuenen and others in Holland ; Graf, Wellhausen, Nöldeke, Dillmann, Kautzsch, Stade, Budde, Holzinger and others in Germany; Westphal and others in France; Robertson Smith, Cheyne, Driver, Addis, Bennett, Ball, Ryle, Estlin Carpenter and Harford-Battersby in Great Britain ; Briggs and Bacon in America, have all made detailed analyses of the whole or of parts of the Hexateuch; and their conclusions have been adopted, or independently verified, by others who have not published detailed analyses but have studied and written on the subjects contained in the Hexateuch: as for instance a large band of contributors to Hastings's *Bible Dictionary*[1] and to the *Encyclopædia Biblica*. It cannot be of chance nor by arbitrariness that among so large a majority of experts, working independently of each other, and in face of continual criticism from scholars on the other side, there should result an agreement of opinion so strong, so surely growing, and so widely based on the phenomena of the sacred text itself. Every position asserted has in turn been contested: in every case the evidence has been several times analysed ; and one by one conservative scholars like Delitzsch, who had at first resisted

---

[1] See especially the article ' Hexateuch ' by F. H. Woods.

the conclusions, have in the end expressed their adherence to them. From the nature of the materials much uncertainty, of course, must prevail. Purely philological evidence, where it alone is available, is often ambiguous: but as we shall see in the next section of this Lecture, the philological is only one department of the evidence. Difference of style or of language is in most cases accompanied by difference of substance, and the judgements which arise on the latter cannot be due to modern literary tastes or standards.

We have seen [1] that the theory of the composition of the Hexateuch from four documents had one rival, the theory of composition from many fragments. There was also another theory, that of expansion; or the enlargement of a small kernel of tradition by successive additions and revisions from later stages of the national memory and religious development. Both of these theories have received some justification from the more recent elaboration of the documentary theory. For within each of the four documents further examination has discovered certain smaller variations of language, but still more of substance, which make it probable that the documents contain later additions in the style characteristic of each, and that thus they represent not the work of the same author so much as that of the same

[1] Above, p. 36.

school of tradition and religious conception.[1]
Then, as there are four documents, and as it is
evident that two of them, the Jahwist and Elohist,
were combined before the others were added, this
implies more than one editor, whose additions
and modifications are to be expected and, where
possible, distinguished. Of the presence of such
minor distinctions, the present state of the text
affords many clear signs; and that the process
of revising and adding continued a very long
time is proved by a comparison of the Hebrew
with the oldest versions into other languages.
Here the work of the critic is necessarily extremely delicate, and the results are often un-

[1] To go into the details of this more delicate and therefore precarious criticism of recent years is impossible in the limits of a
single lecture. But some particulars may be given in a note. For
fuller details the English reader may be referred to the article
' Hexateuch ' in Hastings's *Bible Dictionary;* and, so far as Deuteronomy is concerned, to Driver's introduction to his *Commentary*
and to the forthcoming edition by the present writer of the text and
translation of that book in Haupt's *Sacred Books of the Old Testament.* In the Jahwist document the stories of early humanity and
the growth of civilisation contain some discrepancies which betray
different sources.—In Deuteronomy there has long been a division
of opinion as to how much, if any, of the prefatory introductions,
I–II, belong to the same author as that of the legal codes ; and
within the latter parallel and slightly differing laws are found on
the same subject. In the year 1894 the analysis of Deuteronomy
took a new direction on the publication of Stärk's and Steuernagel's investigations into the use of the singular and plural forms of
address in that Book. In some passages Israel is addressed as
thou, in some as *you.* The data are extremely puzzling because
the text is often uncertain where those pronouns occur, and because the Hebrew idiom permits the same writer or speaker to pass
from the one to the other. But where the change coincides with

certain.   But the uncertainties do not involve
more than the fringes of the four main documents
and their principal constituents.   Upon these, by
facts which are obvious to every student, by
methods that are thorough and exact, through
much debate and jealous revision, there has
gradually been produced among critics a most
remarkable unanimity.

So much for the analysis of the first six Books
of the Old Testament.   The Historical Books
stand next in order.   Some of them, for example
the Books of Kings, explicitly assert that they
have been composed from several sources; all of
them present on the surface the same features as

other changes in the style or religious conception, there is manifestly a strong reason for supposing a difference of author.   Not
only is such coincidence frequent in Deuteronomy both in the
hortatory sections and the laws, but while both the passages in
the singular address and those in the plural have terms and conceptions in common, they have some consistently different term
for the same event or object, and each in addition has a list of
words peculiar to itself and a list of favourite interests different
from that of the other.   It seems to me, therefore, that the
case for two sources in Deuteronomy, thus distinguished, is, if
not proved, very probable; and that it will supplant the older
distinction between the hortatory and legal sections on which
critics were always divided.   But Stärk and Steuernagel, while
striking on a true distinction, have not corrected their analysis
of it in Deuteronomy by comparison with its appearance in the
contemporary Jeremiah and other writers.   The same objection
seems to me to be valid against Mitchell's simpler analysis in
the American *Journal of Biblical Literature* for 1899. — In the
Priestly Legislation, Lev. i. 17–26 has long been regarded by
critics as distinct in character and style from the rest of the code.
(See Driver, *Introd. to Lit. of Old Testament*, 49 ff.): and in the
latter many obviously later additions appear.

the Hexateuch: that is to say, not only differences of style but the presence of double accounts
of the same event. In the Books of Samuel this
latter feature is present to a still greater degree
than in the narratives of the Hexateuch; but it
is not so possible to discern in the Books of
Samuel all the main documents which run
through the history from beginning to end.
What is clear is, that the historical Books
contain many records and traditions, some of
them treating the same events with differences
both of style and substance.[1] Equally evident
is the hand of the editor or editors who compiled
them, and who not only added various statistics
and recurrent formulas designed to frame them
into a continuous history, but placed the whole
of that history under a certain moral judgement,
to which expression is given in language distinct
from that of the materials he employed.[2] And
again, as in the case of the Hexateuch, these
conclusions have been reached only as the result
of long research and debate by many critics, who,
differing in details, have gradually approached
unanimity upon the main lines just indicated.

The analysis of the prophetical and of the
poetical Books presents us with greater difficulties. The process is not so old nor quite so

[1] *E.g.* the accounts of the institution of the Kingdom, of the
meeting of Saul and David, and of the end of Saul.
[2] See further below, pp. 65 f.

thorough as in the case of the Hexateuch, and upon some of the results there is a still wider divergence of opinion. Within the last ten years the dissection of several prophetical books has been carried to an extent which represents rather the ingenuity of a few critics than the settled consensus of the majority. But, excepting these latest proposals as still under judgement, we observe the same tendency in criticism as we have already noted: the steady approximation to the belief that many of the larger books of prophecy are compilations from several sources. For this the evidence is partly that of language and style — it has become very clear that many terms and grammatical forms were not in use till towards the Exile — but the most cogent proofs are drawn from the expression of opposite religious tempers. Both in the larger and smaller prophecies there are obvious interpolations. Generations subsequent to the original prophet made qualifications of, or additions to, his oracles, in order to adapt them to the changed circumstances or altered tempers of the people, and so to perpetuate their religious significance. To this subject we shall return in a later Lecture.

The critical analysis of the Old Testament is therefore not only a movement of considerable age, and pursued by a long and varied succession of experts; but by rational methods and upon

intelligible evidence, derived from the sacred
text, it has produced certain large results on
which the vast majority of critics are more and
more approaching to unanimity. There is, therefore, no ground either for those who attack the
science of Old Testament criticism as hasty
and its conclusions as raw; or for those who
predict a reaction from the conclusions as
certain as the reaction which arose in New
Testament criticism against the theories of
the extreme Tübingen school. The Tübingen
theories were largely deductions from the principles of a certain philosophy of history. But
the proofs of Old Testament criticism are not
à priori : the argument is inductive and the facts
are furnished by the Old Testament itself.[1]

II. *The Criticism of the Old Testament mainly Historical.*

The criticism of the Old Testament, however,
is not merely literary ; and here we have to meet
the second charge which its opponents have
preferred against it.[2] In their recent writings
Professors Sayce and Hommel have, with con-

[1] It is indeed striking that the attempt to prove the late date of
the Levitical legislation from principles of the Hegelian philosophy, which Vatke made in 1833, should have been ignored in the
history of criticism ; and that that late date should not have been
accepted till Graf and others proved it by *inductive evidence* in
1866 and following years.

[2] See above, p. 31.

siderable persistence, represented the Higher
Criticism as if it were only the analysis of the
text of the Old Testament into different documents upon the evidence of language and style.
And they assert that the evidence alleged cannot
but be precarious, because estimated by scholars
with very different tastes and standards from
those of the people among whom the Old Testament arose.   Nothing could be further from the
truth.   Look at what we have already seen with
regard to the discrimination of the documents.
We have seen that this depends not only upon
differences of vocabulary, phrase and idiom, but
still more upon differences of fact and substance
in narratives which relate the same events.

Take the different stories of the origin of the
name of Bethel.[1]   It is impossible to believe that
these came from the same hand.   Or take the
Book of Joshua.   Throughout its chapters there
are visible two differing accounts of the conquest
of Western Palestine by the Israelites.   One of
them represents the conquest and division of
the land to have been thorough and effected in
one generation by the whole people acting together; the other represents it as the work of
the tribes acting separately, and as being far from
complete.   Here are differences of fact, which
are not dependent for their distinction upon
differences of phrase and idiom; yet are corro-

[1] See above, p. 38.

borated by these, for the parts of the Book which
represent the Conquest as complete under Joshua
are composed in the language of the Deuteronomic and Priestly writers,[1] while those who report it
to have been incomplete are written in the style of
the Jahwist.[2] But that is not all. I have already
said that a linguistic analysis is often unable to
distinguish between the Jahwist and the Elohist,
and this is especially the case in the Book of
Joshua. All the more striking therefore are
certain differences of fact in this double document. For instance, in the story of the crossing
of the Jordan, as told in Joshua iii. and iv., there
are two accounts of the monument set up to
commemorate the passage. One of them builds
it at Gilgal on the west bank with stones taken
from the river-bed by the people;[3] the other
builds it in the bed of the river with twelve
stones set there by Joshua.[4] Similarly, in chapter vi. two stories have been interwoven, but
are still distinguishable : one which relates how
Israel marched round Jericho on seven successive
days, the first six they marched in silence, but
on the seventh they shouted *at the word of*

---

[1] *E.g.* x. 28–43, xi. 2, 3, 6, 9–12, 14–23, xii. xiii. 2–12, 14,
xxi. 43–45, xxii. 1–15, xxiii. — Deuteronomic: and xiv. 1–5, xv.
(except 13–19 and 63), xvi. 4–8, xvii. 1*a*, 3–7, 9 (partly), 10,
xviii. 11*a*, 12–28, xix. 1–46, 48, 51 — Priestly.

[2] xv. 63, xvi. 10, xvii. 11–18, with which agrees the account of
a partial conquest in Judges i.

[3] iv. 1–8, 20.   [4] iv. 9.

Joshua and the walls fell ;[1] and another which
relates that a portion of the armed men marched
round the city seven times on the same day,
having in their midst the ark, and that on the
seventh round the people shouted *at the signal
of the trumpets* and the walls fell.[2] Similarly
in chapter viii. we find two accounts of the
ambush against Ai, according to one of which
the ambush consisted of 30,000 men and was
despatched to its position by Joshua either from
Gilgal or soon after the main army left Gilgal;
while according to the other the ambush consisted of 5000 men and was not detached from
the army till the latter had arrived in the neighbourhood of Ai.[3] The existence of all these
' doublets ' is not, I repeat, proved by differences
of vocabulary or of style, for we are generally
unable to say which is from the Jahwist and
which from the Elohist; it is proved by difference
of facts in the substance of the narrative.

Hitherto I have dealt only with the proofs
of the presence of different documents in the

[1] Verses 3, 7*a*, 10, 11 (partly), 14, 15*a*, *and it came to pass . . .
manner*, 15*b*, 20, *and the people shouted*.

[2] Verses 4 (partly), 5, 7*b*, 8, 9, parts of 13 and 15, 16*a*, 20*b*.
Cf. especially verses 16 and 20 : in the latter the people shout
both before and after the trumpets, though verse 16 enjoins on
them not to shout till the trumpets give the signal. Wellhausen
was the first to point out the distinction.

[3] The first account can be traced in verses 3–9 ; the second in
verses 10–14. For the analysis of the two accounts through the
rest of the chapter, see Bennett's 'Joshua' in Haupt's *Sacred
Books of the Old Testament*.

D

Hexateuch. But now let us look at the problem
of the dates of these documents. Here again
the evidence for the critical solution is not altogether that of language and style. On the contrary, historical evidence has been predominant
at every step of the argument: and in particular
has decided almost by itself the principal change
of opinion which criticism has made on this
subject. At first the Jahwist-Elohist and the
Deuteronomic documents were assigned, on account of their historical allusions, to a date after
the beginning of the Monarchy; but the Priestly
Document, which has many archaic features
and which betrays no allusion to the later
history, was considered the earliest of the four.
It was the introduction of other phenomena,
historical in character, which forced critics to
abandon this opinion and to seek for the Priestly
Document a much later date. The change came
about upon two lines of reasoning. The first
was this. When the collections of laws which the
documents contain were compared, it was seen
that they exhibited different stages of what was
fundamentally the same legislation; the simplest
of these stages is found in the Jahwist-Elohist,[1]
the next in Deuteronomy,[2] the most complex
and elaborate in the Priestly Writing.[3] Or, as this
way of putting the matter does scant justice

---

[1] Ex. xx.–xxii., xxxiv., 14–26.   [2] Deut. xii.–xxvi.
[3] Ex. xxv.–xxxi., Levit., Num. i.–xix.

to the differences, we may say that while the legislation in the Jahwist-Elohist is suited to a purely agricultural people, the Deuteronomic meets the necessities of a community more highly organised and equipped, with foreign relations and subject to religious temptations to which in the days of the early kings Israel was not exposed; while, besides, there is in Deuteronomy's modification of the Jahwist-Elohist laws evidence of the influence of the eighth-century prophets. The Priestly Legislation on the other hand cannot be understood in many of its provisions except in the light of the Exile, and of the greater influence which the priesthood assumed in Israel after the return from Babylon. / On the subjects of sacrifice, the priesthood, the gifts due to the priests and kindred matters, there is an almost perfectly consistent increase of elaboration and rigour from the laws of the Jahwist-Elohist, through those of Deuteronomy to those of the Priestly Legislation.[1] I am not now defending the conclusion to which most critics adhere, that therefore the Jahwist-Elohist is the earliest of the Documents, and the Priestly the latest, Deuteronomy coming in between: I am only showing that critics reached that conclusion on historical evidence. Again, critics remarked the

[1] For details see Driver's Commentary on Deuteronomy, chaps. xii.–xxvi.; or the present writer's notes to the same chapters in Haupt's *Sacred Books of the Old Testament*.

fact that the early history of Israel exhibited
no traces of the influence or existence of any of
the three legal codes, but that, on the contrary,
the religious leaders of Israel from Gideon to
Elisha behaved as if there were no such laws in
existence as those (at least) of Deuteronomy and
the Priestly code.   Again I have no room to go
into the detailed proof,[1] and my purpose is simply
to point out the character of the evidence of
which it consists.

On both these lines of proof for the date of
the documents, the evidence, therefore, is historical and is supplied by the Old Testament
itself.   It is, of course, supported by philological
evidence.   The language and the style of the
Jahwist-Elohist are earlier than that of Deuteronomy; and both the ordinary vocabulary and
the lists of proper names in the Priestly Writing
exhibit many traces of a late date.[2]   But all this
is only corroboratory of a conclusion reached
independently and upon the evidence of the
sacred history itself.   Let me repeat, this principal conclusion of modern criticism, — that the
written Law of Israel, in the three forms in which
we possess it, cannot have been the work of
Moses or of the Mosaic, or immediately post-
Mosaic, age, but must be assigned to a much

---

[1] See the introductions to Driver's Commentary on Deuteronomy, and to Addis's *Documents of the Hexateuch*.

[2] G. B. Gray, *Studies in Hebrew Proper Names:* London, 1896.

later date, — has been reached not by the methods of literary analysis, but on lines of historical evidence furnished by the earlier chronicles of Israel themselves.

Let us now take a similar instance from the prophets. The opponents of criticism have often alleged that the conclusion, by which Isaiah xl. and following chapters are taken from Isaiah himself and assigned to a prophet on the eve of the Return from Exile, is due to a dogmatic prejudice against the capacity of Isaiah himself to predict events so far beyond his own time, and is supported mainly upon grounds of language and style. Neither of these allegations is correct. What has compelled critics to date Isaiah xl. and following chapters from the close of the Babylonian Captivity has been the historical evidence furnished by the chapters themselves. These chapters nowhere claim to be by Isaiah, and do not present a single reflection of his time. But they plainly set forth, as having already taken place, certain events which happened from a century to a century and a half after Isaiah had passed away: the Babylonian Exile and Captivity, the ruin of Jerusalem and the devastation of the Holy Land. Israel is addressed as having exhausted the time of her penalty, and is exhorted to leave Babylon, because the door of her deliverance is immediately to open, and as if her return to the Holy Land depended now upon

herself.   Cyrus is named as her deliverer, and is
described as already called upon his career and
blessed with victory by Jahweh.   Nor is all this
predicted as if from the standpoint of a previous
century; but it is taken for granted as the very
basis of the prophet's argument.   Cyrus himself is not merely represented to be above the
horizon and upon the flowing tide of victory, as
a prophet might possibly realise him to be before
he actually appeared.   But he and his victories
are appealed to as the unmistakeable proof that
former prophecies of Israel's deliverance from
Babylon are at last being fulfilled.   Would it
have been possible for the prophet to make such
an appeal, either to Israel or to the heathen, unless Cyrus had been within the ken of them both?
Unless Cyrus and his early victories were already
historical facts, the whole argument in Isaiah xl.–
xlviii. is unintelligible.   You observe, then, that
all this criticism which assigns these chapters to
the eve of the Return from Exile is historical,
and is independent of the literary analysis of
the text, which, however, greatly corroborates it.
Moreover, except for the date of Cyrus, which
is determined by the cuneiform inscriptions, the
historical evidence in question is drawn entirely
from the Bible itself.

Let us take from the historical books one other
example of the same method.   There is no Book
in the Old Testament, whose place in the Canon

and whose value as a record of historical fact have
been rendered more precarious by criticism than
the Books of Chronicles. These two books,
which are really one, include the same period,
whose history is related in the Books of Samuel
and of Kings. They treat many of the same
episodes and of the same personalities. But they
treat these with a great difference. For the
details I must refer you to the article by
Professor Francis Brown in Hastings's *Bible
Dictionary*.[1] For our present purpose it is
sufficient to point out that, when the parallel
narratives in Samuel-Kings and in Chronicles
are compared, it is found that the Chronicler
has increased the numbers of the troops engaged in the campaigns described, of the men
slain, and of the slaves, the cattle and the
objects of value taken captive or brought as
tribute to the victors; that he has enhanced
the characters of some of the leading personalities, like David and Solomon; and that he
has imputed to the period of the Monarchy the
establishment and elaboration of all the ritual
and the law enforced by the Priestly Document.
This comparison with Samuel-Kings makes it
at once evident that we cannot accept the
Chronicler as an authority for the pre-exilic
history of Israel, but must consider his Book

[1] See also the article in the *Encyc. Biblica*; and Robertson
Smith, *The Old Testament in the Jewish Church*, pp. 140 ff.

as a homiletic treatment of that history from
the standpoint of generations after the Exile,
when the Priestly Legislation had so long been
in force that it was impossible to imagine any
part of Israel's history as without it.[1]

These are such fundamental and such obvious
instances of the results of modern criticism upon
the Old Testament that I am almost ashamed
to bring them before you. But the repetition
of them is rendered necessary, not only by the
common opinion of a large portion of the Church,
but by the assertions of scholars I have named
and of a number of other writers, that modern
criticism is mainly dependent upon the precarious methods of literary analysis. How amply
the instances quoted disprove this, and how fully
they discover the main conclusions of critics to
be based upon historical evidence derived from
the Old Testament itself, I do not require further
to demonstrate.

III. *Criticism and Archæology.*

Hitherto we have looked only at the evidence
which criticism finds within the sacred records of
Israel. But our century has been one not only of
Biblical research, but of the discovery and examination of the histories and religions of the peoples
who surrounded Palestine and who were one

---

[1] Cf. Robertson Smith, *op. cit.*, p. 140.

with ancient Israel in blood, custom and mental equipment. Sixty or seventy years ago almost our sole record for the history of the world, of which the kingdom of Israel formed a small province, was the Old Testament. But now — in Babylonia, Egypt and Phœnicia; in Bashan, Moab, Edom and Sinai; in Central and Southern Arabia — there have been unearthed and deciphered a vast multitude of monuments which not only afford us the most ample material for testing the chronology of the Old Testament, and defining the exact nature of many of the historical events in it, but which have uncovered to us the civilisation and religion of the tribes who were Israel's neighbours and Israel's kinsmen according to the flesh. With all this evidence we can compare, in Arabia and Syria, the still current life of tribes of the same race in the same natural environment. It will be obvious how all this archæology and ethnology must enable criticism to attack the chief of the problems bequeathed by the New Testament: the problem of tracing throughout the Old Testament a progressive revelation. That, however, forms the subject of another lecture; and I will now consider only the general attitude of recent criticism to all the historical and archæological evidence which has been gathered from fields outside the Old Testament.

Of recent years the conclusions of the Higher

Criticism have been attacked in the name of
archæology, and by none with more persistence
than the two eminent scholars I have named:
Professor Sayce and Professor Hommel. They
have asserted that ' archæology is on the side of
tradition and not of the critics,' [1] upon the cardinal
question of the Old Testament: the dates and
composition of the Hexateuch. And, as proof of
this, they have alleged what they call ' the re-
luctance of the critics to accept the discoveries
of the archæologists.'   Let us inquire what
grounds there are for these charges.

Criticism, as we have seen, has discovered four
main documents in the Hexateuch, which it has
assigned to various dates from the ninth or eighth
to the sixth or fifth centuries before Christ.
Professor Sayce's argument appears to be that
this conclusion is largely due to the critics' belief
that the art of writing was not practised in Israel
till about David's time, or the end of the eleventh
century before Christ, and that till then legislation and tradition were only oral. In disproof
of such a belief Professor Sayce appeals to the
so-called Tell el Amarna letters. These clay
tablets, which date from about 1400 B.C., or more
than a century before the commonly received
date of the Exodus, represent a frequent and
detailed correspondence between the court of
Egypt on the one hand and its representatives

[1] Sayce, *Cont. Rev.*, vol. lxx., 1896, p. 730.

in Palestine and the rulers of the kingdoms of Mesopotamia on the other. The writing is in the cuneiform character, and the language that of Babylonia. The tablets, therefore, prove that some of the culture of Babylonia, perhaps even including its literature, had spread across the whole of Western Asia, at least a century before the Exodus. From this Professor Sayce infers that the Israelites, when in the land of Goshen and upon their wanderings through the Desert, must have known how to read and write, must have been acquainted with Babylonian literature, and must have been able to appreciate and make use of Babylonian documents, the translation of some of which he thinks can be identified in portions of the Book of Genesis.

Now, in the first place, it is necessary to note that the Tell el Amarna letters are only the documents of high Egyptian or Mesopotamian officials, and of chiefs of settled tribes in Palestine ; and that to argue from their habits to those of a semi-nomadic race, such as Israel were still in Goshen and the Desert, is not very safe.[1] But

[1] As has often been pointed out, the tribes which live to-day on the borders of Egypt and Canaan, half-settled and half-nomadic, do not, for all their contact with the civilised and half-civilised populations of these lands, learn to read and write. Reading and writing are arts, of which the Bedawee tribes do not see the need, and frequently despise. From the culture and habits of correspondence of the court of Egypt and its representatives in Canaan, it is very little less difficult to infer that the Israelite shepherds could write, than to employ the existence of the postal system

suppose we admit that the chiefs of Israel were
in official contact with the Egyptian authorities
during Israel's residence in Goshen, and that they
did learn from their employment in the building
operations of Pharaoh the arts of reading and
writing which were so highly developed in Egypt.
Suppose that we grant (and I for one am not
inclined to deny this) that there were leaders in
Israel at the time of the Exodus who could write,
or have writings made for them, just as Abd-hiba
of Jerusalem and other petty chieftains of Palestine
did.   We have not, therefore, proved that the documents which compose the Pentateuch were written
in the time of Moses.   We have not secured one
iota of evidence to counterbalance the proofs,
derived from the history of Israel itself, that the
Pentateuchal legislation was not in existence in
the time of the Judges or of the earlier Kings.
Few critics have committed themselves to the
absolute negative, that early Israel did not know
how to write; nor do any of the arguments for
the late date of the Hexateuch rest upon a reason
which, even if it were probable, is so impossible
to prove.

The other discoveries of archæologists which
have to do with the Pentateuch are the Babylonian tablets — with stories of the Creation and

and telegraph in the Turkish Empire and the dominions of the
Khedive to illustrate the culture of the nomads in the deserts
which lie on their borders.

Flood, or with annals which cover the events
described in Genesis xiv. — and the Egyptian
monuments which depict the conditions of life
reflected in the story of Joseph. We have not
now to consider how far the evidence furnished
by all these proves the historical value of the
Pentateuch. That question will come up in next
Lecture. Our present inquiry is, how far the
Babylonian and Egyptian monuments affect the
conclusions of critics with regard to the dates of
the Pentateuchal documents.

The Babylonian stories of the Creation and
Flood were probably in existence by a very
early date.[1] At the Oriental Congress in Paris
in 1897 it was announced that Father Scheil had
discovered on a tablet from Sippara of date
about 2250 B.C. a recension of the Babylonian
story of the Flood. This has evidently been
copied from a still older tablet, for here and
there the scribe has inserted the word 'lacuna.'
The story of the Flood may, therefore, be carried
back as far as 3000 B.C. But however early be
its date or the dates of the various versions of
the Creation-Epos, it is evident that they can

[1] In the British Museum we find them on tablets from the
Royal Library at Nineveh of the eighth and seventh centuries B.C.
See the newly issued *Guide to the Babylonian and Assyrian Collections* (1900), pp. 36 ff. For translations see *Records of the Past*,
new series, vol. i. 122 ff., by Prof. Sayce; Gunkel's *Schöpfung u.
Chaos*, pp. 401 ff. by Zimmern; and *Authority and Archæology*,
ed. by D. G. Hogarth (London, 1899), pp. 10 ff.

have no bearing on the question of the dates of
the Hebrew documents, — whether the Jahwist-
Elohist or the Priestly, — which contain accounts
of the Creation and Flood founded on the Babylonian. We are ignorant of the time at which
the Hebrews received these stories; while in their
Biblical form they exhibit so many differences
from the Babylonian as to make it probable
that the materials were used by the writers of
the Pentateuchal documents only after long
tradition within a Hebrew atmosphere.

Nor in the light which the monuments throw
upon Genesis xiv. is there any evidence as to
when that chapter was written. We are still without the proof that its accounts of Babylonian
campaigns are confirmed by Babylonian annals
dealing with the same events; and even if we
had this proof, there would remain the possibility, for which there is some evidence, that
Genesis xiv. is a Hebrew fragment from the
Exile based on Babylonian materials. In any
case this chapter cannot be used in the discussion
of the critical conclusions as to the date of the
four main constituents of the Hexateuch, for it
lies outside them all.[1]

Again, the portrait of Egyptian life presented
by the story of Joseph in the Jahwist-Elohist

[1] Full statements and discussions of the Babylonian evidence
as to the names, etc., in Gen. xiv. will be found in Driver's
Authority and Archæology, pp. 39 ff., and in article ' Chedorlaomer '
in the *Encyclopædia Biblica*. See below, p. 100.

document has been appealed to, as proof that the writer lived at a time when Israel, from their long residence in Goshen, were still familiar with Egypt. But the life, which the story of Joseph portrays, was the life of Egypt not only in Joseph's time. In the same moulds it persisted for centuries after the Exodus, and under the Monarchy Israel had many opportunities of becoming acquainted with it. So that the vivid and accurate descriptions of Egypt, which surround the figure of Pharaoh's Hebrew vizier, are no conclusive proof of the ancient origin of the document which tells the story. On the contrary, the only Egyptian data in that story to which archæologists can attach an approximate age, appear to offer some confirmation of the late period to which critics have assigned the Jahwist-Elohist document. The Egyptian names Zaphenath-Pa'aneah, Potipherah, and Asenath belong to types of names which do not appear, or are not frequent, on the Egyptian monuments till some centuries after the Exodus.[1]

---

[1] The type to which Zaphenath-Pa'aneah belongs occurs first under the Twentieth Dynasty in the thirteenth century B.C., and is frequent only under the Twenty-second in the tenth century. The type to which Potipherah belongs appears in one instance under the Eighteenth Dynasty, though not then attached to a native Egyptian, and otherwise occurs first under the Twenty-second Dynasty, but is not frequent till the Twenty-sixth, 664–525 B.C. The type to which Asenath belongs has a few early instances, but is frequent only under the Twenty-first Dynasty, in the eleventh century and later.

From these facts, reached in complete independence of criticism, the Egyptologists ' Steindorff, Brugsch, and Ebers all agree in inferring that the names in question did not originate before the Ninth Century B.C.' [1] But if this be so, the only archæological evidence which proves anything with regard to the dates of the Hexateuchal documents points in the same direction as the critical arguments which assign the Jahwist-Elohist to the ninth or the eighth century.

Before we leave the Hexateuch let me call your attention to the fact that the critical theory of its compilation from several sources receives one strong confirmation from the archæological side. Professor Sayce himself admits that such a compilation is ' fully in accordance with the teachings of Oriental archæology,' which has shown us that the ancient writings of the neighbours and kinsfolk of Israel were also of a composite character. Let me quote his own words: ' The composite character of the Pentateuch, therefore, is only what a study of similar contemporaneous literature brought to light by modern research would lead us to expect.' [2] And it is remarkable that Professor Sayce, who has so strenuously assailed the conclusions of critics with regard to the Pentateuch, should admit that

[1] Driver, article 'Joseph' in Hastings's *Bible Dictionary*, ii. 775.
[2] *Monuments*, pp. 31, 34 ; cf. *History of the Hebrews*, p. 129.

the Book of Joshua, the supplement and appendix of the Pentateuch, is a composite document with conflicting accounts of the conquest and settlement of Canaan.[1]

Beyond the Hexateuch there is little necessity to follow the critics in their attitude to archæology. The critics cannot be charged with neglecting the long series of Assyrian annals which bear upon the history of the Kings of Israel and Judah, from Omri to Zedekiah. I need only point out how far these annals confirm the critical estimate of the Books of Kings. The earliest Hebrews named on the Assyrian monuments are Omri and Ahab; from them onwards we have among others the names of Ben-hadad, Ahab's Syrian contemporary, of Jehu, Hazael, Pekah, Ahaz and Hezekiah. Pestilences and eclipses are recorded, the tremors of which vibrate through the early prophetical books. We have an account of the invasion of Palestine by Tiglath Peleser, *when he brought into contempt the land of Zebulun and the land of Naphtali, by the way of the sea across Jordan, Galilee of the Gentiles*; the overthrow of Samaria by Sargon; Sennacherib's invasion of Syria, his appearances before Jerusalem, the tribute he exacted, and his disappearance northwards. But criticism has never doubted those

[1] *History of the Hebrews*, ch. iv. ; see above in this Lecture, pp. 47 f.

E

names or these facts. It has recognised that
the Books of Kings were compiled from true
and in many cases contemporaneous annals.
What critics have judged to be late and probably of less historic value has been certain
narratives, for which archæology has no evidence
to offer, as well as the framework, in which
the editor has bound the whole history and
supplied, out of a general scheme, a chronology, and, from the standpoint of a later age,
a religious sentence on each monarch's reign.[1]
Now, remarkably enough, archæology has confirmed this judgement of criticism on the Books
of Kings, so far as regards the chronology. For
while testifying to the reality of Omri, Ahab,
Jehu, and some of their successors, as well as of
the leading events of the history, it has shown
from the contemporary Assyrian data that the
chronology, approximately correct so far as the
distance of one man or event from another is
concerned, has been placed by the editor from
one dozen to twenty years too early — obviously
in order to fit it into the general system, adopted
by the Hebrew editors, of reckoning the years
from the Exodus to the fall of the first Temple
and the Return from Exile.[2]

[1] For this chronology see next Lecture. The moral and
religious judgements of each reign are from the standpoint of
Deuteronomy, which, as we have seen, did not come into force
in Israel till 621 B.C. under King Josiah.

[2] See Kampfhausen, *Chronologie der hebraischen Könige*, 1883;
Robertson Smith, *Prophets*, pp. 144 ff.

So much for archæology and its relations to criticism. ' The fact is,' as Professor Driver says,[1] 'the antagonism which some writers have sought to establish between criticism and archæology is wholly factitious and unreal. Criticism and archæology deal with antiquity from different points of view, and mutually supplement one another. Each in turn supplies what the other lacks; and it is only by an entire misunderstanding of the scope and limits of both that they can be brought into antagonism with one another. What is called " the witness of the monuments " is often strangely misunderstood. The monuments witness to nothing which any reasonable critic has ever doubted. . . . A great deal of the illustration afforded by the monuments relates to facts of language, to ideas, institutions, and localities; but these as a rule are of a permanent nature; and until they can be proved to be *limited* to a particular age their occurrence, or mention, in a given narrative is not evidence that it possesses the value of contemporary testimony.'

The alleged refutation of criticism by archæology may therefore be dismissed, and we pass to another which has been drawn from the sphere of geography. It is often maintained that the accuracy of the topographical data on the Book of Genesis is proof of the truthfulness of the

---

[1] *Authority and Archæology*, p. 150 f.

narratives in which they appear. 'But,' as I have said elsewhere,[1] 'that a story accurately reflects geography does not necessarily mean that it is a real transcript of history — else were the Book of Judith the truest man ever wrote instead of being, what it is, a pretty piece of fiction. Many legends are wonderful photographs of scenery, and therefore let us at once admit that while we may have other reasons for the historical truth of the patri- archal narratives, we cannot prove this on the ground that their itineraries and place-names are correct.'

On the other hand, for the same reason — that the topography of Palestine changed so little during the course of the history of Israel — it will be obvious that geography cannot be of much use in the support of the critical conclusions as to the dates of the documents. The only cases in which it can afford any evidence of these, are where documents, judged by critics to be late on other grounds, contain geographical names, or applications of geographical names, which are themselves of a late origin. For instance, the mountains of Moab are called in the Priestly Document, which recent critics date after the Exile, *the mountains of the Abarim*. Abarim means 'the men or things on the other side,' and there is some evidence that before the Exile the name was applied to the whole mountain-range

---

[1] *Historical Geography of the Holy Land*, p. 108.

east of Jordan.[1] But the post-Exilic writer limited
it to the mountains of Moab, because in his day
these were the only part of the eastern range
which was opposite the shrunken territory of
his people. Again, it appears that the name
Euphrates occurs first in the writings of Jeremiah;[2] in the historical and prophetical books
before his time we hear only of 'the River.'[3]
Now look at the documents of the Hexateuch.
In the Jahwist and Elohist, which critics date
before Jeremiah, the stream is called 'the River';
in Deuteronomy (from Jeremiah's time) and in the
Priestly Writing[4] (from the time of the Exile) it
is called Euphrates. Such is the kind of small
symptoms, which geography supplies, of the
truth of the critical conclusions as to the date
of the Hexateuchal documents. With regard to
the literary analysis of these documents, the
geographical evidence, though still not large, is
quite as decisive. The same localities are called
in the different documents by different names,

[1] Jer. xxii. 20, R. V.; Ezek. xxxix. 11 (reading with Hitzig and
others 'Abārîm' for 'Oberîm'). See further article 'Abarim'
by the present writer in the *Encyclopædia Biblica*.

[2] Jeremiah xiii. 4–7.

[3] 2 Sam. viii. 3 (Kethibh), x. 16; 1 Kings iv. 21, 24 (Heb. v. 1,
4), xiv. 15; Isa. vii. 20; and even Jer. ii. 18, and Micah vii. 12.

[4] 'The River,' Gen. xxxi. 21 (J. E.); Exod. xxiii. 31; Num.
xxii. 5; Josh. xxiv. 2 f. (all E.). 'The great River, the River
Euphrates,' Gen. xv. 18 (D.) (Red, according to Ball); Deut. i.
7; Josh. i. 4 (D.); cf. Deut. xi. 24; 'Euphrates,' Gen. ii. 14
(P.); cf. Jer. xlvi. 2, 6, 10, li. 63; 2 Kings xxiii. 29, xxiv. 7; the
gloss to 2 Sam. viii. 3; and in Chronicles and Apocrypha.

and this with a remarkable consistence to which there are but one or two exceptions.[1]

The geographical evidence, then, so far as it goes, does not contradict but supports the critical analysis of the documents and the critical conclusions as to their dates.

We have now examined the various charges made against the modern criticism of the Old Testament and have found them baseless. That criticism does not depend mainly on linguistic analysis, but still more on historical evidence furnished by the Old Testament itself: the con-

---

[1] *E.g.* for instance in the Jahwist and Priestly Documents the mountain of the Law is always *Sinai*, but in the Elohist and Deuteronomist always *Horeb*, as it is also in a narrative of 1 Kings, ch. xix., which is from the northern kingdom like the Elohist; and in Mal. iv. 2, in which prophet the influence of Deuteronomy is often felt. Notice that Deuteronomy xxxiii. 2, in which Sinai occurs, is assigned on other grounds to the Jahwist. Again, the mountain which Moses ascended in Moab is called *Pisgah* by the Elohist (Num. xxi. 20, xxiii. 14), and by the Deuteronomist (Deut. iii. 17, 27, iv. 49, xxxiv. 1 (?), Josh. xii. 3). Once perhaps the Priestly Writer uses the name (Josh. xiii. 20), but this instance may be Deuteronomic. The Priestly Writer names it *Nebo*. Again, the glen beneath Pisgah, in which Israel camped, before descending into the valley of the Jordan, is called *the glen that is in the field of Moab* by the Elohist (Num. xxi. 20), but in the Deuteronomist *the glen that is opposite Beth-peor* (Deut. iii. 29, iv. 46, xxxiv. 6). The Elohist calls the site of Israel's camp before crossing the Jordan *the field* or *territory of Moab* (Num. xxi. 20), but the Priestly Writer always speaks of it as the *plains* or *steppes of Moab*. Again, the Elohist gives one list of stations on Israel's route through Moab (Num. xxi. 13–20), the Priestly Writer gives another (Num. xxxiii. 44–49).

clusions are not refuted, but to a remarkable extent corroborated, by the evidence of archæology and geography. We have examined the methods and the general course of criticism. We have seen how thoroughly tested and how firmly based are its main results. But in truth no general account of the critical movement can do justice to its argument. In the case of the Hexateuch we must take the text itself and prove the critical analysis verse by verse. If we do so, we shall often indeed be puzzled by details, for which there is no complete explanation on any theory whatsoever. But gradually the characteristic phraseology, favourite interests, religious conceptions and historical traditions of four main documents will fall apart, all the more distinct that they often present the same subjects or events in different ways; and we shall be convinced that we are in touch, not with phantasms of modern scholarship, but with ancient realities — the original constituents of our curiously composite Scriptures. Discrepancies, fatal to the traditional theory, will explain themselves: the history, instead of being full of contradictions, will fall into the lines of a reasonable development, and the Divine education of Israel become more apparent than ever. The other subject of criticism — the exact dates of the different documents, *in the form in which we have them* — may not be so clear to us: we will sympathise with the difference of opinion about these that exists among critics themselves; and we will even keep in mind what some critics forget, that having fastened the present form of a document to an approximate date, we have not therefore prejudiced the question of the earlier origin of some of its contents.

Reviewing the whole of this Lecture, we may say that Modern Criticism has won its war against the Traditional Theories. It only remains to fix the amount of the indemnity.

LECTURE III

THE HISTORICAL BASIS IN THE OLD TESTAMENT

In last Lecture I said that the battle of modern criticism with the traditional theories of the Old Testament had been fought and won; and that it only remains to discuss the indemnity. What do the results of criticism cost? To this question we must now address ourselves.

We have admitted the liberty and duty of criticism. We have found its methods reasonable and carefully wrought. We have seen that its main conclusions rest upon literary and historical facts furnished by the Old Testament itself, and are supported by the evidences of archæology and geography, so far as these go: that, in short, they are as solid as the results can be of a science at work upon so remote a period of history. We have now to ask, what does criticism leave to us in the Old Testament: how much true history and how much Divine Revelation? Of these two questions the chief, of course, is the latter, but as the answer to it partly depends on the answer to the former we must take that first: how much true history has criticism left to us in the Old Testament?

Though this is actually the less important of the two questions (for Revelation is not coincident with actual history [1]), I suspect that it is the one which the preacher or teacher of to-day finds the more urgent and embarrassing. He remembers how through the Old Testament our fathers pursued their expositions and homilies, unhampered by any doubt of the events or personalities which they encountered. To them men behaved and spoke exactly as the sacred text describes. And hence, he will say, sprang not only the dramatic power of the best preaching from the Old Testament, but the greater part of its spiritual influence. Let us put aside in the meantime the cardinal facts of Israel's national history, whether what we call miraculous or not, for on these the greatest Christian preachers did not linger, and let us take the inimitable portraiture which the Old Testament contains. From the time of the author of the Epistle to the Hebrews onwards to the generation before our own, it has been among the personal characters of Israel's history that the greatest preachers in the English language have found much of their richest material and strongest inspiration. Men of such various schools as Sterne — for the author

[1] See below, p. 89, and in Lecture VIII. on Job.

of *Tristram Shandy* was also among the prophets — Butler, Foster, Maurice, Kingsley, Newman, Robertson of Brighton, Candlish, Arnot,
Spurgeon, and Beecher, have all used the Old
Testament chiefly for its characters. Who does
not remember how searching Butler is upon
Balaam, and how impressive Newman is upon
Saul! Some of Sterne's sermons, which he
characteristically offers to his fashionable sub-
scribers as a few reflections on the present state
of society — and, by the way, Sterne's sermons
are worth reading for their unconventional style
and frequent fitness of phrase — are clever ex-
posures of the weaknesses of that human nature
which patriarchs, prophets and kings shared
with ourselves. Robertson of Brighton, whose
strong moral sense and power of analysis found
full scope in the Old Testament, was busy with
its dramas of character to trace the endlessness
of sin and to illustrate how the Divine forgiveness
does not necessarily remove the earthly consequences of human crime. So with a host of
other men. It was, I say, not the miracles of
Old Testament history nor the national events,
upon which the preaching of our fathers fed and
grew strong, but the personal elements; the
development of character, the moral struggles,
checks, catastrophes and recoveries, in which so
many Books of the Old Testament are so very
rich.

'But we,' the modern preacher may say; 'how are we to imitate our predecessors? The strong, confident preaching you describe was all achieved before the influence of modern criticism had reached the pulpit. With perhaps some slight exceptions in the case of Maurice, who felt the issues raised by Colenso but was not greatly affected by them, none of the preachers you have named can be examples to us in the altered conditions of Old Testament study. We know that doubt has been cast by criticism upon large portions of the history to which these moral dramas have been assigned by the Old Testament records. We have heard that some of the stories are as legendary as those of Prometheus and Hercules, and that many of the characters portrayed are but the personifications of the genius and temper of the tribes of which they are represented as the ancestors.' It is not too much to say that such considerations have led to a kind of panic among preachers; and that some have abandoned incontinently whole provinces of their subject, in which in days gone by the Christian pulpit found many of its noblest themes and strongest motives.

In this somewhat disorderly retreat from the great sources of our art, the first thing to rally our minds is to remember how small a portion, after all, of the Old Testament has been affected. I shall be careful in the following estimate to go

not merely to the limit of my own opinion of
what actual history has been left to us, but as far
as the majority of advanced critics have ventured
within the last ten years; because it is needful
that the possible worst should be clearly defined.
Even then the amount of the history and narrative, which criticism has rendered uncertain, is
by no means so great as is usually feared.

Let us leave the Pentateuch till afterwards, and
begin now from the settlement in Canaan. There
are few critics who doubt the authenticity of
Deborah's song, and none who refuse to take it
as a reliable account of the events which it cele-
brates. So will the main facts of Gideon's
career, for the account of which more than one
story has been used; [1] the story of Abimelech; [2]
the occupation of Laish by Dan,[3] and part of the
tragedy in Benjamin.[4] Except some eccentric and
unfollowed critics, no one doubts that with the
time of Samuel we at last enter real and indubitable history. This very great man's influence on
Israel; his genius in swaying the new prophetic
movement, so strange to the sober traditions of
his own office, in selecting Saul and in launching
the large but sluggish powers of the son of Kish
upon so powerful a movement, are not only facts,
but facts of obvious value to the preacher. It
is quite true (as I said in last Lecture) that the

---

[1] Judg. vi–ix.　　　　　[2] Judg. ix.
[3] Judg. xviii.　　　　　[4] Judg. xix–xxi.

Books of Samuel and Kings are composed of
narratives of very various worth. Some are
plainly of an age long subsequent to the events
they describe; there has been time for later
conceptions to mingle with the facts on which
they are based. But others are contemporary,
or nearly contemporary, documents, and in selecting these, as any modern translation or commentary will enable him to do,[1] and in employing
them, the preacher may be as sure that he is
dealing with facts as his predecessors of a less
critical age. Nay more, he will find that criticism
has brought him a certain amount of relief from
difficulties which embarrassed his fathers in their
study and presentation of the sacred history.
That relief is of two kinds, both of which I may
illustrate from the story of David.

We who have reached middle life can remember what time and anxiety the pastors of our
boyhood used to expend upon the double and
sometimes contradictory stories of David's life ;
for instance, the two very different accounts of
his first introduction to Saul. Their attempts
to reconcile these involved — even when one
thought that they succeeded — so much intricate
explanation as to distract them from the clear

---

[1] Like Kautzsch's German translation, for instance, or those
in English, edited by Haupt in the *Sacred Books of the Old Testament;* or the volumes of the *International Critical Commentary*,
by Professor H. P. Smith on Samuel, and by Professor Francis
Brown on Kings (the latter not yet published).

presentation of the moral issues, which it was their first duty as preachers to present and enforce to their people. But they did not succeed. The stories are irreconcileable. What an advantage, then, has the preacher of to-day who can frankly say: 'These are two different traditions of the same event,' and confine himself to the rich material and moral issues of the one or the other!

Or take an instance where the relief afforded by criticism to the preacher is of a moral rather than of an intellectual kind. The character of David was one of the most complex ever possessed by man. His temper was not only ambitious and cruel. It was disfigured by some of the most ferocious traits which are characteristic of his race; for ferocity the Semites have always been notorious. But in the large heart of David there also stirred emotions of an opposite quality: the feeling for greatness in others, even when they hunted him as did Saul, whom he spared, and on whom, though Saul had been his persecutor and implacable foe, he wrote the greatest of all elegies; [1] his generosity and quickness to forgive, as in Saul's case and Shimei's; his noble penitence when his sin was brought home to him; the carriage of his soul in the days of disaster; his chivalry towards the captains who brought him water from the well of Bethlehem at the risk of their lives. Criticism finds no

[1] See Lecture V. on 'The Spirit of Christ in the Old Testament.'

objection to many of the priceless narratives which
have rendered such virtues immortal. Moreover,
it has cleared the old age of David from a blot
by which, if you adhere, with tradition, to the
truth of every part of his biography, all these
victories of his character are robbed of their
splendour.[1] You remember the second chapter of
First Kings, and David's charge to Solomon, when
the days drew nigh that he should die: how he,
a dying man, commanded his son not to let the
hoar head of Joab, his lifelong comrade and lieu-
tenant, go down to the grave in peace; and, in
spite of the oath by which he had generously for-
given Shimei, to slay that spiteful and cowardly person. *Behold there is with thee Shimei son of Gera,
the Benjamite of Bahurim, who cursed me with a
grievous curse in the day when I went to Maha-
naim; but he came down to meet me at Jordan and
I sware to him by Jahweh, saying, I will not put
thee to death with the sword. Now therefore hold
him not guiltless, for thou art a wise man: and
thou wilt know what thou oughtest to do with
him — thou shalt bring his hoar head down to
the grave with blood. And David slept with his
fathers, and was buried in the city of David.*

These are horrible words to be the last of such
a life: horrible words clothing a horrible spirit.
But this is just one of the passages in David's

[1] 1 Kings ii. esp. 2–9: cf. Cheyne, *Aids to Devout Study of
Criticism*, 63 ff.

biography, which, upon linguistic and other grounds, criticism has taught us to doubt. It is a late passage; it betrays the temper as well as the dialect of a legal school in Israel, which enforced the extermination of the enemies of the pious.[1] We have much reason, therefore, to let it go, and letting it go we remove, from the most interesting of Old Testament stories of character, a termination which saddens every charm and blights every promise revealed by its previous progress.

These instances must suffice for the reigns of Saul, David and Solomon, as recounted in the Books of Samuel and Kings.[2] I have already shown that criticism accepts the official annals of their successors, but that personal narratives have mingled with these, and that the religious judgement passed on each reign has been entered by an editor writing from the later standpoint of Deuteronomy.[3] Among the personal narratives which thus mingle with the official annals, the greatest are those of Elijah and Elisha.

The story of Elijah (1 Kings xvii.–xix., xxi.,

[1] Verses 2–4 are plainly, from their language, by a Deuteronomic Redactor, therefore later than the seventh century. The king, as pictured in verses 5–9, is quite incompatible with the picture of him given in the previous chapter ; and the author of the rest of the chapter, verses 13–46, could not have known of verses 5–9, for he gives other grounds for the slaughter of Joab.

[2] The late and less trustworthy accounts in Chronicles have already been treated. See Lecture 11., pp. 55 f.

[3] See pp. 65 f.

F

and 2 Kings i., ii.), cannot be much later than a century after Elijah himself.[1] If some of the colossal elements of this prophet's fame be of posthumous growth, they not only prove how immense the man and his work must have been, but they reveal one of its chief qualities and they do not disguise the rest. The God of Elijah appears in overwhelming physical manifestations — as the Lord of drought and famine, of the cloud, the rain and the fire. He calls his prophet from the solitudes of nature and His hand makes His servant run and leap before the King's chariot across the whole length of Esdraelon. Such elements in the prophet's sympathy are conspicuous in other Semitic religions and are those on which the popular imagination would most naturally fasten. But they do not submerge other and higher religious interests. Elijah's jealousy for his God is not accounted for by explaining the contest of his time as one between the nearly equal religions of two Semitic tribes. Elijah's zeal is inexplicable unless it was inspired by a conviction of the unique character of Jahweh; his intolerance of foreign deities must have had ethical reasons. Such a conclusion is not only

---

[1] For the Northern Kingdom from which it sprang — (notice especially how Elijah goes to seek Jahweh not where the Judæan Amos hears his voice in Jerusalem, but at Horeb)—came to an end in 721, and was in dire trouble by 735. Elijah flourished *c.* 860.

in line with the general development of Israel's
religion [1] and supported by all we know of the
rival Semitic faiths, but sustained by the story
itself. According to this, Elijah enforced the
claims of Jahweh in independence of the nation ;
not only against the deities of Phœnicia but
against Ahab and Israel themselves. He predicted the employment of a foreign nation by
Jahweh to punish His own people. Finally, he
defended the rights of the common man against
the avarice of the king. The religious interest of
the narrative is of supreme significance. It is
the emphasis, by one who felt all the physical
wonder and force of the deity, of the indispensable ethical in religion. The former was
common to all the Semitic religions ; the latter
was the character of Israel's God alone. No
one therefore can doubt the historical reality of
Elijah or the quality of that service which
stamped him as the greatest prophet since
Moses. Elijah was great enough to combine
the physical and ethical significance of the
Godhead. But he is represented as arriving
only gradually at the full meaning of his message, and learning, through doubt and pain,
that the ethical is the greater.[2] From this,
too, we may infer the essentially historical
value of his story : it is further supported by
the saying attributed to him, *How long will*

[1] See next Lecture.　　　　　[2] Chap. xix.

ye limp between two opinions, and his sarcasms upon the Phœnician myths of Baal.[1] We would be foolish, indeed, to doubt the originality of these. For the rest, there is not a single feature in the story which can be identified as late, or which does not reflect, in some way, the religious conditions of Elijah's time.

No school of criticism denies the reality of Elisha, or of his services to Israel in the disastrous days of the border wars with the Arameans and their raids up to the very walls of the capital. It was his ceaseless vigilance upon the enemy, his unbroken hope for his people through their worst defeats, which won for the aged prophet from his king the high name of the *Chariot of Israel and the Horsemen thereof*.[2] But it would be equally impossible to prove the historical reality of the series of curious marvels attributed to Elisha from sources outside the annals of the Kings of Israel. These, however, are practically of no importance to the Christian preacher.

Such instances must suffice for the period of Israel's history from Samuel to the eve of the great prophets of the eighth century. From this onwards, the student of Scripture traverses

[1] xviii. 27.

[2] 2 Kings xiii. 14. Some critics have suggested that the name is a mere imitation of that already bestowed upon Elijah; but Elisha's services were such that more probably it was original in his case.

ground still more certain. The exceptions are
trifling so long as we keep to the Books of
Kings and the Prophets. Consider how all else
lies before us unquestioned by criticism. Unquestioned? I should rather say fortified, explored, illuminated, made habitable for modern
men. The labours of the prophets, the doom
and fall of Northern Israel, the carriage of Jerusalem through her awful crisis upon the solitary
faith of Isaiah; his victory; the reaction under
Manasseh, and the recrudescence of heathenism; the discovery of Deuteronomy and the
reforms of Josiah; [1] the confidence of the people
in an external righteousness and their disillusion-
ment by Josiah's tragic death at Megiddo; the
second reaction to heathenism under Jehoiakim;
the story of Judah's decline and fall; the story
of the Exile and of the Return; [2] the brilliant
hopes and their disappointment; the struggle,
with foreign tyrants and native traitors, for the
nation's purity and loyalty to God; the growth
of legalism and of the sweet personal piety
which grew behind the Law like a garden of
lilies within a hedge of thorns; the story of
the Diaspora and of contact with alien systems
of culture and religion; the story of righteous

[1] On the exact amount of these consult a good commentary
on Kings.
[2] On the exact nature of this and the questions which still
divide critics, see *Book of the Twelve Prophets*, vol. ii. chap. xvi.

suffering in meditation upon its meaning; the
rise of speculation and of the schools of teachers,
who applied the fear of Jahweh and the wisdom
which springs from it to the everyday life of
men.   No historical criticism can take away
these fields from the preacher of to-day.   Across
them he may move with all the confidence and
boldness of the fathers — nay, with more fresh-
ness, more insight, more agility, for the text is
clearer, the discrepancies explained, the allusions
better understood, and all the old life re-
quickened out of which those prophets and
reformers, those psalmists and wise men, with
all their literature, originally sprang.

Before we go back to the Hexateuch there
are two questions about the historical character
of portions of the literature which we have been
surveying that demand some special notice —
the authorship of the Psalms and the character
of the Book of Jonah.

On the former of these this is not the place
to go into details.   But I may say summarily,
that while it is impossible to conceive of so
mobile and vibrant a heart as David's, so bold
and musical a skill, as never stirred to the
praise of his nation's God in an age when the
secular and the religious were one; and while
the King's fame as the father of sacred min-
strelsy appears inexplicable unless he actually
composed some hymns; yet recent criticism has

tended to confirm the impossibility of proving any given psalm in our Psalter to have been by David.[1] 'The Psalter is the hymn-book of the second Temple' at least five hundred years after David passed away. No reliance can be placed upon the titles which its editors have prefixed to individual psalms.[2] And although it is possible, and I think on the whole certain, that the Psalter contains pre-Exilic elements — for it is hardly conceivable that lyrical expressions of the teaching of the great prophets were not preserved in Israel — yet, like all other religious poetry, that of Israel suffered such changes in its tradition and in its adaptation to use in public worship, that we cannot with any certainty trace its various constituents to their personal origins.

But if such conclusions be inevitable, does the religious value of the Psalter suffer from them? I venture, from practical experience, to think that it does not. The criticism of the Psalms may rob the preacher of the right to use many of the

---

[1] See Robertson Smith, *Old Testament in the Jewish Church,*[2] vii.

[2] Some of them, like that of the 52nd, are so plainly unsuitable to the verses below them as to throw discredit on the rest; and as a matter of fact we know, from the titles given to the concluding Psalms in the Greek version but not found in the Hebrew, that the manufacture of titles was a process always going on, even after the Hebrew Canon closed, and based on pure conjecture. For a discussion of the whole subject see Robertson Smith, *op. cit.;* Cheyne, *The Origin of the Psalter*; Driver's *Introduction,*[6] chap. vii.; and on the other side Robertson's *Poetry and Religion of the Psalms:* Edinburgh, 1898.

incidents and personal experiences which have
lent picturesqueness to his preaching.   But, after
all, much of this is the mere confectionery of the
pulpit, fit only to spoil the appetite of the hearers
for the sincere milk of the word.   No denial of
Psalms to David or to Moses can diminish their
spiritual value as authentic expressions of the
human spirit on every level and under every
shadow of the Church's experience.   The detachment of the Psalms from this or that famous
figure in Israel's history will only leave us the
more free to appreciate their essential and un-
mitigated humanity, under the influence of God's
Spirit.   This is true even of such a Psalm as
the Fifty-first.   There is every reason to believe
the Psalm to be Exilic.[1]   Further, it is not the
acknowledgment by a single individual of an
extraordinary and revolting crime against some
fellow-creature, but the confession, on behalf
of the whole Church, of her inherent sinfulness
before God, and of her neglect of her mission to
the world.[2]   I do not ask you to accept this view

[1] The last two verses plainly fix the composition of the Psalm
in the days before sacrifices had been resumed on the Temple
altar and the walls of Jerusalem were still unbuilt.   For the proof
that these verses are from the same author as those which precede
them see Cheyne, *Origin of the Psalter ;* Robertson Smith, *The
Old Testament in the Jewish Church,* pp. 440 ff.; and compare
The Book of the Twelve Prophets, pp. 276 ff.

[2] Verse 4, ' *Against Thee, Thee only have I sinned and done
this evil in Thy sight,*' could hardly be said by David of his crime
against his fellow-man and woman (cf. also verse 3).   It is suitable
to the lips of the Exilic Church, who were suffering in Babylon

of the authorship and meaning of the Psalm. I
only desire you to perceive that it does not lessen
the religious value of the Psalm to the preacher
or to his people.

The Book of Jonah raises a larger question than
those of its own interpretation, but this is answered for us by Christ Himself. I said above that
Revelation is not coincident with actual history.
Christ has shown this by His parables; and the
only view of the story of Jonah, which does justice
to its teaching and explains its place in a Book
of prophetic discourses, is that which treats it not
as real history but as a sermon, in the form of
a parable, upon the great evangelical truth, that
*God has granted to the Gentiles also repentance
unto life.* This I have elsewhere sufficiently
proved and illustrated.[1]

There still remains the most difficult part of
our present task — the Hexateuch. We all know
that, from the time of the Epistle to the Hebrews
to the present day, the strong preaching from
the Old Testament, of which I have spoken, has
understood the narratives of the Pentateuch as
actual history. How has criticism affected our
materials here?

not because of their sins against that Empire, but because of their
sins against God. For the use of verse 5 by the Church, and not
by an individual, cf. Isaiah lxiii. 16 and John viii. 33 ff. For the
meaning of bloodguiltiness in verse 14*a* see its contrast in 13, 14*b*
and 15, the Church's duty of declaring God to sinners; and cf.
Ezekiel iii. 18 ff.

[1] *Book of the Twelve Prophets,* vol. ii., chaps. xxxiv.–xxxviii.

I propose to take the Book of Genesis, and
to examine first the part which opens with the
Creation and Fall of Man in the second chapter
and closes in the eleventh just before the call of
Abraham.

Here it is obvious that we do not have a transcript of actual history, in the narrower sense
of that word. This need scarcely be argued, but
we may take two points in illustration of it. The
Book of Genesis, by a careful chronology, carries
the human family back by named generations to
the creation of the first man, in 4219 B.C., or —
according to the Greek version which makes
the ages of the Patriarchs much greater at the
birth of their sons than the Hebrew does — to
5408. But recent discoveries, in Babylonia and
Egypt — the first of which we owe to American
and the second to British labours — prove that in
both of these great river-valleys man lived and
had already developed considerable culture at a
date long anterior to that assigned to his creation
by the Book of Genesis.[1] Again, the Book of

[1] The antiquity of human civilisation may not be so great as
some Assyriologists calculate, but on the very lowest reckoning it
preceded both of the Biblical dates for the Creation. An inscription of the Babylonian King Nabonidus, c. 550 B.C., states that
he restored the temple of Narâm-Sin, built 3200 years previously,
which would fix the date of Narâm-Sin at 3750 B.C., and this is
generally accepted by Assyriologists, who have not only found inscriptions of Sargon I., father of Narâm-Sin, but inscriptions of his
predecessors who, from the more primitive character of their writings, must have reigned about 500 years earlier, or say 4200, and
who had even then reached a stage of civilisation requiring many

Genesis fixes the building of the Tower of Babel in 2564 B.C., or, if we take the Greek data, in 3166, and asserts that till then the *whole earth was of one language and of one speech*. Yet we have discovered inscriptions in three languages, of different families, Sumerian, Babylonian and Egyptian, which are all earlier than either of these dates.[1] Clearly then, on this ground of chronology alone, we cannot regard the early chapters of Genesis as actual history.

In support of this conclusion, archæology provides us with further evidence. In Babylonian literature there are traditions of the origin of man, of Paradise and of the Flood, which bear, even in their details, a remarkable resemblance to the account of the same subjects in Genesis i.–ix. Critics are now generally agreed that the traditions reached Israel at an early age, and that,

previous centuries for its development. The ' 3200 years,' however, of Nabonidus' inscription is a suspiciously ' round ' number. It is a multiple of forty, a usual Semitic reckoning for a generation; eighty forties. If we take it as eighty generations and adopt the juster calculation of thirty-three years for a generation, this would give us instead of 3200 years only 2640; which would fix Narâm-Sin's date, instead of at 3750, at 3190 B.C. Now, no Babylonian sovereigns have yet been discovered between 2900 and the relics of Narâm-Sin. The later date for him is therefore not improbable. But even if we accept it, the beginnings of civilisation in Mesopotamia can hardly be placed after either of the Biblical dates of the Creation. — The inscription of Nabonidus is in the British Museum, No. 91, 109; see *Guide to the Bab. and Assyr. Room*, pp. 171 f. and Pl. xxx. Further see *The Babyl. Expedition of the Univ. of Pennsylvania* (1893, etc.), ed. by Hilprecht.

[1] See more fully Driver, *Authority* etc., p. 34.

along with other elements of Babylonian legend and mythology, they underwent considerable modification and gradually became, when perhaps all memory of their true origin was lost, part of the folk-lore of Canaan. The process probably extended through many centuries before the authors of these chapters of Genesis used them for a higher purpose. But this absence of history from the chapters, this fact that their framework is woven from the raw material of myth and legend, cannot discredit the profound moral and religious truths with which they are charged, any more than the cosmogony of his time, which Milton employs, impairs by one whit our spiritual indebtedness to *Paradise Lost.*

Nor (it is hardly necessary to add) does the legendary character of these stories altogether destroy their historical value. Anthropologists are of opinion that many of the legends and superstitions of a people spring from recollections of tribes who preceded them in the occupation of the land, and who either disappeared in some great catastrophe, or, before dying out, struggled for a time furtively and mysteriously in wilder parts of their ancient domain. Such recollections of early races appear to underlie the genealogies and primitive civilisations described in the first eleven chapters of Genesis; and they are still more apparent in the rest of the Hexateuch: in Israel's traditions of the

aboriginal tribes of Canaan and of the earliest
adventures of the families of Jacob.

Whatever may have been the historical and
literary origins of the narratives in Genesis of
primæval man, their ethical value to the preacher
is beyond all question. Look at the grandness
of the conception which dominates and employs
them. The Epic of Humanity in which they are
arranged begins with a vision of creation. It
traces the Divine purpose from the making of
man. It follows man from the dawn of the
moral sense through the elementary conflict of
passion with conscience, the growth of knowledge,
the necessity of labour, the beginnings of crime,
the rise of civilisation, the separation of the
peoples, the emergence at last of a chosen
people — chosen, be it observed, not for their own
salvation or their own glory but, as the epic
affirms, in order that in them all families of
mankind may be blessed.

Nor is this great epic only thus colossal in
conception. In insight it is equally profound.
I need not speak of the absence of national
narrowness from its account of the origin of the
race. Man is treated as man ; the great human
experiences of temptation and guilt, of desire
and labour and death, are brought before us with
a simplicity which too often hides from us the
depth and volume of their truth. Take the prose
poem of the Fall of Man in Paradise. It is usual

to call the morality of early Israel a purely tribal morality like that of all their Semitic kinsfolk. But the nation which produced this story almost certainly before 700 B.C., had already within it minds far advanced beyond the stage of a tribal morality.[1] The man who composed the third chapter of Genesis was not the simple scribe of some early traditions at which, in our superior wisdom, we can smile as at a story for children. He was the acute and faithful reader of his own heart, and, from whatever source you believe his inspiration to have been derived, you cannot gainsay the essential truthfulness of his account. He had grasped the relation of God to the individual, he was expert in the heart's experience of temptation: the mysterious connection between knowledge and the boldness to sin; the workings of conscience; the relation of guilt, if not to death, yet to the terror and curse of death. After all the centuries of man's acquaintance with himself, after all the analyses of philosophy and ethics, we have hardly reached deeper than this ancient examination of the mysteries and complications of the human heart.

But go a little further in this epic and you discover traces of a remarkable conception of history. Evil is followed out of the individual heart to its effects on the family, on the state and on civilisation. The Fall of the Man in the

---

[1] See below, next Lecture, pp. 133 ff.

garden is not the only Fall in the Book of Genesis, and every one of the others is traced to a similar source: the increase of knowledge and of power unaccompanied by reverence; the opening of the eyes to the desirable things of life which gradually come within reach of us all as the apple came within the reach of Eve. We have this presented to us in the form of several laborious cycles of progress, each ending in a colossal catastrophe. One of them relates the increase of mankind in numbers, their progress in intellectual and national power, their stagnancy in hate and the desire for vengeance.[1] Another tells us how men multiplied, how the pride and beauty of the race wedded with the sons of God, and wickedness became so great that God resolved to destroy man from the face of the earth.[2] Another describes the rise of architecture. Men settle in Shinar, they build cities, their art and their power increase, but their pride and impiety also, till God comes down and confounds the colossal and irreverent ambition of their works.[3] All three stories contain much legendary material from several different sources. Their authors have also been unable to throw off that fear of God, which is cast out only by the perfect love taught by Christ, and under which Pagan races have ever imagined the Deity to be jealous of the intellectual and material achievements of His

[1] Gen. iv.   [2] Gen. vi. ff.   [3] Gen. xi.

creatures. Yet in all the greater relief that they lie beneath so sombre a heaven, the noble and permanent lessons of the inspired author stand forth: that human genius and human wealth, if not accompanied by faith and obedience to God, mean the development of a fatal pride, whose end is the destruction of many individuals and the retardation of all human progress. Has this no inspiration for the modern preacher? Does it not present a truth conspicuously absent from some theories of evolution which inspire so much of the hopefulness and the pride of modern man ? — the truth, namely, that no evolution is stable which neglects the moral factor, or seeks to shake itself free from the eternal duties of obedience and of faith. Take the story which ends in the Song of Lamech in the fourth chapter. Cain has gone forth from the presence of God to the Land of Nod. From this first emigrant spring the civilisations. His eldest son founds a city. A later descendant, Lamech, has two wives, Adah and Zillah, names which probably mean *Light* and *Shadow*, and from them are born Jabal, the father of all who dwell in tents; Jubal, the father of such as handle harp and pipe; and Tubal-Qain, the wielder or forger of all instruments of copper and iron. And these three, the father of the Pastoral Life, the Maker of Music, and the Forger of Weapons, have a sister Na'amah, *gracious* or *beautiful*, whom later Jewish legend calls the mother of singing.

Now, how does the Song of Lamech greet all this progress of the equipment and adorning of human life? With an outburst of praise to God, the giver? With some apostrophe to man's power and skill? With thankful notes for the peace of the pastoral life defended by weapons from its foes? With none of these; but with a savage exultation in the fresh power of vengeance which all the novel instruments have placed in their inventors' hands.

Then said Lamech to his wives Adah and Zillah,
    Hearken to my voice,
    Give ear to my saying :
    I have slain a man for the hurt done me,
    And a young man for the wound of me.
    If seven times Qain be avenged,
    Lamech shall be seventy times seven.

How weird is this: how terrible! The first results of civilisation are to equip hatred and render revenge more deadly. And all the more weird is the little fragment, that out of those far-off days it seems to mock us with some grotesque reflection of our own time. Civilisation finding its apotheosis in enormous armaments; wealth and prosperity leading people to an arrogant clamour for war.[1]

These instances, from that part of the Old

---

[1] On Gen. i.–xi., see Ryle, *Early Narratives of Genesis;* Marcus Dods, *Genesis* (*Expos. Bible*) ; Budde, *Urgeschichte.* Against the above view of Lamech's song, see Cheyne, 'Cainites,' *Encyc. Bibl.*

Testament in which we can be least sure that we are treading historical ground, are surely enough to show you how independent of historical certainty (in the narrower sense of the term) are the materials and inspiration which the preacher may draw for his own times from the ancient Scriptures of his Church.

Let us take the rest of Genesis in illustration of the same truth. With the close of the eleventh chapter we pass from humanity in general to the call of one family and the career of its individual heroes, whose characters have been so largely the source of the confident preaching I have described. After the criticism of the past century, how does it stand with the historical quality of the narratives from Abraham to Joseph? And if that quality be impaired, what is their value for the preacher?

As we saw in last Lecture, the documents in which the narratives are presented to us are of various dates, from the ninth or eighth to the sixth or fifth centuries before Christ. The earliest of them, the Jahwist and Elohist, to which the bulk of the narratives belong, may be approximately assigned to the eighth century, and of the same age are the earliest prophetic references to the Patriarchs; [1] they agree with,

[1] Hosea's to Jacob, xii. 3–5 (Heb. 2–4), 12, 13 (Heb. 11, 12). Cf. the references by Amos to the conquest of Palestine and dispossession of the Amorite by Israel on their coming forth from Egypt (ii. 9, ix. 7, and by Hosea ii. 15 and xi. 1).

and are probably drawn from, the Jahwist-Elohist. But this means that the literature upon which we are dependent for our knowledge of the history of the Hebrews from Abraham to Joseph, is of a date from nine to eleven hundred years later than the personages and events which it describes.

Nor can archæology furnish us with contemporary evidence of the Patriarchs and their careers. Archæology has indeed restored much of the life to which they belonged. It has shown us that in the time of Abraham, whom the documents assert to have come out of Mesopotamia into Palestine, there was constant traffic between these countries. The city, to which the early home of his family is assigned, has been identified and explored. *Ur of the Chaldees* lies on the borders of Arabia and Babylonia.[1] The settlement there of a nomadic Arabian tribe, such as the earliest records of Israel prove them to have been in genius and temperament; their contact for a time with civilisation; their half-weaning from the desert, and subsequent migration northwards along the Euphrates to

[1] Ur is the modern Muḳayyar on the S. bank of the Euphrates, nearly 90 miles (as the crow flies) from the present junction of that river with the Tigris. Harran lay about 550 miles to the NW. of Ur, about 80 miles N. of the Euphrates at Tiphsah or Thapsacus, the ancient 'passage' towards Canaan; and between the Euphrates and the Habur (mod. Khabur), probably the 'two rivers' of the name Aram-Naharaim, given by Gen. xxiv. 10 as the region in which Harran lay.

Harran and then south into Canaan, are all
illustrated not only by archæology but by the
drift of Arabian tribes upon Mesopotamia and
Syria within historical times. These last also
make possible the wanderings of such a half-
settled family as Abraham's upon the desert
borders of Southern Palestine and Egypt. The
four Mesopotamian kings, of whose invasion of
Canaan and pursuit by Abraham we are told
in Genesis xiv., 'were really contemporaries;
and at least three of them ruled over the
countries which they are said in Genesis xiv.
to have ruled'; and their invasion of Palestine
was 'in the abstract, within the military possibilities of the age.'[1] The existence of the names
Jacob and Joseph has been discovered in
Palestine at an earlier age than the Exodus;[2]
the name 'Israel,' as of a people, in touch with
Egypt, has been deciphered upon a stelé of the
Pharaoh under whom the Exodus probably took
place.[3] And not only does the story of Joseph
reflect the social customs, the economic processes,
and the official etiquette of the kingdom of the
Pharaohs;[4] but the settlement of a semi-nomad
tribe in Goshen,[5] at first in favour with the court of

[1] Driver, *Authority and Archæology*, p. 44.

[2] In the lists of cities conquered in Palestine by Thothmes III.
of the fifteenth century, cf. W. M. Müller, *Asien u. Europa*,
162 ff.

[3] Merenptah; cf. Steindorff, *ZATW*, xvi. 330 f.

[4] See above, pp. 62 ff.

[5] This name is apparently identical with Kesem, the twentieth

Egypt and then, on the succession of another dynasty, oppressed and enslaved, has also been proved to be perfectly possible in the history of Egypt between the eighteenth and fourteenth centuries.

But, just as we have seen, that in all this archæological evidence there is nothing to prove the early date of the documents which contain the stories of the Patriarchs, but on the contrary even a little which strengthens the critical theory of their late date,[1] so now we must admit that while archæology has richly illustrated the possibility of the main outlines of the Book of Genesis from Abraham to Joseph, it has not one whit of proof to offer for the personal existence or characters of the Patriarchs themselves. Where formerly the figures of the 'Father of the Faithful' and his caravans moved solemnly in high outline through an almost empty world, we see (by the aid of the monuments) embassies, armies and long lines of traders crossing, by paths still used, the narrow bridge which Palestine forms between the two great centres of early civilisation; the constant drift of desert tribes upon the fertile land, and within the latter the frequent villages and their busy fields, the mountain-keeps with their Egyptian garrisons, and the cities on their mounds walled with broad bulwarks of brick and stone. But amidst all that crowded life we

nome of Lower Egypt. But see Griffith's 'Goshen,' Hastings's *Bible Dictionary*.   [1] See above, pp. 62 ff.

peer in vain for any trace of the fathers of the Hebrews; we listen in vain for any mention of their names. This is the whole change archæology has wrought: it has given us a background and an atmosphere for the stories of Genesis; it is unable to recall or to certify their heroes.

With, therefore, nothing more from archæology than the sense of the possibility of the main events of these stories, we return to the stories themselves; and here we meet with not a little that confirms the scepticism engendered by their late date. We perceive, *first*, that many of the personal names are names of tribes as well; *second*, that the characters described in the individuals are the characters developed in history by the corresponding tribes; and *third*, that the transactions between individuals, who bear tribal names, may often be most naturally explained as transactions between tribes. It is hardly necessary to give instances of the first of these facts: the recollection of the sons of Noah, of Abraham, of Isaac and of Jacob is enough. But take a few illustrations of the second and third. The characters of Ishmael, of Jacob and of Esau were the characters of the historical tribes Ishmael, Israel and Edom. Jacob is the essential Israel; in economy, shepherds settling down to agriculture; in religion, worshippers of Jahweh by descent and covenant, meeting Him at certain famous shrines, but carrying about with them domestic gods, as we see even in the family of David; in temperament and genius, astute, persistent, unbroken by disappointment or hope deferred, capable of excelling their neighbours in the Semitic craft and fraud, but capable too of vision and of struggling with the Unseen. Esau, on the other hand, is the essential Edomite, as we see him in Scripture, as we realise him on his proudly isolated territory, as we touch him to the last in Antipater and the Herods [1] — a hunter, *a man of the field* or wild uncultivated lands, a man with gods but no religiousness; [2] *profane,* impulsive, careless, easily wearied. Similarly, Ishmael with *his hand against every man,* Moab with his drunken and incestuous origin, and Reuben with his unchastity, are reflections of the qualities which the tribes called by the same names appear to have developed in history. Or take the transactions imputed to individuals with tribal names. When Jacob marries the daughters of the Aramean Laban, and after a long and cruel struggle, which proves that son and father-in-law cannot share the same lands, fixes a boundary with Laban that neither shall pass, 'they plainly represent two peoples' [3] at one

[1] See *Book of the Twelve Prophets,* vol. ii. chap. xiv.

[2] Cf. the curious absence of any influence from the Edomite religion on Israel in the midst of constant influences from the religions of all the other neighbours of Israel.

[3] Driver, Hastings's *Bible Dictionary,* ii. 535*a.*

time related, as philology and ethnology alike prove the Bible to be right in stating, but later in history divided — and this on the very line on which Jacob and Laban are said to have set up their landmark. Similarly, when Judah is represented as *going down from his brethren* [1] to Adullam and begetting children by a Canaanite woman, we are not compelled to read that as the story of a scandalous adventure by the son of Jacob. We may much more naturally interpret the tale as an account of the irregular marriages which members of the tribe of Judah, situated within historical times on the Central Range of Palestine, contracted with the Canaanites on the Shephelah below them.

The numerous facts, of which these are sufficient instances, prove that we have in the stories of the Hebrew Patriarchs just what their late date would lead us to expect: efforts to account for the geographical distribution of neighbouring nations, for their affinities, contrasts, and mutual antipathies, and in particular for the composite character of Israel. Perhaps such efforts become most transparent in the derivations offered for geographical names, and the origins claimed for customs and institutions extant in the writers' own day. Finally, this view is confirmed by the undoubtedly late features which can be recognised in the stories, and by

[1] Genesis xxxviii.

the different accounts of the same subject in the different documents according to the characteristic spirit of each. The Blessing of his sons attributed to Jacob in Genesis xlix. not only describes the geographical disposition of the Twelve Tribes after their settlement in Palestine; but, in verses 22–26, reflects the experiences of Northern Israel during the Aramean wars of the ninth century; another edition of the same Blessing is attributed to Moses in Deuteronomy xxxiii. In the Jahwist, or Judæan Document, Judah is the chief of his brethren; but in the Elohist, Reuben.[1] On the whole, the religious atmosphere of the Jahwist and Elohist stories throughout Genesis is that of the early kingdom of Israel.[2] The Patriarchs sacrifice in many places, like Elijah and Elisha, but chiefly at the shrines to which in the eighth century, as Amos and Hosea tell us, the Israelites resorted: Beer-sheba, Bethel, Gilgal by Shechem — *the terebinth of Moreh* — and Mizpeh of Gilead. In the eighth century there was yet no Deuteronomic veto on sacrifice at places other than the *one*, where Jahweh should set His name. The Priestly Writers, on the other hand, with their strict views

---

[1] For this and other differences in the combined narratives in Genesis xxxvii. see the analysis by Addis, *Documents of the Hexateuch*, i. 70 ff.

[2] See Robertson Smith's trenchant review of Renan's *History of Israel*, vol. i., in the *English Historical Review*, vol. iii. (1888), pp. 128 f.

of the confinement of ritual to the central sanctuary, never make any allusion to the licence of
sacrifice which the Jahwist and Elohist impute to
the Patriarchs, and do not localise the appearances of the Deity to Abraham or to Jacob at
any of the shrines famous in the eighth century.[1]
Surely this clinches the proof that the stories
of the Patriarchs have reached us, as told by
later generations, who reflected upon them their
own conditions, experiences and beliefs.

It is extremely probable, however, though
impossible of proof, that the stories of the
Patriarchs, thus replete with the circumstances
and conceptions of a later age, have at the heart
of them historical elements. The oldest literary
portions of the documents are songs and poems,
some of which, although (as we have seen in the
case of Genesis xlix.) they also bear late marks,
may have grown round a contemporary kernel,
while a few others may be altogether from the
age to which they are assigned. A more significant symptom is the presence in the names,
characters and deeds of the Patriarchs of much
which cannot be interpreted racially, but which
is distinctly individual. It is always possible, of
course, to regard this as the addition of an age, in
which the tribal meaning of the stories had been
forgotten, and they were conceived as purely

[1] See the Priestly Document as separately set forth in Addis's
Documents of the Hexateuch, vol. ii. pp. 207 ff.

personal narratives. But it is equally just to take some of the individual elements to have existed in the tradition from the beginning, and to this we are further moved by two considerations: *first*, that it is impossible to attach any tribal quality to some of the names, like Abraham; and *second*, that a great religious advance such as Abraham is said to have made has always an individual character and experience as its starting-point. With critics there has been a distinct reaction of late in favour of admitting the personal reality of Abraham;[1] no one has ever doubted that of Moses; while Joshua's personality rests to-day on surer grounds than in the earlier stages of criticism.[2] With regard to the more difficult cases of Jacob and Joseph, the sane and expert arguments of Canon Driver in his articles in Hastings's *Bible Dictionary* will be felt to be conclusive by all who have not incontinently abandoned the task of tracing Israel's history behind the Exodus.

Such is the case for the narratives of the Patriarchs. On the present evidence, it is impossible to be sure of more than that they contain a substratum of actual personal history. But who wants to be sure of more? Who needs to be sure of more? If there be a preacher who

---

[1] Cf. Cornill, *Geschichte des israelit. Prophetismus.*

[2] See article 'Joshua' by the present writer in Hastings's *Bible Dictionary*, ii. 786 f.

thinks that the priceless value of these narratives
to his work depends on the belief that they are
all literal history, let him hold that belief if he
can, and confidently use them. Or if he cannot
believe that Genesis is literal history, and yet
thinks it must needs be, in order to be used as
God's Word, let him seek his texts elsewhere:
his field is wide and inexhaustible.

Than these extremes there is, however, a
nobler way: and the honest student who is
ready to accept the evidence and example of
Scripture itself will surely find this. He will see
that the sacred writers aimed at something higher
than the bare reproduction of primitive history
— in itself an impossible task; that, possessed
by the experience of God and the human
heart, which subsequent ages of the Divine
education had delivered to them, they read all
that into the traditions of the remote past; and
so achieved the creation of types of character
essentially historical, not only in this, that they
portray with wonderful fidelity the tempers,
aspirations and experiences of Israel and her
neighbours, but because they discover human
nature, as it is in every race of mankind, and
clearly tell of the reality of God, as they themselves had been inspired by His Spirit to find
Him. To the sacred authors of these stories we
cannot refuse a licence of dramatic and ethical
expansion which we, more consciously, permit

in our own preaching, and which every powerful preacher of the traditional school has fearlessly employed. As preachers, we cannot refuse to follow the narratives of Genesis till we refuse to follow the parables of Jesus.[1] If criticism, with the help of archæology, has failed to establish the literal truth of these stories as personal biographies, it has on the other hand displayed their utter fidelity to the characters of the peoples they reflect, and to the facts of the world and the Divine guidance in which these peoples developed. The power of the Patriarchal narratives on the heart, the imagination, the faith of men can never die: it is immortal with truthfulness to the realities of human nature and of God's education of mankind.

[1] See below, on Job, in Lecture VIII.

LECTURE IV

THE PROOF OF A DIVINE REVELATION IN THE OLD TESTAMENT

WE have now reached the most important of the questions with which these Lectures have to deal. Does the criticism — whose historical results are estimated in last Lecture — leave to us unimpaired our belief in the Old Testament as the record of a Divine Revelation? It is true that, if this question had to be answered in the negative, there would still remain in the Hebrew Scriptures matter of extraordinary value to him who seeks to lead his fellow-men to the knowledge of God. Some contain parts of the argument which we call Natural Theology; others illustrate how belief in God is consonant with experience and indispensable to conduct; others test the former of these conclusions amid the apparently hostile facts of life: while all exemplify the truth that whatsoever religious beliefs be shaken, faith in God and His goodness are the invariable starting-point and inevitable return of the far-travelling hearts of men.[1] Yet precious as such human argument and experience by itself would be, it is all of less interest to us than the question whether Israel's knowledge of God was due to the authentic, personal action of God Himself. This is the testimony of the writers of the Old Testament, and it is confirmed by our Lord. Here, then, we touch the very crisis of our inquiry.

Before we examine what effect modern criticism has had on the answer to the question of Revelation, we must see whether we understand the statement of the question, or in other words what are the exact claims to Divine inspiration which the Old Testament makes for itself. These have been strangely misunderstood both by their assailants and by most of their defenders.

In the first place the Hebrew Scriptures — in contrast to the timidity of many of their apolo-

[1] 'As Scripture nowhere contemplates men as ignorant of the existence of God, it nowhere depicts the rise or dawn of the idea of His existence in men's minds. . . . The Hebrew came down from his thought of God upon the world, he did not rise from the world up to his thought of God. . . . His contemplation of nature and providence and the life of man was never of the nature of a search after God whom he did not know, but always of the nature of a recognition of God whom he knew. . . . The singer of Ps. xix. only saw repeated on the heavens what he already carried in his own heart.' . . . Isa. xl. 25 ff. ' teaches nothing new or unknown, it recalls what is known, reburnishing the consciousness of it, in order to sustain the faith and the hopes of the people. There is, however, in one or two passages an approximation to some of the arguments of Natural Theology,' e.g. Ps. xciv. 5 ff. — Dr. A. B. Davidson, article 'God' (in Old Testament), Hastings's *Bible Dictionary*, ii. 196.

gists — emphasise the origin of human valour and justice, skill, art, and wisdom — all common virtue and common knowledge [1] — as by the inspiration of Almighty God. This is irrespective of the use of these qualities in the service of Israel. *The earth is Jahweh's and the fulness thereof; the spirit of man is the candle of Jahweh. By Him kings reign and princes decree justice. Have we not all one Father, hath not one God created us?* Of course men have imaginations and thoughts which are not God's thoughts. But courage, wisdom, justice, wherever found, are of His Spirit. Even upon civilisations alien to Israel and doomed to destruction, like those of Egypt and Phœnicia, Isaiah pours his regrets and his hopes, [2] as if their powers were divine and might yet serve the purpose of Jahweh. But the writers of the Old Testament give even more practical proof of this generous belief by their adoption from sources beyond Israel of cosmogonies, traditions, legends and even conceptions of Deity. In our present inquiry, therefore, we need not encumber our-

---

[1] See especially Isaiah xxviii. 6, 23–29, and Robertson Smith's remarks in *Old Test. and Jew. Church* [2], p. 340: 'According to Isaiah xxviii. 23 ff. the rules of good husbandry are a "judgement" taught to the ploughmen by Jehovah, and part of Jehovah's Torah (verse 26). The piety of Israel recognised every sound and wholesome ordinance of daily and social life as a direct gift of Jehovah's wisdom. Accordingly Jehovah's law contains, not only institutes of direct revelation in our limited sense of that word, but old consuetudinary usages, which had become sacred by being taken up into the God-given polity of Israel and worked into harmony with the very present reality of His redeeming sovereignty.'

[2] Isa. xix. and xxiii.

selves with the question of the inspiration of other literatures than that of Israel. Whatsoever things are true, honest, just, pure, lovely and of good report, are of God. His providence, too, is universal. *Are ye not as the children of the Ethiopians unto me, O children of Israel? saith Jahweh. Have I not brought up Israel out of the land of Egypt and the Philistines from Kaphtor and the Syrians from Kir?*

But, in the second place, the Hebrew writers claim for Israel a special choice and providence by God in order that He may make known to them, as He directly does to no other people of mankind, Himself: that is to say not in His metaphysical substance, for of this there is no definition in the Old Testament, but in His character and in His ethical purposes for all mankind. In contrast to some modern theories, which regard Revelation as the communication by supernatural means of many kinds of truth — which, as we have just seen, Israel did not hesitate to borrow from the traditions of other peoples — Revelation by the Hebrew writers is limited to the Revelation of God Himself: and that not of the fact of His existence, which the Old Testament takes for granted, but of His ethical character and will for men. This Revelation they represent as unique to Israel, and with equal emphasis assert that it has not been discovered by human efforts unaided, but that God Himself has ' taken the initiative,'[1] and made Himself known to Israel.

In the light of these two aspects of Old Testament doctrine of the Knowledge of God, our question as to its Revelation is not therefore primarily one as to its origins, but one as to its contents. Are these unique ? Do we have in the Old Testament a true knowledge of the character and ethical purpose of God which we do not find original to any race except Israel ? But then, secondly, is this knowledge all explicable as impressions of God received through the people's physical environment, or by their merely intellectual inferences from the facts of their history, or by their remarkable combination of the conceptions of God which they received from nations with whom they came into contact ?[2] Or, while all these may have been used, does the evidence justify the claim of Israel that God in His Love and Holiness drew near to this people and impressed Himself personally upon them through the events of their history and through the consciousness of their great men ?

I think it can be shown that criticism, so far from throwing doubts either upon the uniqueness

[1] A. B. Davidson, *op. cit.*, p. 197.

[2] It is one of the great services of Budde's *Religion of Israel before the Exile* to show how much Israel benefited religiously during that period from her contact with other Semitic peoples. See especially p. 71 (but cf. below, p. 132 of this Lecture).

of Israel's true knowledge of God, or upon the personal influence of God as producing this, certainly proves the former, and leaves us with the latter as its most natural and scientific explanation. Or to put this otherwise — the most advanced modern criticism provides grounds for the proof of a Divine Revelation in the Old Testament at least more firm than those on which the older apologetic used to rely.[1]

Modern research has achieved this service for us, first by changing the whole arena upon which the question of the uniqueness of Israel's religion

[1] It would be very easy to prove the compatibility of belief in Revelation in the Old Testament with the results of modern criticism by simply citing the personal dicta of some of the most eminent critics. There is an idea abroad among Christians that the whole critical school are hostile to belief in Revelation. For this some critics, who avoid the question of Revelation even when their discoveries lead them to the verge of it, are partly to blame; but it would be readily dispelled by the explicit confessions of such a belief by other critics, and these among the most able and advanced. Kuenen in his collected Essays approaches the question of Revelation in the Old Testament, yet never addresses himself to it. I stated this in a review of the German translation of the Essays (Kuenen's *Gesammelte Abhaendlungen*, 1894) in the *Expositor* (July–Dec. 1895), and the translator, Professor Budde, a pupil of Kuenen, and one of the most eminent of German critics, wrote me that the observation was right, but that as for himself his belief in 'a genuine revelation of God in the Old Testament remains rock-fast.' That belief has been shared and stated by a number of advanced critics. The late Professor Robertson Smith affirmed again and again his belief in the Divine Origin of the Old Testament, and in the last of his Burnett Lectures (unfortunately unpublished), proved 'the uniqueness of Hebrew prophecy and the impossibility of accounting for it by natural or historical reasons' (from an MS. report of the last Burnett Lecture). Cf. also *The Old Testament in the Jewish Church* [2], p. 297.

has to be fought out.   Fifty years ago the apologist
for the Old Testament could determine the character of its religion only by comparison with those
of the nations of classical antiquity.   But there
was always something unsatisfactory, something
impossible, in this comparison.   The Greeks and
the Romans were Aryans, Israel was Semitic;
there did not appear to be any ground common
to them all from which you could start the contrast of their respective developments.   The older
apologetic for the Old Testament was, therefore,
more or less unreal.   But this has been changed
by the researches of the past fifty years.   The
discovery of the monuments of Babylonia, Syria
and Arabia, the study of the pre-Mohammedan
literature of the Arabs, the observation of current
life in the Arabian deserts, have disclosed to us
the ritual, the institutions, the conceptions of God
and the world, which prevailed in the race from
which Israel sprang.   We are able to contrast
the religion of Israel with those of peoples who
were of the same stock, who inhabited similar
geographical conditions, who were modified by
the same political forces, who exhibited the same
genius and temperament, and who exercised
strong religious influences upon Israel at various
periods in her history.

At first it appeared as if this recovery of the
Semitic race as a whole were to result in the
proof of a physical origin for the religion of Israel.

From their native deserts the race seem to have derived a capacity for detachment from the things of sense, and a capacity of vision. In what we may call the religious temperament, and in the qualities required for the propagation of religion: the powers of intuition, of introspection, of self-denial, of patience under hope deferred, of zeal even to the pitch of fanaticism, the Semite in history has been supreme. Under the fascination of the unfolding of the complete picture of the race, derived from so many periods and areas, it was asserted that the religion of Israel was simply the flower of the natural religiousness of the Semitic peoples.

Others went further. Besides deriving the religious temper of the Hebrew from his racial origin, they essayed to trace his religious creed to the same source. The hypothesis naturally started from the fact that the three great forms of monotheism, Judaism, Christianity and Islam, have all sprung from Semitic peoples. Does this prove, in the Semites, or in the history of the world they inhabited, a native tendency to such a form of faith? In saying that religion is a quality of the Semitic temper, are we able to narrow our terms and assert that monotheism was a necessary notion of the Semitic mind? You can see of what importance the question is at the point which we have reached. On the answer to it depends the answer to our question about a real revelation in the Old Testament. It requires, therefore, a detailed examination.

The thesis, that monotheism was native to the Semitic mind, has been chiefly maintained by Renan. More than forty years ago he asserted that 'monotheism summed up and explained all the characteristics of the race.' The origin of this he found in the desert, the birthplace and, to a large extent, the home of the Semites. 'Nature,' he says, 'plays a small part in the Semitic religion, because she plays a small part in the Semitic world.' 'The desert is monotheist: sublime in its immense uniformity it has revealed to man the idea of the infinite; but not the sense of that life incessantly creative which a more fertile nature has inspired in other races.' And from this 'austere, grandiose influence' he deduces, upon the lines of natural development, all the contents of Israel's monotheism.[1]

I do not propose to spend much time in proving to you, in contradiction of these statements, that all Semitic tribes were originally polytheists, for we have more important matters in hand than the proof of so certain a fact. Since Renan formed his confident opinions, a large number of monuments have been discovered, not only in Babylonia

---

[1] See 'De la part des peuples Sémitiques' in the *Journal Asiatique*, 1859: *L'Histoire Générale des Langues Sémitiques*, 1863 (third edition), pp. 5 ff.; and the more modified statements in the *Histoire du Peuple d'Israël*, i. pp. 8 ff.

and Phœnicia (whose nations he always asserted to be exceptions to the Semitic rule), but in the territories of the Arameans, Moabites, Edomites, and even in Central Arabia, which bear witness that polytheism was the religion of every one of these tribes. Sinai and Mecca, from which two of the great monotheisms took their rise, were both of them desert sanctuaries, and both of them were pantheons. We do not see anything different when we shift our gaze from Mecca and Sinai to Jerusalem. Palestine repeats the religious record of Hauran, Moab and Arabia. As was to be expected where nature is lavish, agriculture the staple, and men drink wine; where the land is broken up into well-defined provinces, and cities multiply, and the political side of religion is developed with its differentiation of many deities—where, in fact, on the seaboard of the Mediterranean we find physical and political conditions similar to those of Greece—the polytheism of the Semite becomes luxurious and rank. Baalim abound everywhere: Baalim of the underground waters, and Baalim of the waters above; Baalim of the mountains and Baalim of the plains; Baalim of the sun and Baalim of the stars; Baalim of the cities and Baalim of the tribes. Every nation has its own god, and believes in the reality of the gods of its neighbours. Every power in nature is worshipped, till altars rise *on every high hill and under every green tree*, with a mythology which is not only almost as elaborate as the Greek, but many of the grossest forms of which the Semitic peoples of Canaan are justly supposed to have conveyed in early times to the Hellenic world.

Such was the race to whose natural tendencies and geographical environment Renan traced the origins of Israel's monotheism. They were polytheists, and nowhere did their polytheism become more rank than in the very province in which Israel's monotheism culminated.

Before, however, we can dismiss Renan's assertions, we have to ask whether Semitic polytheism contains anything which points either to a primitive monotheism or to an ultimate monotheism. Do we find in it any recollections of a habit of regarding the Deity apart from the various gods, or can we trace in the Semitic world, outside Israel, Christianity and Islam, any signs of a development towards monotheism?

Of the former of these the evidence is extremely meagre. Virtually it consists only in the possession by all Semitic peoples of a common word for God, *'el*, which proves that the Semites were able to form the abstract conception of Deity, but does not prove that outside Israel any of them had ever regarded a single deity as universally sovereign, or comprising in Himself the functions and attributes of the various local gods. On the other hand, Professor Robertson

Smith has shown how the basis of all Semitic faiths, as we find them in history, appears to be the physical kinship of gods and men. According to that notion each tribe of men was descended from a divine father, whose blood flowed in their veins, and who was lord and ruler of the tribe alone.[1] There are no clearer facts about Semitic religion than these two: that every tribe had its own god, and that between a tribe and its god there existed a congenital solidarity, so to speak, which could never be dissolved, nor have substituted for it a solidarity between the tribe and any other deity. This does not look like a religion which has descended from a primitive monotheism.

Turning to our second question — was there in the Semitic form of religion any tendency *towards* monotheism? We cannot deny that in the singular relation between each tribe and its deity there lay what we may call a great opportunity for monotheism. To have one God singled out for the tribe as supreme; to believe that no other was his equal within a certain territory and for a certain number of men — this surely gave room and time for a purer faith to develop. It meant a habit and direction of the mind which might be employed in the interests of unity. But in itself it was no more than this; and we can see that unless there were present in that space, from

[1] *Religion of the Semites*, p. 31.

which the supremacy (if not the reality) of other gods was excluded, and at work upon that habit of worshipping one as the governor of life, some influence superior to limits of space and capable of employing that habit for a spiritual end, the opportunity would be lost and the habit rendered barren.

Such an influence, not only capable of sustaining the habit of worshipping one god within the territory of the tribe, amid all temptations to divide his worship with that of others, but strong enough to extend this habit wherever the tribe travelled or the thoughts of the tribe travelled, might be one of three kinds — intellectual, political, or moral.

Of the intellectual forces which make for monotheism, the two most powerful are the ability, by comparing several gods, to form an abstract conception of the deity common to them all; and the conclusion from the observation of the course of nature, that this is a harmonious and consistent whole, derivable from a single cause. Both of these powers are found among the Semites; but, outside the influence of Israel, neither of them led to monotheism. Of the former we have a proof in the possession, already noticed, by all the Semites of a common name for God — *'el*. But *'el*, if ever used as a proper name, appears to have been regarded as that merely of one other god, in addition to the national and local deities. Again, some of the Semites developed a cosmogony, but outside the Old Testament this appears never to have been accompanied by, or to have led to, monotheism. Gods in the plural and of both sexes assisted at every stage of it.

Of more probable influence for monotheism than these intellectual tendencies were the political forces of the Semitic world. In the growth of a single tribe to power over its neighbours there lay the possibility of its deity being raised to a higher rank than all their deities. Did experiences of this kind never develop that opportunity to monotheism which we have found inherent in the characteristic form of Semitic religion? The answer is that minor conquests within the Semitic world, so far from always extending the conqueror's notion of the power of his god, constantly brought him under the temptation of adding to his worship of the latter the worship of the gods of the land which he had taken and occupied. An instance of this is found in the history of Israel, who, after the settlement of Canaan, frequently fell under the fascination of the local Baalim, with their supposed patronage of the fertility of the soil. No general conquest by one tribe of all the others took place before the great advance of the Assyrian Empire in the eighth century before Christ. This discredited, as we see from

the prophecies of Isaiah, a number of the local
and tribal deities in the Semitic world, who did
not enable their worshippers to resist it.   It
helped to shatter, as Robertson Smith has pointed
out, the tribal limits of religion, and so far was
undeniably a new opportunity for the development of monotheism.   Yet, in the long-run, the
Assyrian conquests only substituted among the
Semites a small number of new gods for the crowd
of discredited deities; and by divorcing religion
from the local interests and everyday life of the
tribesmen and throwing it back into association
with the forces of nature, those conquests did
religion more harm than good.[1]

This brings us to the last of the possible forces
which make for monotheism — the ethical.   In
the fragmentary condition of the monuments and
traditions, upon which we depend for our knowledge of the pagan Semitic religions, it is difficult for us to appreciate the ethical contents of
the latter.   This, however, is certain.   The fact
that the gods were tribal brought religion into
touch with the practical conduct of life, with the
discharge of justice, and with public emergencies.
But there the ethical virtue of it appears to have
ceased.   The duty of the god, the help he could
afford, were identified with the selfish interests
of the tribe.   Not justice nor mercy was the
supreme care of the deity, but the victory and

[1] See Robertson Smith, *Religion of the Semites*, pp. 35, 65.

prosperity of his people. On the one hand, there can have been no idea of humanity as a whole; on the other, little sense of the value of the individual in himself.[1] The awe and sanction of religion kept a man in his place as part of the tribal organism; but ethically it did not develop his individuality beyond his public duties of courage, and devotion to the interests of the tribe. The god, who (as several scholars have pointed out) was simply the glorified sheikh of the tribe, had a moral interest only in the fulfilment of the individual's social obligations and due performance of the ritual, but had no concern with his spiritual character. In short, it may be said, reversing the well-known words about Jahweh, that the Semitic god saw as man seeth; he looked not upon the heart. Wellhausen says of the heathen Arabs, even after some influences of Judaism and Christianity had come upon them, that religion did not work with any energy upon the thinking or doing of the individual. No doubt the individual was affected by the fear of God. But even in the days when, under foreign influence, the heathen Arabs had slightly anticipated Mohammed in the conception of one God, He affected them only in one way. The highest moral name they gave Him was El-Wāz', the Restrainer.[2] That is to say, the thought of God

---

[1] This is very apparent from the early religion of Israel.

[2] Wellhausen, *Reste arabischen Heidentumes*, p. 191.

kept them from sin, but was powerless to inspire
them to new ideals of virtue. For the rest, the
Deity moved above the individual, an inscrutable
yet easily irritated Fate: God that was force and
not character.

This has been a somewhat long survey, but
your attention will not have been wasted if it
has led you to understand that, while there existed
in the fundamental form of Semitic religion and
at various crises in Semitic history certain opportunities for the development of monotheism, and
also some influences which make for monotheism,
yet outside Israel those influences were not powerful enough to make use of the opportunities.

How, then, was it that monotheism appeared
in Israel alone of all ancient Semitic nations ?
How was this member of the race alone able
to take advantage of opportunities which all the
others shared with her; and in a physical environment, very fertile in polytheism, not merely to rise
above this to a stage of religion subordinate only
to the Christianity of Christ, but to exhibit
throughout her whole history a religious progress
which Christ affirmed to be the gradual preparation for Himself ?

To this unique exception in the history of
Semitic religion it is my firm belief that only
one cause can be assigned, and that is, that in
the religion of Israel, as recorded in the Old
Testament, there was an authentic revelation of

the One True God: of which thesis the rest of this Lecture is offered as a proof on the lines of modern criticism. And as the proof is most difficult with regard to the earlier stages of Israel's history in which we see their religion not yet far removed from the ordinary Semitic levels, I propose to limit the inquiry to the period before the greatest prophets. If we can prove the possibility of revelation among the religious conditions which then existed, the pure monotheism of the prophets which followed, and the culmination of the whole process in Christ, will complete and vindicate our argument.

There is no necessity to prove in detail the Semitic origins of the Hebrews and their religion.[1] The traditions of the people affirm not only these but the close kinship of Israel to certain tribes of the race which still clung to the ancestral desert, or had not drifted beyond its borders: Ishmael, Ammon, Moab and Edom. Israel were at first a loose confederacy of clans descended from a common ancestor, and cursed with the incoherency of all Semitic society. They came out of the desert into Palestine, and through the formative period of their history not only were affected by the neighbourhood of the desert to their territory; but portions of them intermarried with

---

[1] I have given detailed proofs in the first of the Jowett Lectures on the Religion of Israel in the Eighth and Seventh Centuries, which I hope soon to publish.

desert tribes or continued in close alliance with
these. Their fathers had been nomads; and
the characters of their typical men, as for instance
Jacob, are essentially, in their good and bad
elements, the characters of the desert herdsmen.

It is in their religion, however, that their
Semitic origin is most apparent. The god of
early Israel was a tribal god; and His relation
to His people is described in the same way as
Israel's neighbours describe the relation of their
gods to themselves. Israel looked to Jahweh as
the Moabites looked to Chemosh, for leadership
in war, for decisions upon justice — including the
detection of criminals and lost property and the
settlement of questions of inheritance — and for
direction as to the ritual of worship. They
prayed to him to let them see their desire on
their enemies, ascribed their victories to His
love for them, their defeats to His anger, and
they devoted to Him in slaughter their prisoners
of war, and the animals they captured from
their foes; all exactly as their Moabite neighbours
are reported, in very much the same language,[1]
to have done to Chemosh, the god of Moab.
Moreover, they regarded the power of Jahweh as
limited to their own territory, and His worship
as invalid beyond it.[2] Though, like all Semites,
they felt their duty to one God as the supreme
Lord of themselves, they did not deny the reality

[1] The Moabite Stone.   [2] 1 Sam. xxvi. 19.

of other gods.¹ Again, like other Semites, early Israel associated their God with certain physical forces. The manifestations of Jahweh took place in the rain, the thunderstorm, the lightning and the fire; His voice was heard in the stir of the trees before the wind.² Again, the ritual of Israel is full of exact analogies to the ritual of Semitic sanctuaries from Cyprus to Southern Arabia. The sacrifice of certain animals at certain seasons of the year; the smearing of lintels and other objects with blood; the anointing of pillars in honour of the Deity; the presence of human sacrifices with as much infrequency and sense of the awful crisis that demands them as elsewhere in the Semitic world; the worship of images by Jacob's family, by David, and at the sanctuaries of the Northern Kingdom; the discovery of the Deity's will through dreams, in ecstasy or by lot; the attestation of the Divine word by physical signs accompanying it; circumcision;

¹ Not even by the Second Commandment, which is not a declaration of monotheism, but only the obligation to have Jahweh, of all the gods, as their sole god. It is difficult to say when the sense of the reality of other gods died out in Israel. It is confessed by David: it is implicit in the absence of all missionary effort in pre-prophetic times, and the remembrance of it lingers even in so monotheistic a Book as Deuteronomy; one of the verses in which, iv. 17, is a curious compromise between the belief in the reality of the heathen gods and that in the divine sovereignty of Jahweh. Not till Jeremiah and the second Isaiah do we find language used of the idols which expresses unambiguously the writer's belief in their nothingness.

² Genesis iii. 8; 2 Sam. v. 23 ff.

I

the law of blood-revenge and its mitigation by the rights of sanctuary; the sacrifice of spoil of war to the Deity: all these things have not only for the most part the same names as in other Semitic languages, but — except for a higher moral character which, however, only sometimes distinguishes them — they are the same as among other Semites, in intention and details of execution. And finally (as we shall see in another Lecture, so that we need not go into detail upon the subject now), early Israel had as little religious interest as other Semites in a future life. Except in the case of one or two heroes [1] this was not connected with the Deity: if men inquired of it they did so not by religion but by magic and necromancy. The reason of such a separation between religion and the future life was precisely that which accounts for it elsewhere in the Semitic world. The unit of religion was the living tribe : they were the interest and care of the Deity; with whom the individual had no part or portion except in his place as a living member of the tribe.

It is plain, then, that to whatever heights the religion of Israel afterwards rose, it remained before the age of the great prophets not only similar to, but in all respects above-mentioned identical with, the general Semitic religion ; which was not a monotheism, but a polytheism with an

[1] Enoch and Elijah.

opportunity for monotheism at the heart of it — each tribe being attached to one god, as to their particular Lord and Father.

Our next question is whether any of the forces which could take advantage of this opportunity for monotheism[1] were present in Israel to a greater degree than we have found them among the other Semites.

To begin with the *political,* — we find that up to the eighth century the history of Israel was largely one of conquest. In the belief of the people this history had been started by the victories of their God over one of the great empires of the world. Jahweh had brought His people out of Egypt, divided the sea, led them through the desert and dispossessed the nations of Canaan before them. These experiences must have lifted Israel's ideas of Jahweh very much above the level of the respect entertained for their deities by nations who remembered nothing of their own history except as transacted within the narrow bounds of their territories. We have more than one proof that the faltering faith of early Israel in the power of Jahweh was wont to refresh itself by the memory of those great events. This, however, as we have seen, did not cure even the leaders of the people of their belief in the reality of other gods; and indeed the settlement in Canaan, so far from extending,

[1] See above, p. 122.

in their regard, Jahweh of Sinai's power over that land, brought them under the fascination of its native gods, the patrons of its agriculture. With such experiences others conspired, especially when, under Solomon and Ahab, Israel entered into commerce with foreign peoples and concluded political alliances; for such relations involved the erection of shrines to alien gods side by side with the altars of Jahweh. It is certain, then, that without the presence of other influences, Israel's political history would have been powerless to produce her monotheism.[1]

Nor can we describe these influences as *intellectual*. Early Israel does not seem to have had more of the power of sustained speculation than her Semitic neighbours. As we have seen, there is little argument in the Old Testament for the being, and none for the unity, of God. The cosmogony of the first chapter of Genesis belongs to the youngest of the Pentateuchal documents, and is of date subsequent to that at which the ethical foundations of monotheism

[1] Professor Budde has acutely remarked in his recent lectures on *The Religion of Israel before the Exile*, (p. 71), that the contact with other gods did not altogether mean religious loss for Israel. They probably learned in Canaan to associate the more beneficent forces of nature with the Deity, as they saw them exemplified in the native gods, and they transferred the attributes of these to Him. This is true, but the transference would not have taken place, or at least would not have been unaccompanied by the grosser features of those gods, unless from other sources Israel had been convinced of the higher ethical character of Jahweh.

were already laid by the prophets. The eighth chapter of the Book of Proverbs, sometimes called 'the only metaphysic in the Bible,' is probably of a still later origin. And whatever the date of the Book of Job may be, its arguments on God are not those of the head, but those of the heart and conscience.

We turn, therefore, to Israel's *ethical* attainments before the eighth century, and here, in the opinion of all critics, we at last find proofs of the distinction of her religion from that of other Semites, and the sources of the monotheism which culminated in her prophetical writings.

By the beginning of the pre-prophetic period the Jahwist and Elohist documents[1] were extant in Israel. We have already seen the high conceptions which govern the Jahwist's account of the origin and early civilisation of man. In the stories of Jacob and Joseph we are presented with portraits of character which display great powers of ethical reflection, and in the story of Joseph reveal the purest and most tender of moral ideals. The responsibility of the individual to God in matters deeper than those of a tribal morality is taken for granted. *How can I do this great wickedness and sin against Jahweh?* says Joseph in answer to the chief

[1] With the exception of some later strata, which I shall avoid in the following ethical estimate of the documents.

temptation of his life; [1] and again he explains the motive of his treatment of his brethren in the words, *for I fear God*.[2] Throughout these early documents God's care of the individual is beautifully illustrated.

Now it may be, as some critics hold, that these documents, in the form in which we possess them, were composed after the teaching of the eighth-century prophets had begun to work in Israel. Yet even allowing this, we must assign to the processes of ethical reflection which blossomed in them a considerably earlier date. The possibility is confirmed by those stories of David which cannot be much later than David's own time. In those we have already found [3] the records of a character whose essentially Semitic features do not show more real to nature than the higher qualities which dramatically mingle with them. This lofty ethic appears in connection with the national God. David's sin is discovered to him by a prophet of Jahweh: it is before Jahweh that the guilty king repents and humbles himself. A century and a half later we have confirmatory evidence of the morale of Israel's religious leaders. Micaiah ben Imlah breaks from the racial idea, that the tribal God must necessarily give his tribe the victory, and at the risk of martyrdom proclaims

---

[1] Gen. xxxix. 9.
[2] Gen. xlii. 18.　　　　[3] See Lecture III., pp. 79 ff.

from Jahweh Ahab's defeat.[1] As we saw in last
Lecture,[2] the zeal of Elijah for Jahweh is inexplicable except on the belief that Jahweh's
character is absolutely different from that of
other deities. The prophet's intolerance of the
latter must have had ethical reasons; and this
view is confirmed by the manner in which
Elijah enforces Jahweh's claims, not only against
the Phœnician deities but, in the teeth of Ahab
and Israel themselves; predicts the employment
of a foreign nation by Jahweh to punish Israel;
and champions against the injustice of the king
the rights of the subject in the case of Naboth
and his vineyard. We see, then, that before the
eighth century the ethics of Israel had already
burst the bonds of a tribal morality within
which other Semitic religions were still confined.
This is what we should have expected from the
appearance of so largely developed an ethical
monotheism in the prophets of the eighth century. It would be unscientific to wholly doubt
their testimony that the principles they enforce
were not new in Israel. A religion such as theirs
is no isolated creation.

We have now to ask, what were the sources
of those ethical features in the religion of early
Israel, which so largely prepared the way for
the monotheism of the prophets and helped to

[1] 1 Kings xxii.
[2] Pp. 82 f.

render the creed of Israel so conspicuous an exception in the religion of the Semites?

Among modern critics there is virtual unanimity in carrying back the origin of Israel's ethical distinction to the time of Moses, and in regarding him as its instrument. Kuenen, for instance, who is so careful to claim the prophets as the creators of ethical monotheism, admits that, though Jahweh of early Israel and Chemosh of Moab (for example) were branches of the same stock, 'sons of the same house,' there must have been in the Jahweh religion from the very beginning the germs of that development which it afterwards achieved in such marvellous distinction from all the other faiths from whose level it had started. But though the origins of Israel's distinction are thus generally assigned to the Mosaic period, there is some difference of opinion as to what was their exact cause. Israel in the time of Moses enjoyed the same motives to ethical development as we have seen existing in other Semitic tribes. The close association of the deity with the tribal morals and public justice presented many opportunities of reflection on his character, which the honest and able minds among his accredited representatives can scarcely have failed to employ, with the result of raising the tribal conception of the divine commands, and the ethical ideal generally. How did Israel alone succeed in taking advantage of such opportunities? It is not enough to answer that her intellect must have been quicker and more reflective than that of other Semites; nor, as we have seen, that Israel's political history, which so powerfully assisted her religious development, was itself the cause of that.

A more probable origin for the ethical superiority of Israel has been sought in another direction. Historians of the world's faiths have learned to distinguish between nature religions and historical religions; between those which represent the original connection of a deity with his worshippers as physical, and those which describe the deity as drawing near to his people and becoming known to them through events in their history. The faith of Israel was of the latter kind. The people's memory traced their relations with Jahweh to what their earliest historians call a *covenant* between Him and them. Their prophets appeal to what has evidently been a long-established belief among the people, that Jahweh had not always been the god of Israel, but that He found them at a crisis in their history, and offered His help in return for their obedience. He had chosen them, and they had taken Him as their lord and god. The true metaphor for this relation was not paternal but conjugal: it rested on a contract. In Israel's belief in this transaction some historians of her early religion find the

germs of her rapid ethical development.[1] It does
not seem to me, however, to exhaust the secret
of which we are in search. For Israel alone did
not recognise reciprocal duties between themselves and their God; other peoples, however
physical they conceived the origin of their
relations with their deities to be, interpreted
these relations as involving mutual responsibilities between each god and his nation. Their
histories gave them also opportunities of reflect-
ing on the meaning of their god's anger with
them as experienced in their defeats and the
devastation of their lands. Nevertheless, they
were not thereby inspired to the ethical development which we see in Israel. Or look within
Israel. The popular religion which the prophets

1 Professor Budde has given a very able and reasonable statement of this hypothesis in the first of his American Lectures on
The Religion of Israel up to the Exile. 'Israel accepted Jahve's
offer to be its god; and relying on his promise through Moses to
deliver it found he kept his word and felt that it owed him
gratitude and fidelity in return for the boon.' 'He was unknown
to it before. It knew, however, this much from experience, that
he was a great and powerful god who could help if he would. It
could adopt his worship only with fear and dread, always in doubt
whether it had fathomed the depths of his nature, whether its
actions found favour with Jahve and would be regarded as
sufficient proof of fidelity. Whenever things went badly with the
people, it was far from thinking that Jahve had not power to
help. On the contrary, its conscience awaked each time to the
questions: "Wherein have I deserved the displeasure of Jahve?
What must I do to ensure his favour?" Thus arose a really
living force whose operation tended to the ethical development of
Israel's religion. . . . The germ of this whole development took
place at Sinai. . . .'

attacked, itself contained the idea of a contract between the nation and Jahweh, and was
conscious that His fulfilment of that contract
demanded obedience and gratitude from His
people.[1] Yet the popular religion of Israel did
not therefore become ethical: on the contrary,
the prophet's charge against it was that it was
devoid of morality, and was inspired only by
formal and superstitious notions of what Jahweh
required of the people.

Hence the prophets who combat the popular
religion of Israel declare that the people must
form new notions of the terms on which Jahweh
made His covenant, or, which comes to the same
thing, that they must form new notions of Jahweh
Himself. The prophets constantly complain of
the people's ignorance, and urge them *to know
Jahweh* Himself. If we believe the prophets, as
everybody does believe them, when they say that
Israel's relation to her God was based not on
physical connection with Him, but upon a historical covenant, we ought not to refuse their
further testimony that this covenanting Deity
had from the first revealed His moral attributes.
This is confirmed by all we can gather from
the genuine records of Israel's history before
the prophets. Although we are uncertain
whether any written law has reached us from

[1] This is plain from the account which Amos gives of the
zeal of the popular religion in his day.

Moses himself, we cannot but believe, on the
evidence at our disposal, in the existence in
Israel from his time onwards of what was a
more powerful factor of ethical development
than any written code could have been: a consciousness of the character of the Deity such as
no other Semitic people possessed. In other
words, the covenant itself was not the factor
which told in early Israel's ethical development, but knowledge of the God behind the
covenant, and appreciation of His moral attributes.

It is true that early Israel's view of the Divine
character is limited and disturbed by those
ancestral conceptions of Deity which were
common to themselves and their Semitic kinsfolk. The first beginnings of the higher faith
had to express themselves in the language,
through the symbols, and even in the intellectual
conceptions, with which the men to whom they
came were already familiar in connection with
religion. The development, therefore, of whatever new ethical principles or influences met
Israel in the time of Moses could only be
gradual. And thus the Jahweh of early
Israel shared much of the same character, and
was believed to reveal Himself in many of the
same forms which the other Semites associated
with their gods. Yet from the first Israel must
have seen in Jahweh attributes of a higher kind

than any of their neighbours attributed to the Divine character.

We must observe, too, this remarkable fact: that the rapid moral growth of early Israel never runs away from the character of the national God. Other ancient nations achieved ethical progress at the expense of their religion. Their gods were left behind and laughed at as the conscience of the worshippers developed. But Jahweh was never found wanting by Israel, and never discredited by any new conception of truth or by any strange experience in their history. Every fresh moral ideal is confessed by the people as the impression of His character and will; and for each new problem raised by their contact with the world their faith in Him is found sufficient.

Such are the facts of the early religion of Israel which the critical[1] study of it, in comparison with other Semitic religions, presents in answer to our question about the Old Testament as the record of a Divine Revelation. Are they sufficient to prove the claims of Israel, that God Himself spoke directly to this people in the events of their national history from the begin-

[1] That is, based only on such parts of the Old Testament as are admitted by the textual and historical criticism of the Old Testament to be evidence of the pre-prophetic religion of Israel.

ning, and by the mouths of their leaders from
Moses to Elijah? We have seen how thoroughly
Semitic the religion of early Israel was in frame
and fibre; and not less how in it alone of all
Semitic faiths there dwelt an ethical spirit —
the only promise in all that Semitic world of a
true monotheism, and a promise which was actually fulfilled by the great Hebrew prophets.
We have seen how all attempts to account for
this religious uniqueness of Israel by their
physical or historical conditions have failed,
because these conditions were equally shared
by Israel's Semitic kinsfolk. We have seen
that the gradual ethical development, which
thus differentiated Israel from her neighbours,
appears to have begun with the introduction
to the nation of Jahweh as their God; and
that every stage of its progress was achieved
in connection with some impression of His
character.

It seems to me that there are here the lines
of an apologetic, for a Divine Revelation through
early Israel, more sure and clear than any which
the traditional interpretation of the Old Testament ever attempted to lay down. That is all
I seek to prove. There are those who refuse
altogether to believe in the possibility of the
Christian idea of Revelation; and with them
other arguments must be employed. But if we
are Christians, and hold that man's education
in the knowledge of God is not exclusively a

human process, that the Mind which our minds, and the Heart which our hearts, seek behind the phenomena of nature and history, cannot be less urgent or forward than our own in the desire and effort to meet, then we cannot doubt that the history of early Israel, as critically interpreted, was an authentic and a unique stage in the process of Revelation — that Israel were receiving through their national God real impressions of the character and mind of the Deity.

Obviously this could not flash upon them all at once. The Revelation of the Unity of God and of His perfect Holiness, as we know it, would have been no real revelation to a people on the level of Israel from the fourteenth to the ninth centuries before Christ. It would have hovered in the air, out of reach of their primitive conceptions and undeveloped conscience: impalpable, impossible. Had one dreamed it, there was no language capable of its tradition. The character of God had to be proved upon the only floor on which men then expected to see the interest of the Deity in morals: that is to say, within the narrow limits of the tribal life and through the tribal institutions. The will of God, in order to be understood, had to be expressed, not merely in the spoken dialect of the people, but in the dearer language of religious symbol and sacrament, already consecrated by the use of many generations. The mind of God had to make its way to the mind of man through older intellectual conceptions of the Deity, which, as we have seen, clung about the people's notions of Jahweh for centuries after Moses. But just because of its adoption of the practical realities and religious symbols of the life on which it descended, the new Spirit secured a habitation in the mind of the people and the means of tradition and development. Among all the errors and limitations which the past had bequeathed, the impressions of the righteous character of God worked as a leaven. They elevated gradually the great body of unwritten custom and legislation which Israel had derived from their Semitic fathers; they moulded the nation in discipline and taught them gratitude and loyalty to their Head; they proved themselves active beyond the tribal territory and life; they helped the mind of Israel to rise to every problem which its widening horizon presented.

But the divinity of the process is vindicated beyond itself. It carried Israel through the crises of the eighth century, when every god of their neighbours was discredited, but Jahweh by the moral character, slowly revealed as His through the previous ages, was trusted by His people as the wielder of the world's forces. It produced the monotheism of the Prophets. And finally Christ confirmed it as the gradual preparation by God for the full revelation of Himself in the life and death of His Son.

LECTURE V

THE SPIRIT OF CHRIST IN THE OLD TESTAMENT

THE older theologies approached our present subject in a way different from that which I ask you to follow. Of Christ in the Old Testament they have mainly treated under the heads of Typology and Messianic Prophecy. These are departments of Biblical Doctrine for which we have the warrant of the New Testament. As usually treated, however, they are either too wide or too narrow for the illustration of the Spirit of Christ under the Old Covenant.

Too wide — for to the preacher, as the history of the Christian pulpit has painfully proved, their vagueness has been a constant temptation to overdo them. In their elastic range, and the ambiguous quality of many of their details, the spoiled children of the pulpit have taken a larger licence than even among the predictions and apocalypse of the New Testament. Venturing beyond the furthest hint of the Apostolic writers, preachers have spun their allegories of Christ out of every plausible character and transaction in Old Testament history and poetry; or

K

have assiduously polished each rite and institution of the Jewish Law in the attempt to make it a mirror of our Lord and His Sacrifice. It would not be unjust to call those mere flatterers of their Lord, who, without moral insight or real devotion, have heaped upon Him indiscriminately all the titles of Old Testament History, and symbolised every detail of Jewish worship as if it were the ingenuity of their efforts and the quantity of their results which were well-pleasing to Him, or capable of convincing the doubter of His Divinity. The fancy, that to discover some type or predic- tion of Christ where nobody else had seen one before was to honour Christ and confound His enemies, has been the besetting sin both of mediæval and of Protestant styles of exegesis; and nothing has been more guilty of rendering sermons on the Old Testament artificial and un- real. How different is the liberal and patient temper of Calvin! He examines every alleged type and prediction. He says this is 'too forced'; that 'too fine.' 'In these things we require not cleverness but *quid solidum*,' some- thing reliable, something sane. And therefore, when he does admit a type or prophecy of Christ, he makes us sure of it. We know that he seeks to learn what God means rather than to find what his own ingenuity can prove. He is jealous to serve his Lord with truth.[1]

---

[1] The same spirit, struggling with far heavier difficulties, is seen

But if Typology and Messianic Prophecy are in some directions too vague to show us Christ aright in the Old Testament, in others they are too narrow. There are many passages which breathe His Spirit, and which have never been included among 'the types' or Messianic predictions. I do not suppose, for instance, that under one or other of these heads either the Song of Deborah or the Elegy upon Saul and Jonathan was ever gathered by a theologian ; and indeed Matthew Henry, on the ground that the Elegy does not name the Name of God, calls it 'a humane composure,' a piece of non-religious literature. I hope to show that both of those early poems breathe the Spirit of Christ, and that this Spirit is shared by many other passages, which no system of Typology or Prophecy has ventured to include.

Again, every one, who is familiar with the efforts of Christian preaching to illustrate or explain the Sacrifice of Christ from the Old Testament, is aware how the emphasis of the argument is almost always laid upon the animal sacrifices of the Levitical legislation, and how the human sacrifices of Old Testament history — the sufferings of the righteous and the vicarious strife and agony of the heroes of Israel — are

in Theodore of Mopsuestia (d. 429 A.D.), the greatest Old Testament exegete among the early fathers : cf. the just title accorded him in Sieffert's work, *Theod. Mopsuestenus Vet. Test. sobrie interpretandi Vindex* (1827).   See below, **Lecture VII.**

either forgotten or used only for the peroration. An equal error has been made in the Old Testament argument for our Lord's Divinity: the proofs have been sought in strained interpretations of the essentially human attributes and offices of the Messianic King, instead of in those affections and struggles for the salvation of men which the Old Testament imputes to God Himself.

The following Lecture is the attempt to place the whole subject of the prophecy of Christ in the Old Testament and the presence of His Spirit in the history of Israel upon historical and ethical lines, in place of those so largely followed by theologians and preachers in treating of Typology, Messianic Prophecy and the Argument from the Old Testament for our Lord's Divinity and His Sacrifice.

I. *From the Earliest Times to David.*

We will most suitably start upon our task from the point which was reached in the close of last Lecture. We saw that the main factor in the development of the religion of Israel was the impression upon the people, through the events of their history and the consciousness of their greatest men, of the character of God. This it was which separated the people from the heathen around them, quickened within them a new moral sense, sifted and qualified the mass of custom and unwritten law which they had inherited as children of the great Semitic family, and finally produced both prophecy and the legal codes, in which the principles of prophecy and the hereditary practice of the nation were together precipitated.

But we must not suppose that this revelation of the character of God was confined to His righteousness, or was even predominantly that of His righteousness. That is one of the most widespread fallacies about the Old Testament. Mr. Matthew Arnold, who is almost as brilliant an instance of the method of writing history by intuition as Renan himself, never made more manifest the perils of such a method than when he defined the essence of Israel's religion as a tendency or force, not ourselves, which makes for righteousness. More patient workers in the field have fallen into the same error. Nothing is more certain about the object of Israel's faith than first, that it was a Person; and second, that the character of this Person was by no means only or predominantly righteousness. Jahweh is as effectively a God of grace as He is a God of justice; and although our meagre information requires us to speak with caution of the earliest period of Israel's religion, it is sufficiently well-established that during that period His grace was (to say the least) as manifest to His people's hearts, and as operative in their lives, as His

Justice: for the full expression of which we have to wait till the prophets. In this connection criticism has done no disservice to the Christian preacher by removing from the pre-prophetic stage of the religion the vast bulk of the Law; for it has thereby left him the more free to appreciate throughout these long centuries the love and faithfulness of Israel's God. Our information, as I have said, is meagre, but it is enough. We cannot doubt the servitude of Israel in Egypt, nor their deliverance under Moses, in obedience as they believed to the impulse of Jahweh ; nor their sojourn in the Desert, when, as water is spilled upon the sand, so Israel's distinctive character might have passed from them, and except for the patience and watchfulness of their God they might have sunk back into the nomadic life from which their fathers had sprung. No one doubts their arrival in a land, where again their unity might have been dissipated amidst the geographical conditions, but a national career and destiny became possible by their trust that Jahweh, in spite of their frequent unfaithfulness to Him, continued to preserve and to lead them. The notes of grace — of Divine redemption and guidance — were thus in the religion of Israel from the very first. We may not have many, or any, authentic expressions of this from the period itself; but after it, in a number of the most ancient frag-

ments of the Old Testament, the remembrance
appears. In Deborah's song Jahweh's people are
his *lovers*.[1] The good-will of Jahweh to help His
nation against their foes comes as an inspiration
to Gideon.[2] In the movement of ecstatic prophecy
which broke out in Israel under Samuel, we see
the power of the sense of the 'Rûᵃḥ' or *Spirit
of Jahweh*, — His personal energy — granted to
His people to inspire them to victory over their
Philistine oppressors. The movement is the
passion of a people for their God, who affects
them not only by His righteousness, the full force
of which they obviously did not yet comprehend,
but by His redemption of them from servitude,
His patience with their disloyalties, His faithfulness to them in face of their foes. It is the
early Jahwist (or Elohist) who gives the proclamation to Moses: *Jahweh, Jahweh a compassionate
and gracious God slow to anger and plenteous in
mercy and truth*.[3] Such words may be a more
explicit sense of the Divine Law than the Mosaic
Age in Israel had achieved; but in any case
the germs of the higher consciousness of God,
which, as Kuenen admits, were present in the
Mosaic Age, were germs of the consciousness
not of His justice merely but still more of His

---

[1] Judges v. 31*a*. E. Meier, Winter and Budde reckon this
verse to be a later addition to the Song of Deborah: 'in the
style of the Psalms' (Budde); but, in my opinion, on insufficient
grounds.

[2] Judges vi. 11 ff.   [3] Ex. xxxiv. 6.

mercy and faithfulness. The long poem in the
thirty-second chapter of Deuteronomy, which is
probably not later than the eighth century, and
which so accurately represents the passage of
early Israel from the nomadic life of the desert
to the agriculture of Canaan,[1] as beautifully
ascribes it to Jahweh's fatherly providence of
the nation when

> *In a wilderness land He found him,*
> *In the waste and the howling desert;*
> *He encompassed him, yea kept His eye upon him*
> *As the apple of His eye, so He watched him.*
> *As an eagle which stirreth his nest,*
> *And fluttereth over his young,*
> *And spreadeth his wings to catch them,*
> *And beareth them up on his pinions,*
> *Jahweh alone was his leader,*
> *And never a strange God was with him.*

The prophets of the eighth century are full of
wonder at Jahweh's love for Israel and His choice
of them to be His people; at His long patience
with them and constant forgiveness of their
rebellion and sin. The elements of this wonder
cannot be wholly from the prophetic age; the
same sense, however dim, must have stirred
Israel from the first.

So at least we seem to see in the very early
Song of Deborah. The attraction of such a God,

---

[1] See *Historical Geography of the Holy Land*, pp. 85–90.

and the loyalty which His loyalty calls forth, are there represented as the factors of the national unity. These dozen desert tribes, cursed with the incoherence of Semitic life, were brought together and kept together by their common trust in their Deity. When, after the settlement in Palestine, among the diverse opportunities which the broken geography of the land so remarkably affords, they were tempted to separate from their common interests upon widely divergent lines of culture,[1] it was, as the Book of Judges testifies, not by a return to the Law that they were united but by the recollection of their debt to Jahweh. In Deborah's as in Gideon's case, memory was the nurse to faith, and the conviction of His unfaltering desire to help them rallied the people against their foreign tyrants. The opening verse of Deborah's Song gives us the whole secret of the national inspiration in a tribute of glory to Jahweh:

For that the leaders took the lead in Israel,
For that the people offered themselves willingly,[2]
Praise ye Jahweh!

In the end of the Song which thus grandly opens, we are repelled by the savage exultation of a woman over the treacherous murder of a defeated foe. And rightly; for Christ has given

[1] Judges iv. 15*b*–17.
[2] The exact meaning of these two lines is obscure; but their intention is plain.

us the right to judge. But do we pay as much attention to the virtues which are manifest in the Song? Nowhere do we find a more scathing exposure of those who prefer the material ambitions of life, however legitimate, to the call of national need in the name of the religious ideal;[1] and nowhere is self-sacrifice more finely celebrated.

> *Zebulun was a people that jeoparded their lives to the death,*
> *And Naphtali on the high places of the field.*[2]

Whatever views we have of war — and we are those who themselves owe their religious liberty to the virtues of the battlefield — let us remember what war did for Israel. *By war*, says Jahweh elsewhere, *I took you*,[3] and we may extend the meaning of these words beyond the mere fact that so He helped them to freedom, to the moral assurance that by the call to fight He redeemed them from selfishness, from servitude to material aims, from schism and disloyalty to Himself. The battlefield was the Golgotha of early Israel. It was there that Zebulun and Naphtali laid down their lives for the brethren; and there that the Spirit of Christ which was in Israel from the beginning won its earliest triumphs. When we hear a Psalmist sing (in a Psalm for which there are more reasons for

---

[1] Judges iv. 15*b*–17.   [2] Verse 18.   [3] Deut. iv. 34.

a pre-exilic date than for any other in the
Psalter) —

> *By thee do I break through a fence,*
> *And by my God do I leap over a wall —*
> *He maketh my feet like hinds' feet*
> *He teacheth my hands to war,*
> *So that a steel bar is broken by my arms.*
> *Thou hast enlarged my steps under me*
> *So that my ancles swerve not* [1] —

we ought to remember the issues at stake in
Israel's wars, and the virtues which these evoked.
In the next verse the Psalmist gives the secret
of it all: *Thy gentleness hath made me great.*[2]

The heroism, the self-sacrifice, the loyalty to the
nation and to Jahweh were the warrior's devotion
to the tender and faithful character of his God.

The poem next earliest to Deborah's Song,
David's Dirge upon Saul and Jonathan, is another
illustration of the same Spirit. It is all the more
valuable to our present purpose that it is one of
the few specimens of the popular poetry of early
Israel. The Dirge is not religious in the narrower
sense of the term. It is without the name of
God: it says no word of the service of the dead,
whom it praises, to the religion of their nation.
And above all, it does not commit their spirits to
God, nor express any hope of a future life.[3] On
these grounds the great Puritan commentator,

---

[1] Psalm xviii. 29, 33, 34.   [2] Verse 35.
[3] This will be dealt with in the next Lecture.

Matthew Henry — a man of firm belief in the inspiration of the Bible and of rare insight into its meaning — has called the Dirge, as I have already said, 'a humane composure,' an extract from a book of popular ballads with the authorship of which the Holy Spirit has had nothing to do. But Christ has said, *Not every one that saith unto me, Lord, Lord ;* and again, *By their fruits shall ye know them.* Judged by that standard, the absence of the Divine Name from this poem will not prevent us from appreciating its truly Christian spirit. The Dirge is by a man upon his dead enemy and his dead friend. But for the former there is no word save of generosity and admiration. Saul had relentlessly hunted David, and upon more than one occasion had attempted his life. Latterly he had been a bad king to Israel, and his death, with the defeat it brought upon the nation, had been due to his own errors. David is not only silent upon these, but remembers nothing of the persecutions to which Saul had subjected him. That the poem is animated, not merely by a poet's heart for the virtues of a great man, but by the spirit of personal forgiveness for very cruel wrongs, is proved by the whole attitude of David to the living Saul and his house. David spared his hunter's life, and showed kindness to his children. Criticism has no doubt to cast upon the story, according to which the service of David's youth had been the attempt to win the king from his evil moods by skilful playing on the harp. Here was the secret of David's attitude to Saul through the persecution which he suffered from him. The life of his tormentor, which he spared when he had the power to take it, and which he praised when the king by his own error lay dead on Gilboa, had once been intrusted to him by Jahweh to redeem from the powers of evil for the service of God and the people. But this is the Spirit of Christ. Though the Dirge upon Saul finds no place in any theologian's system of 'types,' it is yet one of the most beautiful anticipations which the Old Testament has to offer us of Christ's teaching : *But I say unto you, Love your enemies, bless them that curse you, do good to them that hate you, and pray for them that despitefully use you and persecute you.*

These instances from the early history of Israel are enough to prove to you and me, as preachers of the Gospel, that, accepting the results of modern criticism, we shall yet be sure of finding across that whole stretch of the Old Testament — upon which its effects have been most feared, and where we must confess the life to be very rude, the ethics to be primitive, and monotheism itself to be undeveloped — the presence of Divine Grace, of the Spirit of Christ, and of the virtues of forgivingness and self-sacrifice which these call forth in men.

II. *The Prophets.*

The teaching of the Eighth-Century Prophets foreshadows the gospel of Jesus upon its great texts of Forgiveness; Repentance; *the Kingdom of Heaven is at hand;* and the coming of the Perfect King or Messiah.

Upon the two first of these themes Hosea has all the essence of the evangel; which indeed quotes his great saying: *I will have mercy and not sacrifice.* Through terrible personal suffering inflicted by one whom he loved, Hosea was led to understand how men's sins cost God more pain than anger.[1] From that moment the Gospel of Divine Forgiveness was assured. And just because she, whom the prophet was himself moved to forgive and redeem, was an individual, we may believe that, while the nation still continued with Hosea to be the unit of religion, he planted in Israel's faith the seeds which Jeremiah developed of the confidence that God too in forgiveness deals with the single souls of men. Upon Repentance Hosea's teaching is startlingly evangelical. The care with which he follows every symptom of it in his people;[2] the ethical sternness with which he repels their easy optimism regarding it;[3] the labour he takes to distinguish its true character from the sorrow of this world,[4]

---

[1] Chaps. i.–iii. [2] v. 15, vii. 1, xi. 7 ff., xii. 6, xiii. 7, xiv. 1.
[3] Ch. v. 15–vi. 6. [4] *Ibid.* and vii. 14.

and founds it on a new Knowledge of God and of His love,[1] in short, on a real change of mind — all this anticipates in a wonderful way the Metanoia of the Gospels and Epistles.[2]

Unlike his younger contemporary, Amos cannot be called an evangelical prophet: it is Law rather than Love in the Divine Nature on which he dwells ; yet he too had his part in the evangelical preparation. That passage, which least of all Old Testament literature looks like Gospel, the first and second chapters of Amos, is a real intimation that *the Kingdom is at hand.* It is the proclamation of the truth that all men are morally equal, and that to the righteousness of Jahweh not only Israel, but every one of her heathen neighbours, is responsible. Such is the necessary ethical basis for the preaching of repentance and forgiveness to the Gentiles. The missionary spirit of Israel will take centuries yet to awaken ; but this is its womb: this sense, for the first time expressed in the Old Testament, of the moral equality of all men before God.

In Isaiah's prophecies we meet with the first of those descriptions of the coming King which Christian theology regards as direct predictions of Christ. The Greek version of the very difficult prophecy of Immanuel is quoted by St. Matthew

[1] iv. 6, vi. 6, xi. 3-4, xiii. 4.

[2] A full exposition of Hosea's teaching on forgiveness and Repentance will be found in *The Book of the Twelve Prophets*, i. chaps. xxi.-xxiii.

as the statement of the Birth of Jesus from the
Virgin:[1] *Behold the Virgin shall be with child,
and shall bring forth a son, and they shall call
his name Emmanuel.* The Hebrew original[2] is
indefinite, and means *some marriageable woman.*
Isaiah meant no more than that some one should
be born whose character and hopes should be proof
that God was with His people. Whether the
promised Unborn was an individual, or a future
generation of Israel, it is difficult to make out ; but
probably the latter is what Isaiah intends. This
would not impair the legitimacy of Matthew's
reference of the prophecy to Jesus, to whom
prophetic descriptions of the people of Jahweh
are equally transferred with the predictions of
their coming King.[3] Against the authenticity
of other Messianic passages, of the Prince with
the Four Names and the Ideal Ruler, strong
reasons have been adduced[4]; but these cannot
be regarded as conclusive. The premises of
the passages — the firm hold which the Davidic
dynasty had secured in Judah, the memory of
David himself as an ideal king, the need in
the time of King Ahaz for a monarch strong,
just and loyal to Jahweh — were all present
in Isaiah's day. The tasks assigned by the

[1] Matt. i. 22, 23.

[2] Isaiah vii. 14.

[3] Cf. Matthew's application (ii. 15) to Jesus of Hosea's description of Israel's call out of Egypt (xi. 1).

[4] Isaiah ix. 6 f. ; xi. 1-5.

passages to the victorious Prince and righteous Judge are exactly those on which the whole ministry of Isaiah was bent, while they are not such as were necessary in the Exilic Age to which the passages have been relegated by some critics.[1]

In any case the application of these prophecies to Jesus Christ must be made with discrimination. They have been too hastily used as predictions of the Godhead of the Messiah. But not even do the names in Chapter ix. 6 f. imply Deity; while all the functions attributed to the Promised King are human. Isaiah's Messiah is an earthly monarch, of the stock of David, and with offices that are political, both military and judicial. He is not the mediator of spiritual gifts to his people : forgiveness, a new knowledge of God, and the like. It is only in this, that he saves the people of God from destruction and reigns over them with justice and in the fear of God, that he can be regarded as a type of Jesus Christ.[2]

[1] Against the authenticity of Isaiah ix. 6 f. and xi. 1–5, see Hackmann, *Die Zukunftserwartung des Jesaia*, 1893; Cheyne, *Introduction to the Book of Isaiah*, 1895; and for the historical theory which relegates all predictions of the Messiah to the Exilic Age, cf. Marti, *Geschichte der Israel. Religion*, p. 190; and Paul Volz, *Die vorexil. Prophetie u. der Messias*, 1897. On the other hand, Driver, Kirkpatrick, Duhm, Skinner, Budde and a majority of critics leave the passages in question with Isaiah. For the arguments on both sides, and the conclusion that those for the authenticity are the stronger, see the present writer's article on 'Isaiah' in Hastings's *Bible Dictionary*, ii. pp. 487 ff.

[2] So the present writer in Hastings's *Bible Dictionary*, ii. 491.

In the belief that chapters xl.–lxvi. of the Book
of Isaiah were from himself, Isaiah has been
called by Christians the Evangelical Prophet.
These chapters, however, we now know to be by
the great evangelist of the Exile.[1] To a gospel
for the spiritual life of the individual, Hosea
makes a far closer approach than his greater
contemporary; yet even in the genuine work of
Isaiah we find the elements of the doctrines
of Grace. Jahweh forgives sins, even the most
heinous and defiling.[2] His love and pity never
fail His people's penitence.[3] He is their well-
beloved, and constantly cares for them.[4] It is His
passion for them which is the spring and assurance of all their deliverance.[5] Of these truths
Isaiah became himself convinced through his individual experience of pardon and of cleansing.[6]

 Isaiah, however, was too much engaged with
the fate of his nation to become the preacher
of that personal religion, of which the proofs
were given him in his inaugural vision. Even
in the following century, in the great Law-
book which codifies the teaching of the eighth
century prophets, the unit of religion is still
Israel as a whole. Deuteronomy is the most
perfect example the world has seen of a system of national religion, but it addresses itself

---

1 See above, pp. 53 f.   2 Isa. i. 18.
3 Isa. xiv. 32; xxxvi.–xxxvii.   4 Isa. v. 1 ff.
5 Isa. ix. 7, etc.   6 Isa. vi. 5 ff.

to the nation. The individual is treated only as a member of the nation, and there is no promise for humanity beyond, nor conscience of Israel's ' missionary' duty except to the *strangers* who settle in the land.   Yet the high monotheism of the Book, along with its tenderness and humanity; its enforcement (in dependence on Hosea) of the love of God, based on a true knowledge of His character, and its care for the education of the young, secure for Deuteronomy a place in the evangelical preparation.   Its influence on the domestic and personal religion of Israel in all ages has never been exceeded by that of any other Book in the Canon.   Our Lord not only quoted from it the expression of the essence of the Law,[1] but sustained upon its words His own soul in the conflict with Temptation.[2] There are few books in the Old Testament, the regular exposition of which will more profit a Christian preacher and his people.

This brings us to Jeremiah, who, beyond every other in the old dispensation, was the forerunner of Jesus Christ: and that both in his teaching and in his personal experience.[3]

Jeremiah began his career as a prophet about 627, before the discovery of Deuteronomy in the

[1] Matt. xxii. 37 f.; Mark xii. 29 f.; Luke x. 27.

[2] Matt. iv. 4 and 7; Luke iv. 4, 8; cf. Deut. viii. 3; vi. 13, 16; x. 20.

[3] He was expected by the Jews of our Lord's day to return to earth: cf. Matt. xvi. 14, *some say . . . Jeremias.*

Temple, and he watched the progress of the reforms which it inspired under the reign of Josiah. With many of these he must have sympathised; and he frequently quotes from the letter of the Book. But besides his hostility to the formal obedience which his contemporaries showed to *the Law*, Jeremiah's ideal of religion was in advance of that of Deuteronomy. His monotheism was more free of the older conceptions of the Deity: to him at last the idols are *vanities* or *nothingnesses*, empty of reality: in Deuteronomy they are still subordinate deities whom Jahweh has *assigned to all the nations under heaven*.[1] We have evidence also of another attitude than that of the Deuteronomist to sacrifices and burnt-offerings. Jahweh, according to Jeremiah, gave no commands to the fathers of Israel concerning these; His commands were ethical only.[2] We have here a more explicit repetition of Hosea's text quoted by Christ: *I will have mercy and not sacrifice*. Hence it does not surprise us that before the end of his ministry Jeremiah proclaimed *a New Covenant* (the Deuteronomic being the old), in which there is no word of ritual or sacrifice, but man's communion with God, and God's forgiveness of man, depend on the inward knowledge, and acceptance, of God's ethical revelation. This is the Covenant which Christ said was sealed in His blood.[3]

[1] Deut. iv. 19.   [2] Jer. vii. 22.   [3] Luke xxii. 20.

It is, however, in his experience of the relation of the individual to God and to the community, that this greatest of the prophets becomes likest to Christ. The experience came to Jeremiah from the earliest moments of his career; but it was developed by antipathy to the people's formal fulfilment of the Deuteronomic ideals of national religion; it was confirmed by the collapse of these with the death of Josiah; and it was slowly articulated in the gradual decay of the nation and in the cruelties which the lonely prophet suffered under Jehoiakim and Zedekiah. The community, which Isaiah had described as inviolable, upon its historical site of Zion and in its political form as the kingdom of the house of David, was about to be broken up. The individual was being left to his own resources: there was a call to each man to save himself. The monarchy, the nation, the ritual, the Temple, were certain of destruction: Jeremiah could promise to his disciples only their bare lives.[1] And to a man like Jeremiah, such leadings of Providence were enforced by a number of religious considerations. As almost none before him had felt, Jeremiah knew how God can single out the individual and deal with him apart from his family, his citizenship, or his priesthood: *Before I formed thee in the belly I knew thee, and before thou camest forth of the womb I consecrated*

[1] Jer. xlv. 5; cf. xxi. 9; xxxviii. 2; xxxix. 18.

thee.[1] By temper the man was solitary, intro-
spective, greatly concerned about himself. His
nation, too, deserved nothing of him; they had
betrayed his God, they refused to listen to his
word, and they cast him off. What a conspiracy
of temptation was here to break away from the
community, to assert a purely individual religion,
to save one's own soul out of so manifestly
doomed a dispensation! Jeremiah tells us how he
felt the strain. At one time he prayed for some
far-off caravanserai of wayfaring men, where he
could be separate from his own people and no
longer responsible for their life.[2] At another, his
countrymen put him in prison lest he should
desert to the Babylonians;[3] and at another the
Babylonians offered him a place among themselves.[4] But God kept Jeremiah to a more
excellent way, and he had scarcely found his
position before God as an individual, independent
of every rite and relation, or realised his opportunities as an individual, when there descended upon
him a sense of his oneness with his people far more
stringent than ever prophet had felt it before — a
sympathy with their sufferings which breaks out
in the most pathetic cries in all literature; and
a conscience of their sins, which astounds and
perplexes him beyond the power of articulate
expression. *Jahweh, thou hast beguiled me and*

[1] Jer. i. 5.   [2] Jer. ix. 2.
[3] Jer. xxxvii. 13 ff.   [4] Jer. xl. 4 ff.

*I am beguiled: thou art stronger than I. Why
is my pain perpetual and my wound incurable?
Art thou altogether become to me as a liar, and as
waters that fail?* [1] His perplexity is his personal
experience of the sufferings of the righteous
through the wrongdoing of the wicked. *Only let
me put before Thee certain questions of justice:
Why is the way of the wicked fortunate, and how
are they happy who deal treacherously? Thou
plantest them: they take root and flourish and
bring forth fruit. Thou art familiar in their
mouths, but very far from their reins. Yet Thou,
O Jahweh, knowest me: Thou seest me and triest
my heart towards Thyself.* [2] It is a darker, a more
bewildered heart in Gethsemane: though it says
Thy will be done in its own way, *Thou hast right,
O Jahweh,* [3] it does not understand the meaning
of its burden and its cross.

A later generation, however, awoke to the
virtue of Jeremiah's pain. Whether the figure of
the Suffering Servant in the fifty-third of Isaiah
be intended by the writer as an individual (as it
seems to me we ought to conclude), [4] or (in the
opinion of most modern critics) as a personifica-
tion of the righteous and suffering remnant of
Israel, there is no doubt that the vision is partly
inspired by the nation's appreciation of the

[1] Jer. xx. 7; xv. 18.   [2] xii. 1–3.   [3] xii. 1.
[4] Both from the grammar and by the fact that Jeremiah's individual experience is reflected in it.

meaning of Jeremiah's life. They had awakened
to this through their own experience. God's
doom had fallen on a generation not more guilty
than their fathers; it had covered the righteous
as well as the sinners. Innocent children had
been born into it, and a whole generation had
grown up in exile under a curse which they
had not earned.

> *Our fathers have sinned and are not,*
> *And we have borne their iniquities.*[1]

It was out of this actual experience of the
reality of vicarious suffering as part of life
and of the providence of God, that the great
evangelical truths of the fifty-third of Isaiah
were developed. The Exile had brought Israel
face to face with the heathen world, and while
they received chastisement from their tyrants
they were conscious of their religious superiority
to these. In their despair before the world, there
gradually awoke the sense of a capacity to serve
it; there was aroused a new appreciation of
an old call. Israel was Jahweh's Servant and
Messenger to mankind. His exile was the
punishment of his refusal of this mission.[2]
But it was also a new opportunity for obedience ; and in so far as those upon whom the
exile had fallen were, as individuals, innocent,
could it not be said that the pains of the Exile

[1] Lam. v. 7.
[2] Which thought is developed by the later Book of Jonah.

fulfilled some higher religious end than the punishment of Israel, and were themselves part of
Israel's work for the world? Israel had been
blind and deaf,[1] and therefore Jahweh had given
him to the spoilers. But now *my Servant is
wise :* he understands his mission and the meaning of his sufferings, and (so the pregnant phrase
implies) shall succeed.[2] Thus in the meeting of
the old memory of a call to the service of
Jahweh, and the fresh experience of the sufferings of the righteous, there was born that conception of One sent from God, righteous and
blameless; misunderstood by the world and
deemed to be lying under God's displeasure;
by whose sufferings sinful men are redeemed,
and by whose stripes they are healed.

Side by side with these beliefs in the efficacy
of vicarious suffering, which were derived by
Israel from her experience of life, there grew
up a reconstruction of the ritual and the priesthood, in which the ideas of atonement and
cleansing for sin replaced to a large degree those
more peaceful and joyous feelings of communion
with God which govern the conception of sacrifice in Israel's earlier codes. The fifty-third of
Isaiah speaks of the human Servant of Jahweh
as bearing the sins of the people, efficaciously
removing them, and so giving his life a guilt-
offering for many. This guilt-offering was the

[1] Isaiah xlii. 19.　　　[2] Isaiah lii. 13.

central rite of the new system of ritual: in which sin was said to be borne and expiated by the death of beasts representative of those who offered them.

It has been argued by some [1] that there is no idea of substitution in the animal sacrifices of the Levitical Law, but that their offering is simply an act of penitence. The argument is far from conclusive, and its authors have to admit, both that the human conscience has elsewhere (though not universally) associated substitution with animal sacrifice, and that there are at least echoes of this in the Jewish system. Nevertheless, there is a truth underlying the opinion. The idea of vicarious suffering and substitution of the innocent for the guilty, whereby the guilty are redeemed from their sin, is to be traced not to those animal sacrifices of the Levitical ritual, but rather to the nobler source of human vicariousness and its virtue, as learned by Israel from their own experience, and idealised in the Suffering Servant of Jahweh, whose prototypes are Jeremiah and the righteous remnant. In such human instances we get the ethical truth of vicariousness: red with the blood of real life. In the animal sacrifices the expression of the idea is largely mechanical.

Unfortunately, both in Jewish and in Christian theology, it has been the sacrificial animals and not

[1] *E.g.* Schultz, *Old Testament Theology.*

the human Servant, Law and not Prophecy, which have governed the conceptions of atonement for sin. Symbol and ritual were among ancient people the best vehicle for the tradition of ideas, and therefore we can understand why, till our Lord's time, the truths we are treating should find their favourite popular expression in the forms of animal sacrifice, and why Christ Himself should associate His supreme Self-Sacrifice with the Paschal Lamb. But even the author of the Epistle to the Hebrews, who dwells more than any other New Testament writer upon the Levitical antitypes of Christ, shows their insufficiency, and precedes his exposition of them by majestic emphasis on the humanity of Christ — as distinct from an official priesthood — and by illustration of this from those human aspects of vicarious service in the Old Testament which fill his opening chapters. This example, unfortunately for Christianity, has been misunderstood — not by the greatest theologians but by the smaller ones, and by generation after generation of popular preachers. It is because Christian divines have dwelt too much on the Old Testament system of sacrifices and too little upon the figures of Jeremiah, the suffering remnant and the Servant of the Lord: too much upon the animal types of the Cross and too little upon the human forerunners of Christ: that their explanations of the vicarious character of the

passion and death of the Redeemer have so
often been mechanical and repulsive. Certainly
in our day, when animal sacrifices have so long
ceased to speak to the imagination and conscience of men, it is the direst blunder a preacher
may commit to dwell upon them except for the
barest of exegetical purposes. If we are to
get our fellows to believe in the redemptive
virtue of Christ's Cross, it will be by proving
to them that vicarious suffering and its ethical
virtue are no arbitrary enactments of God, but
natural to life and inevitable wherever sin and
holiness, guilt and love, encounter and contend.
'Non est dolor nisi de amore amisso, quanto
profundior erat amor tanto altius tangit dolor.' [1]
And in this we shall succeed most readily by
proving, as we can do from the history which
we have been traversing, that the figure of a
Sufferer, holy and undefiled, by whose stripes we
are healed, by whose bearing of our iniquities
we are justified, was desired and confidently
expected by men, not because Heaven had
arbitrarily proclaimed it, but out of their own
experiences of life and death, the very elements
of which provided them with their marvellous
picture of Him.

The Levitical system, however, was not wholly
animal or mechanical. The head and centre of
it was human, the *Great* or *High Priest* who first

[1] Hugo St. Victor, on Gen. vi. 6.

appears in Hebrew history with the Return from the Exile. In the visions of Zechariah,[1] he carries the guilt of the whole people before God and receives their pardon; in the Levitical Law he enters within the veil as their representative on the Day of Atonement.[2] At first of equal rank with the native governor of Israel,[3] the High Priest assumed gradually much of the civil and judicial power, till he became King as well as Priest, and thus besides gathering upon his person the virtue of the sacrificial system, represented also the political Messiah of the earlier prophets. It is unnecessary to follow in detail the influence of this Figure upon the theology of the New Testament and the constitution of the Christian Church. We shall see in a later Lecture, how a merely official and unhistorical interpretation of the double office was employed to defend the temporal government of the Popes.[4] How infinitely different is the human and ethical High Priesthood claimed for Jesus by the author of the Epistle to the Hebrews! Here there is nothing official, nothing of a secular sovereignty. Jesus, though the Son of God and natural head of mankind, enters upon His priesthood through the voluntary assumption of human nature and fellowship with all its suffering and temptation. The name of His great office is borrowed from

[1] Ch. iii.   [2] Levit. xvi.
[3] So in Haggai and Zechariah.   [4] See Lecture VII.

the Law; but its character and virtue are drawn
from the prophet's picture of the suffering servant
of the Lord.

But the Spirit of Christ in the Old Testament
is not exhausted even in its greatest human
figures; whether the Messiah of the earlier prophets, the Suffering Servant of the later, or the
High Priest of the Levitical system. We must
seek another line than these supply for the full
prophecy of the Incarnation. Parallel to that
prospect of the blessed future, which finds its goal
in the appearance of a human Saviour now reigning over His people and now suffering with them
and bearing their sins, there runs through all the
Prophets another line of vision the end of which
is the appearance of God Himself and Alone —
either undertaking His people's deliverance from
their enemies or reigning over them in visible
majesty. The human Messiah, whom the earlier
prophecies of Isaiah predict, disappears from the
later and God is all in all.[1] In Jeremiah, Jahweh
Himself is His people's *Righteousness*,[2] that is
their full and manifest vindication in history.
In the prophecy which most critics assign to
some disciple of Isaiah *Jahweh will be for us in
majesty. For Jahweh is our Judge, our Lawgiver,
our King: He will save us.*[3] At each great crisis
in Israel's history, the Eternal will appear, as for

---

[1] See article 'Isaiah' in Hastings's *Bible Dictionary*, vol. ii.
[2] Jer. xxxiii. 16.   [3] Isa. xxxiii. 21, 22.

instance He is pictured in an exilic or post-exilic vision [1] treading the wine-press of battle, and the blood of His people's foes stains all His raiment. With such theophanies we may take the very numerous passages of the Old Testament which attribute to the Deity effort and passion of the most violent kind, describe Him in the similitude of a man of war, Israel's champion and protagonist, and do not even hesitate, as in one instance,[2] to picture Him as a woman in travail. All these anthropomorphisms, as they are called, are not to be interpreted as the mere effort of their writers' art to make the unseen vivid to the imagination of a rude people. We are to see in them the expression of what all the Prophets felt to be the essence of the Divine: the truth that God makes His people's salvation His own concern and effort, and accomplishes this not in power only but in pain and self-sacrifice. The sins and sorrows of men are not only set in the light of His countenance, but He bears them upon His heart.[3] His righteousness is not only regnant but militant. He *rises and comes down*, entering His people's war with their enemies on a level of struggle equal with themselves. His love is not only complacent but sympathetic, passionate, self-sacrificing: *in all their affliction*

---

[1] Isa. lxiii. 1–6.   [2] Isa. xlii. 13, 14.

[3] Isa. xl.–lxvi. uses the same verb סָבַל *to bear*, meaning *to bear with pain and difficulty* of God and of the Servant of God.

He is afflicted. He *pleads* for their loyalty; *reasons* with them in their sins; travails for their new birth and their growth in holiness; and is *longsuffering* with their sinfulness and their ignorance.[1]

It is very evident, therefore, that the essence of the truth about God's love and the perfection of that love in suffering, which Christ manifested and which is the glory of the Christian doctrine of the Incarnation, was already conceived and expressed by the Prophets.

The Spirit of Christ in the Old Testament is not confined to its human heroes and ideals: the length and the breadth, the height and the depth of it belong to the Old Testament's revelation of God Himself.

---

[1] The substance of this passage will be found in an article by the present writer on 'The Messianic Prophecies' in a little volume of aids to Bible teachers, published by Messrs. Collins of Glasgow.

LECTURE VI

THE HOPE OF IMMORTALITY IN THE OLD TESTAMENT

WE now turn to as fascinating, and at first sight as perplexing, an aspect of our subject as we have yet encountered: the attitude of Israel and their Scriptures to a future life.

Every one knows, at least in outline, what that attitude is. For the most part the writers of the Old Testament display towards the future of the individual beyond the grave a steady indifference; which is the more striking that it persists among lavish and brilliant hopes for the earthly future of the nation. The references to a personal immortality in the presence of God are exceptional. In the historical Books they are limited to two heroes of the nation; in the prophets they do not occur; in the Psalms and the Book of Job they consist of a few cries of confidence that the believer in God can never be separated from Him. Otherwise, the life beyond the grave is pictured as a cheerless, dusty, underground reflection of the mere surface of

human existence, but without God or hope; from
the ultimate certainty of which the believer
seeks a respite by prayers for a long earthly life,
and the fulness of God's favour so long as this
lasts.

Such is the impression which the Old Testament makes upon those who search it for a
gospel of immortality. It is our first duty to
discover, by an examination of the details,
whether this impression is a just one. If we
prove it so, we have next to inquire what are
the historical reasons for so singular an attitude
towards the life to come. And finally we must
determine the practical value of Israel's faith in
this matter to the preacher of to-day.

I. *The Old Testament Data.*

In the historical portions of the Pentateuch —
which it is not necessary to separate into their
various strata, for towards this subject their attitude is remarkably alike — death is as busy as
elsewhere in the world, and men are as busy
caring for their dead. When Sarah dies Abraham
buys a sepulchre of the sons of Heth, and in
time is himself buried there with Isaac his son.
Jacob loses Rachel by the way, and by the way
lays her to rest *as thou comest to Ephrath.* His
own body is embalmed in Egypt and buried
in Macpelah. Joseph's body is embalmed and
carried by Israel all over the wilderness that it

too may lie in the Promised Land. Aaron and
Moses come to the end of their long years and
are laid, the one in a known, the other in an
unknown, sepulchre. These are the great personalities, yet neither for all their greatness do
they project themselves beyond death, nor for
all their closeness here to God do they crave
from Him another life, nor in spite of the affection and reverence which surround them to the
last, and the scrupulous care which is taken for
their proper burial, is there any hope expressed
of their continued existence. Abraham, when
God promises to be his great reward, is anxious
only for an heir of his own body; [1] and when his
wife dies is busy only to procure her a grave in
the soil promised to his descendants.[2] A living
seed and a land for them to dwell in — that is all
that Abraham's story contains of gospel for the
future.   Similarly, the last words imputed to
Jacob are fraught with hope only for the tribes
which have sprung from him, and for their settlement in Canaan: *Lo, I am dying, but God will be
with you and bring you back to the land of your
fathers.*[3] For himself there is the prospect of
Sheol; he is eager that he be not brought down
there in grief. The inference is that the state in
which a man enters Sheol is his state for ever-

[1] Gen. xv. 1 ff.

[2] Gen. xxiii.; see especially verse 8: *to bury my dead out of my
sight.*

[3] Gen. xlviii. 21; cf. xlix.

more.[1] For Joseph the last hope is a grave with
his people in Canaan,[2] and for Moses a prospect
of Canaan on the eve of the nation's occupation.[3]
Even though God Himself prepares a sepulchre
for the body of the friend who spake with Him
face to face,[4] nothing is said of a future for Moses
with God. All men, small and great, loved or
hated, come under the curse upon their first
parents : *dust thou art, and unto dust thou shalt
return*.[5] There is but one exception, the mysterious story of Enoch,[6] which, however, describes
not life after death, but a translation without
death to the presence of God.[7]

---

[1] Gen. xxxvii. 35; xlii. 38; xliv. 31. [2] Gen. l. 24–26.
[3] Deut. xxxii. 52. [4] Ex. xxxiii. 11.
[5] Gen. iii. 19. [6] Gen. v. 23 f.

[7] I have said above that it is not necessary in this review of
the historical portions of the Pentateuch to distinguish between
the strata from different periods, for the testimony of all is alike.
Here, however, are the exact references. It is the Jahwist and
Elohist who give us the confinement of Abraham's hopes to
descendants from his own body (Gen. xv. 1 ff.); the death of
Rachel (xxxv. 19); Jacob's dread of Sheol (xxxvii. 35, xlii. 38,
xliv. 31), and his hopes for his descendants (xlviii. 21; cf. xlix.);
the burial of Jacob (l. 1 ff.), and Joseph's last charge (l. 24); the
death of Moses: *the time draws near that thou must die* (Deut.
xxxi. 14): *thou shalt sleep with thy fathers* (ver. 16): *this is the
land, to thy seed will I give it, but thou shalt not pass over thither*.
So Moses died (xxxiv. 4, 5); Joshua's death and Joseph's burial
(Josh. xxiv. 29 f.).
 The Deuteronomists add few details relevant to our subject:
Moses must not enter Canaan (Deut. iii. 23 ff., iv. 22); his death
and burial (xxxiv. 5 f.) (it is doubtful whether Jahweh is described
as Himself burying his servant : see Dillmann and Driver on the
passage). The Priestly Writers give us the story of Enoch (Gen.
v. 23, 24); of Macpelah (xxiii.) ; the death of Abraham (xxv. 7 f.);
of Ishmael (ver. 17); of Isaac (xxxv. 29); of Jacob (xlix. 33); his

So, too, in the historical books which follow the Hexateuch. Soldiers on the battlefield, kings in the midtime of their career, the innocent child, the only son of his mother, the friend whose love was wonderful passing the love of women, the righteous man, the faithful prophet, the martyr — they are mourned and bewept, but never a word of hope is spoken regarding them. As in the Pentateuch, there are traces of a popular belief in an underground abode of the dead, where these preserve the characters they bore in life and whence they may be summoned to speak to the living. But that world is outside of religion; the traffickers with it are wizards and necromancers, whom the servants of Jahweh seek to drive from the land.[1] There is again as in the Pentateuch, a single hero, who escapes this subterranean fate by escaping death, and is translated to Heaven:[2] but Elijah in his fiery chariot is no revelation of a future with God for the common man. Some women receive their dead raised to life again. There are stories of prophets who bring back the breath to the bodies

burial (l. 12, 13). Nadab and Abihu die before Jahweh (Lev. x. 2); death of Aaron on the top of the mountain (Num. xx. 22 ff.); death of Moses (Deut. xxxii. 48 ff.) (with the reason why Moses died in Moab before the entry into Canaan), xxxiv. 1b, 2, 7a, 8. It is the Priestly Writer who uses the phrases *gathered to his people* (Gen. xxv. 7 f. 17, xxxv. 29, xlix. 33); *to the men of his people* (Num. xx. 24); *to thy people* (Deut. xxxii. 50).

[1] 1 Sam. xxviii. 7 ff.
[2] 2 Kings ii. 11.

of those who have expired.[1]   But even the faith
that Jahweh's love and omnipotence can work
such miracles provokes no single expression of
hope that He will redeem the dead to eternal
life in His presence.

The darkness is nowhere more impressive
than over the Dirge of David upon Saul.   The
verses of this noble elegy throb with the joy of
life : the flash of the sword, the glint of gold, the
sheen of scarlet, and the beauty and strength
of men.   They praise the services of the dead
to the country and nation.   They are inspired,
as we have seen,[2] with the feeling for greatness
and the spirit of generous forgiveness.   But
none of these light one spark of the life to
come.   The poetry, the reverence, the love of
the elegy are perfect; but it breathes no hope.
We recognise, of course, that the soul has her
hours sacred to grief; when even God in His
great patience stands aside and leaves the broken
heart alone with its dead.   Yet this can hardly
be the explanation of the absence from David's
song of the name of God and of every hint of
another life; for nowhere else in all the story
that surrounds the song do we find any promise,
or even instinct, of immortality for man.   When
Abigail says to David : *May the life of my lord
be bound up in the bundle of life with Jahweh
God*, it is of this life she is talking, for she has

[1] 1 Kings xvii. 17 ff.; 2 Kings iv. 32 ff.   [2] Above, pp. 155 ff.

just said, *Should a man rise up to hunt thee and seek thy life*, and she immediately adds, *but the lives of thine enemies may He sling them out as from the middle of a sling*.[1] Life was here, for Jahweh was here. When men died they were *gathered to their fathers*.[2] It is a sweet phrase; but it had no religious hope till Christ put this into it.[3] Sheol was the abode of the dead, not of God, and as in the Pentateuch, so in these historical books, men went down into Sheol with such sorrow or blood, as fell upon the end of their lives, irremovable from them.[4]

Before we pass from the historical books, one bit of evidence for belief in the continued existence of the dead must be noted. It has been thought by critics that Scripture contains proofs of the existence, in the earlier history of Israel, of the worship of the dead. Both in the Elohist's story of Jacob, and in the life of David, mention is made of certain Teráphim or images of gods, and these are elsewhere described in connection with oracles.[5] They were probably family gods;[6] the inference that they were the ancestors of the

[1] 1 Sam. xxv. 29.

[2] And, as in David's case, to the child that preceded him (2 Sam. xii. 23).

[3] Cf. Ps. xlix. 2 with Matt. xxii. 32 ; Mark xii. 27 ; Luke xx. 38.

[4] Gen. xxxvii. 35, xlii. 38 ; 2 Sam. xii. 23.

[5] Jud. xvii. 5, xviii. 14 ; Hos. iii. 4 : cf. Zech. x. 2 ; Ezek. xxi. 21.

[6] Cf. Laban's statement (Gen. xxxi. 30), and Micah's (Jud. xviii. 24).

family is not unnatural, and is supported by
traces of a habit of sacrificing to the dead which
appear in mourning customs forbidden to Israel
by the later law as alien to the religion of Jahweh.[1]
The evidence is not conclusive, though sufficient
for more than probability.[2] But in any case it
points to a popular belief in the continued
existence of souls after death. These were

---

[1] Deut. xiv. 1; xxvi. 14; Lev. xxi. 5.

[2] See Stade, *Gesch. des Volkes Isr.*, i. 467; Schwally, *Leben nach dem Tode*, 35 ff. in support of the proof of an ancestor cult. For reasonable doubts of it cf. Davidson, art. 'God,' Hastings's *Bible Dictionary*, ii. 200 f.; and for a full argument against it, Frey, *Tod, Seelenglaube und Seelenkult im Alten Israel*, 1898. It seems to me, in spite of what Professors Davidson and Frey adduce, that whether the teraphim were understood to be the images of ancestors or not, the practice of the worship of ancestors in Israel is proved by the laws in Deut. xiv. 1 and xxvi. 14, taken along with the fact that sacrifices to the dead survived in historical times in other ancient religions, and also among the Semites: cf. Robertson Smith, *Religion of the Semites*, p. 217. The shade of Samuel is called a god (1 Sam. xxviii. 13). The same preposition is used in Deuteronomy between such sacrifices and the dead, as between the legal sacrifices and Jahweh. Those are *to the dead;* these are *to Jahweh*. When among the Adwân in Moab in 1891, I questioned them concerning their sacrifices. It was hard for an ear unaccustomed to the Bedawee pronunciation to catch many details. But this was clear. They distinguished certain spring sacrifices, which they make within their camps as minshan el-mawât 'for the sake of the dead,' from those in Mecca at the Great Bairam, which they described as minshan Allah, 'for the sake of God.' — The whole question has been fully argued by Charles, *A Critical History of the Doctrine of the Future Life*, 1899, pp. 20 ff. While I cannot agree with all his inferences from the texts he cites (*e.g.* Ex. xxi. 2–6; 1 Sam. xxviii. 13, 16) his argument as a whole appears to me to be successful for the existence of ancestor-worship in Israel. — Other instances of sacrifices to the dead, in Doughty, *Arabia Deserta*, i. 241, 450.

called by the later literature *Rephā'im*, probably
'the flaccid ones,' but earlier names for them,
when they spoke through a necromancer, are
'ōbhôth; [1] and *yiddĕōnîm*, perhaps 'knowing ones,' [2]
and are proofs of a belief in their knowledge of,
and their influence upon, human life.[3] Still it is
to be noted that they are not represented in any
association with the Deity, and that the religion
of Jahweh from a very early time regarded traffic
with the dead as incompatible with loyalty to
Jahweh Himself.

When we pass to the prophets we find no
relief from the prevailing silence as to Jahweh's
relation to the dead. The prophets have sovereign
beliefs in God's faithfulness and omnipotence, and
sovereign hopes for the future of Israel upon earth ;
but one and all ignore the fate of the individual
man. Some of them have left us the stories of
their personal origins, they have emphasised their
individual relations to the Deity ; but not one

[1] According to 1 Sam. xxviii. 7, the necromancer was called
the possessor of an *'ôbh :* according to Lev. xx. 27 the 'obh was
in the necromancer.

[2] In Lev. xx. 27 parallel to 'ôbh and *in* the man or woman who
mediated between the spirit and the inquirer. Cf. 1 Sam. xxviii.
3, 9.

[3] Dr. A. B. Davidson thinks that the name Rephaim 'and the
fact that the 'obs twittered and muttered and spoke low out of the
ground (Isa. viii. 19, xxix. 4) indicate that they were regarded
as anything but powerful "gods ".' (Hastings's *Bible Dictionary*,
ii. 201). Still they had superhuman knowledge ; and at least
the whole prevalence of this necromancy proves a popular belief
in the real existence of the dead.

has betrayed his feelings about his death or bequeathed any hope which strengthened him in face of it. The great passages on resurrection and the Divine conquest of death which we read in Hosea[1] and in Ezekiel,[2] describe the revival of the nation from disaster and exile. In one very late prophecy[3] there is a cry that the national recovery from exile shall not be enough; those, who have died before it comes, must rise from their graves to share it. But obviously this is not the hope of a life with God beyond the grave. Another cry,[4] which rises with this, is of confidence that God will abolish death. But that confidence sinks again, and the brightest picture of the subject which later prophets leave us is of this life: a Jerusalem from which premature and violent death has been banished, and the city is full of men and women who have reached a quiet old age.[5]

Turning now to the Psalms, we must put aside, as we have done in the case of the Prophets, all expressions of immortality which are manifest metaphors of the revival of the nation, and merely affirm its reconstruction and perpetuity upon earth. After these have been disposed of, there remain very few Psalms which illuminate the destiny of the individual beyond the grave; nor is any of them a reasoned confidence in a future

[1] Hos. vi. 1 f., xiii. 14.   [2] Ezek. xxxvii.
[3] Isaiah xxvi. 19.   [4] xxv. 8.   [5] Zech. viii. 4.

for him with God. At the best they are but
cries flung out in revolt from the thought of a
future without Him, or in passionate confidence
that in death He cannot desert the soul He has
favoured with His grace. Some critics have
denied an individual reference to the Sixteenth
Psalm, and have interpreted its verses of Israel
as a whole; and this is not an impossible interpretation. Yet it seems to me that the ninth
and tenth verses are most naturally understood
of the individual, or at least of his generation;
it was the living generation and not the nation,
actual or ideal, who feared Sheol.[1] And the individual character of the confidence of the Seventy-
third Psalm is still more clear:

> *Nevertheless I am continually with Thee ;*
> *Thou hast holden me with Thy right hand*
> *Thou shalt guide me with Thy counsel,*
> *And afterward receive me to glory.*
> *Whom have I in heaven but Thee ?*
> *And there is none upon earth I desire besides Thee.*
> *My flesh and my heart fail;*
> *But God is the strength of my heart,*
> *And my portion for ever.*[2]

Yet such faith did not always succeed in breaking away from the prospect of that fate for

[1] The reference of the Psalm to individuals is further confirmed if we read *thy pious ones* (or *leal* or *loving ones*) as some
codd. do instead of the singular.

[2] Ps. lxxiii. 23–26.

individuals which we have already seen accepted
by the earlier books, and which is now described
with more explicitness.   In Psalms, if not of the
individual yet of the living generation of Jahweh's
people, before whom death looms inevitable, there
are cries that the suppliants may be allowed to
continue the praise of God in the land of the
living:

> *For in death there is no remembrance of Thee:*
> *In the grave who shall give Thee thanks?*
> *The dead praise not Jahweh,*
> *Neither any that go down into silence.*[1]

Another Psalmist describes himself, or his own
generation, as the temporary guest of God, who
must soon depart from His house and go away:

> *Hear my prayer, O Jahweh,*
> *And give ear unto my cry;*
> *Hold not Thy peace at my tears:*
> *For I am but a guest with Thee,*
> *And a sojourner, as all my fathers were.*
> *O spare me, that I may recover brightness,*
> *Before I go hence, and be no more.*[2]

This is not a prayer for immortality, but for a
little more patience from God, a little more
warming of the hands at the fire of this life
before the door opens and the guest is dismissed
into the night.   From such depression caused by
the shortness of life other Psalms recover hope;

---

[1] Ps. vi. 5, cxv. 17 ; cf. xxx. 9, lxxxviii. 11.
[2] Ps. xxxix. 12 f.

but they do not recover by taking hold of the hope of eternity. The Ninetieth, for instance, which of all others most pathetically illustrates the transitoriness of man's existence upon earth, gives him no expectation of another, but asks for gladness through the days that remain, some little recompense for the evil of the past, some reflection of God's beauty, and the establishment of the work of His servants' hands. Even Job, when every other door of righteousness is closed to him, bursts for only a few moments into the possibility of another life, of the vision of God and the experience of His justice beyond the grave; [1] but then, as if the thought were strange and too daring, he falls back from it upon other lines of search, and the Book closes with the manifestation of God's power on this earth, and the recovery of His servant to an earthly prosperity. The rest of the literature gives us no relief. The wisdom of the Book of Proverbs is for this life alone; and Ecclesiastes, which ends with a funeral, finds the only profit man can have in the enjoyment, under the fear of God, of the fleeting opportunities of life while they last ; for they are soon gone, and all things, youth and love, knowledge and effort, are *vanity* — that is, not worthless while they last, but lasting so little — a breath, a pulse which soon expires. In the very late Book of Daniel,[2] we find, however, one

[1] Job xix. 25 ff.   [2] *Circa* 165 B. C.

explicit prediction of the resurrection of *many
of them who sleep in the dust of the earth, some to
everlasting life, and some to shame and everlasting
contempt, and they that be wise shall shine as the
brightness of the firmament ; and they that turn
many to righteousness as the stars for ever and
ever.*[1]   This prediction stands in very definite contrast to all that we have elsewhere found.   We
may recognise in it a more confident development of the faith, which has already broken
forth in some Psalms, of the impossibility that
God should relinquish to the grave those who
have trusted in Him.   But we must remember
that there had come in, between them and its
particular notes of resurrection and judgement,
certain popular views and imaginations of the
future beyond the grave which do not receive
any other expression in the Old Testament.

These, then, are the essential lines in the attitude of the Old Testament writers to the life
beyond the grave.   They reveal the existence of
a popular belief in a state after death, which the
earlier religion, apparently taking it for granted,
left alone as outside its interests ; but which the
later faced and fought, and to some extent rose
above, in the strength of faith in the God of Israel.
Our next duty is to inquire what were the historical reasons for this popular belief in the state
of the dead, as well as for the various phases of

[1] Dan. xii. 2, 3.

the attitude which the religion of Israel assumed towards it. I believe that, instead of being chilled by the whole subject as so many are, a preacher will find it, when historically explained, one of the most fruitful sources of material and inspiration which the Old Testament has to offer him.

II. *The Historical Explanation.*

We are all probably acquainted with the curious reason which used to be offered for the silence of the earlier Hebrew writings with regard to another life. By Warburton, in his *Divine Legation of Moses*,[1] it was imputed to a design on the part of the great lawgiver to withdraw the mind of his people from the overpowering effect of the elaborate visions of the other world which they had encountered on the monuments of Egypt. No nation has developed ' other-worldliness ' more than have the builders of the Pyramids and vast mausoleums of Memphis, Abydos and Thebes. According to Warburton, Moses intended to purge the mind of Israel of all the morbid influences of this ' other-worldliness,' and so he carefully excluded from his legislation every hint of the life to come. The explanation is ingenious, but it is artificial. It is also inadequate in light of the critical reconstruction of the history. And there is another and more natural reason for the phenomenon which it seeks to explain.

[1] 1738–1741.

We find this in one of the characteristics of the
race to which Israel belonged. The Semites,
or, to be accurate, those nomadic Semites with
whom Israel was more closely connected, have
never been conspicuous for their interest in, or
their imagination of, a future life. The Arabs,
whom early Israel so largely resembled,[1] remember their dead ; and as they pass their graves will
call upon them by name and pour libations of
water on the sandy mounds ;[2] as we have seen,[3]
they also sacrifice to them. Yet this is all. They
have not, and never seem to have had, either
dogma of another life, or any vision of such, unless their beliefs in subterranean *jins* or spirits
spring from their imagination of the dead in the
grave. In Arabic poetry before Mohammed's
time the few sparks of the hope of immortality
are, according to Wellhausen, due to Jewish or
Christian influence.[4] When Mohammed himself,
borrowing from the same sources, preached the
resurrection, his countrymen mocked it as in-
credible ; and even now, after twelve centuries
of the prevalence of his religion in the Arabian
Peninsula, the Arabs, by the witness of several

[1] See above, p. 127.

[2] Wellhausen, *Reste arab. Heidentumes*, p. 161 ; Doughty,
Arabia Deserta, i. p. 241, 448. I have heard my Bedawee guides
in Moab and south of Engedi hail by name the occupants of un-
titled graves which we passed on our way: ' Ya Ahmed ! ' ' Ya
Dhiâb.' Conder (*Heth and Moab*, new ed. p. 318) states that the
Adwan remember nine generations of ancestors.

[3] P. 184, note 2.   [4] *Reste arab. Heidentumes*, p. 164.

travellers,[1] have not formed any clear notion of a future world.

The reasons for all this are not far to seek. One of them may be the notorious incapacity of the Semite, when uninfluenced by foreign civilisations, for sustained speculation. Others are undoubtedly found in the migratory habits of the desert life. The shifting camps, the easily obliterated graves, the want of written monuments and records, impress the imagination rather with the transiency than with the permanence of man.[2] It takes the long occupation of one site, the building of cities, the raising of monuments, the capacity for history, to sustain the memory of the dead and to hand on the tradition of another life. In the poetry of the Bible, the tent, easily folded and carried away, is the type of man's transient life; but eternity is figured in the city which hath foundations. Even Job's daring hope of his vindication in a life to come is uttered along with the passionate cry for the inscription of his cause on some monument or book. *O that my words were now written! O that they were recorded in a book: that they were graven with an iron pen and lead in the rock for ever!* [3]

---

[1] *E.g.* Doughty, *Arabia Deserta*, i. pp. 240 f., 445 f.

[2] ' In the border Semitic countries is a long superstition of the grave; here (*i.e.* at Hayil in Central Arabia) is but the simple nomad guise, without other last loving care or adornment.' — Doughty, *Arabia Deserta*, i. p. 618.

[3] xix. 23 f.

When Semites settled down and built themselves cities, and in consequence sepulchres,[1] they
either developed or, as is probable in Babylonia,
partly borrowed from the race which preceded
them, a certain imagination of life in the grave.
The pictures of man's future home which are
characteristic of Babylonian literature are conceived in the likeness of one of the caves or
underground structures in which the dead were
laid for burial.

> *The house of darkness . . .*
> *The house men enter, but cannot depart from.*
> *The road men go but cannot return.*
> *The house from whose dwellers the light is with-*
>   *drawn.*
> *The place where dust is their food, their nourish-*
>   *ment clay.*
> *The light they behold not; in darkness they*
>   *dwell.*
> *They are clothed like birds, all fluttering wings.*
> *On the door and the gateposts the dust lieth deep.*[2]

This was the universal resort of men and their
everlasting home.   The exceptions to the hopeless,
passionless fate which it contains are few.   So
far as Babylonian records have been deciphered,
they amount to one or two — as many as Enoch

[1] See p. 193, note 2.

[2] From the Assyrian Descent of Ishtar to Hades (German
trans. by Jeremias, *Die Bab. Assyr. Vorstellungen vom Leben
nach dem Tode*, p. 11 ; Eng. in *Records of the Past*, i. 145.

and Elijah in the early history of Israel — who were taken to the abode of the gods and enjoyed immortal life in their presence.[1] For the common man the underworld is inevitable, with its dust, its joyless existence, its silence broken only by the peeping and chirping of ghosts — a conception derived, as all who have explored Eastern sepulchres must admit, from the noises of the bats which throng the sepulchres. The Babylonians called the realm of the dead Aralû; it lay beneath a great mountain of the same name. Some scholars assert that it was also known to the Babylonians as Sheol;[2] others, however, doubt this.[3] Aralû had divine guardians, but lay outside the jurisdiction of the gods of the upper world.[4] It was entered only through the gates of the grave.[5]

Whether the Hebrews borrowed their conception of Sheol from that of the Babylonians, or whether both came from a common source, is uncertain. The latter is the more probable theory.[6] It is, as we have seen, in the later writings that the Hebrew conception of Sheol

[1] Jastrow, *Religion of Babylonia*, etc. 576 f.

[2] Jastrow, *op. cit.* pp. 558 ff.; *American Journal of Semitic Languages*, xiv.; Jeremias, *op. cit.* p. 109.

[3] Jensen, *Kosmologie der Babylonier*, pp. 22 ff., and Zimmern, quoted by Charles, *op. cit.* p. 34, n. 2.

[4] Jastrow, p. 582.

[5] *Ibid.* p. 586.

[6] There are slight differences in the two conceptions. The confirmation of the evidence that the name Sheol occurs in Babylonian would, however, strongly support the first theory.

becomes most developed; and though original to
early Israel, the conception may have been elaborated through Israel's Babylonian connections in
the seventh and subsequent centuries. In the
Book of Job, Sheol is behind *bars* where men *rest
in the dust,* and *spread their couch in the darkness.*[1]

> *There the wicked cease from troubling;*
> *And there the weary be at rest.*
> *The prisoners are at ease together,*
> *They hear not the voice of the driver,*
> *The small and the great are there;*
> *And the slave is free from his master.*[2]

When, then, the nomad Semite became civilised, this is all that his inscribed sepulchres and
monuments, keeping the dead in remembrance,
brought to him. Of immortality in the true
sense of the word — with God and in full enjoyment of life — the Hebrew had no inherent conception. Even nature appears to have made to
him no such suggestions of resurrection as in
Babylonia inspired hope for a heroic individual
or two,[3] but were not extended to the common
man.

The want of hope among the Semites must
not, however, be altogether charged upon their
physical environment: the main cause was the
conception of the individual which prevailed in
Semitic religion. To the ancient Semite, as we

[1] xvii. 12–16.   [2] iii. 17–19.
[3] Epic of Ishtar; see Jeremias, *op. cit.* p. 119, n. 2.

saw in last Lecture, God did not deal with the individual, but with the tribe as a whole. It was the tribal existence which the divine honour was obliged to maintain: so long as that was preserved on earth, the fate of the individual, after he fulfilled his length of days, mattered little. In Old Testament language, the leaves or the branches might perish, if only the stock and stump remained. In another sense than that in which Christ used the words, the gods of the ancient Semites were not the gods of the dead, but of the living. The necessities of a life of almost constant warfare confirmed the tribes-men in these beliefs, and the dead were forgotten in the stress of defending the living. There was no time to brood on the past, and even in the sacred duty of blood-revenge, which other-wise might have been supposed to preserve the memory of the fallen, the responsibility was mainly felt to the tribe whose blood had been spilt, and it crowded out the memory of the individuals for whom the vengeance was piously performed.

The same ideas prevailed in early Israel. Up to Jeremiah's time the religious unit was almost ex-clusively the nation, and the religious problem — not as in Christianity the salvation of the indivi-dual — was the perpetuation upon earth of a people of Jahweh, to serve, praise and bear witness for Him. You remember how we saw that the great ideas of redemption and providence came into the theology of Israel by the redemption of the nation from Egyptian servitude, and by the guidance of the nation through the wilderness. The idea that God cared for and dealt directly with individuals could not, of course, be utterly absent, and we see it illustrated in a great many of the early narratives of Israel.[1] But it is significant that some even of those apparent individuals are, as we learned, personifications of tribes and clans; and at least even the most personal of them all are represented as departing this life with hopes, not for themselves, but for the future of their families. It is not otherwise when we come to the prophets. In spite of their own individual experiences of religion, in spite of Hosea's sense of love for the outcast wife, and Isaiah's assurance of his own cleansing and call by God, the interest of the prophets in the fate of the nation as a whole is too overwhelming to allow them to develop the elements of their consciousness of a personal relation to the Deity. As Isaiah puts it, the great problem of religion, the one end upon which he and his fellows see concentrated the omnipotence and righteousness of Jahweh, is the preservation of a Remnant of Israel; for if Israel utterly perish, none will be left on earth to represent Jahweh, and the knowledge of the true God must disappear. To save

[1] Above, pp. 106 f.

and to purify the Remnant is the whole interest and warfare of religion, to which not only must all others be postponed, but beside the crisis and the glory of which they lose their reality. The future of the nation on which the early prophets dwell with such power and beauty is — till we reach the faint beginnings of apocalypse in Zephaniah — reached along the lines of history and upon the surface of this earth. The early prophets do not think of another world, but of this one, as the scene of Israel's ceaseless life with Jahweh — this world better indeed, freed from war, famine, storm, and lust, but still *this* world — and they do not always promise that the death of individuals shall be absent from it. With such national hopes drawing them on, the prophets do not stop to think — at least, they do not stop to speak — of what becomes of individual Israelites. If one generation fall, God will raise another to take its place.

The indifference of the prophet to the individual is, however, not the most interesting thing : from the Psalms we learn that the individual himself appears to have acquiesced in it. Between his feet and the golden future of his people there lay his own grave : the black, inevitable door to Sheol. Jahweh would continue to guide the nation, but at that point Jahweh ceased to guide him. He fell to the

dead, and Jahweh and Israel left him behind.
Thus, while to us death means to go to God, to
the Israelite death was to leave God. God was
with Israel and in Israel: but with the dead
Jahweh had as little to do as had the Babylonian
gods of the upper world.

We have already seen some proofs that even
the pious adherent of Jahweh accepted this
view,[1] and from the Psalms they might be multiplied. Their date is quite uncertain ; if, as is
probable, they are late, their testimony is all
the more remarkable. They prove that at the
very heart of Israel's religion there were pious
men who cried out against death as the dissolution of their communion with Jahweh, but who
regarded that dissolution as the inevitable end
and prayed only for a reprieve till their years
should be full :

Sheol cannot praise Thee.
Death cannot celebrate Thee.
They that are gone down unto the pit cannot
*   hope for Thy truth.*[2]
I am a guest with Thee,
And a sojourner as all my fathers were.
O spare me, that I may recover brightness,
Before I go hence, and be no more.[3]

But to these acceptances of the popular belief,
which are acceptances of despair, and which we

---

[1] See above, p. 88.   [2] Hezekiah's Psalm; Isa. xxxviii. 18.
[3] Ps. xxxix. 12, 13.

can hardly read without a shudder, individuals (or generations) in Israel sometimes added others that are full of inspiration to ourselves. The Ninetieth Psalm is, even in the Old Testament, the most pathetic description of the drift of the generations of men into darkness. *Jahweh, Israel's dwelling-place in all generations*, alone is eternal.

> *Thou turnest man into crumbling,*
> *And sayest : Return, ye children of men.*
> *Thou carriest them off as with a flood.*
> *They become like a dream.*
> *In the morning they are like grass which*
>   *groweth up ;*
> *In the morning it flourisheth and groweth up,*
> *In the evening it is cut down and withereth.*
> *For we are consumed by Thine anger,*
> *And by Thy wrath are we troubled.*

The reason for this death is the same as that to which the Jahwist assigns it in his story of the origins of man.

> *Thou hast set our iniquities before Thee,*
> *Our secret sins in the light of Thy countenance.*
> *Who knoweth the power of Thine anger,*
> *Or Thy wrath as befitteth the fear of Thee ?*

Against the universal fate which men expect, thus explained and confirmed as it is by the stern ethical principles of Jahweh's religion, the Psalmist fortifies himself and his generation, not by the hope of a life to come, not by a gospel which explicitly gets rid of death as well as sin; but by his faith that Jahweh is the home of all the *living* generations of His people: by beseeching Him to turn their hearts to the value of the days which they are still to have with Him; by a prayer that what remains of these days for himself and his contemporaries may be filled with gladness, according to the days wherein they have been afflicted; and that whatsoever their hands have found to do may be confirmed by Him.

What a noble resolution to turn from the contemplation of death to work and worship! To us it is inexpressibly precious as the proof that Israel's faith, before any hope of a future life broke upon it, had by its native ethical principles and experience of God, conquered the paralysing influences of that intellectual conception of death, which it had inherited as a part of the Semitic race.

The time came, however, when, as we have seen, even so bright and so ethical a faith as that of the Ninetieth Psalm was insufficient, and the individual, who found no victory and no gladness in this life, dared to hope for something beyond. When exactly such a hope emerged we cannot determine; but our ignorance of the date is of little moment beside the fact that we know how the change was caused. As we saw

in last Lecture,[1] there began to brighten, about
the end of the seventh century, the vision of the
religious worth of the individual. The reasons
for this were many and complex. The nation
was breaking up, and the individual was being
bidden to think of himself. New ethical convictions of personal responsibility were born;
both Jeremiah and Ezekiel give expression to
them. But more than all there was the spiritual
originality, the independent experience, the
unique relation to God, of Jeremiah himself. I
cannot but think that his example did more
than anything else to develop in Israel the
consciousness of the spiritual duties and rights
of the individual. At least it must have contributed powerful aid to the other tendencies I
have mentioned; and we find it expressed in
Jeremiah's conception of the New Covenant. In
the time of the Exile, when the political and
religious institutions of Israel disappeared, the
greater stress was laid upon personal qualities as
the means and highest possibilities of religion :
*Thus saith the High and Lofty One who inhabiteth
eternity, whose name is Holy. I dwell in the high
and holy place, with him also that is of a contrite
and a humble spirit to revive the spirit of the humble,
and to revive the heart of the contrite ones.*[2] The
precious fruit of so much sorrow was not lost
when the nation and its ritual were restored.

[1] Pp. 165 ff.   [2] Isa. lvii. 15.

It is the witness of all historians of the post-exilic period, that within the strong nationalism and legalism of the Jews there flourished the most beautiful personal piety; souls feeling, as Jeremiah felt it, their individual relation to God.

It would appear to be from such convictions of the individual's relation to God that the few hopes of immortality spring which emerge in the Old Testament. They start from a revolt of the individual believer in God either against the horrible conditions of Sheol, the expectation of which he had intellectually inherited; or against the injustice, which God's providence of this life does not redress, and so forces the conscience to appeal to His judgement hereafter. We have seen how, even when he had no hope, the pious Israelite shrank from the future which gaped for him in Sheol. It was the utter antithesis of his experience here: it was silence, it was powerlessness, it was devoid of the presence of God. But God loved him, and had made him His own: and God was omnipotent and eternal. God could not have been to the pious what He had been, and made them what they were only to abandon them in death.

I have set Jahweh always before me.

Because He is at my right hand I shall not be moved,

Therefore my heart is glad,

And my . . .[1] rejoiceth.
Even my flesh dwelleth in safety,
For Thou wilt not abandon my life to Sheol,
Neither wilt thou suffer thy pious ones to see the
* pit.*
Thou wilt make me to know the path of life:
In Thy presence is fulness of joy,
At Thy right hand are pleasures evermore.[2]

The other two instances of hope for the individual after death spring from more purely
ethical reasons. The writer of the Seventy-third
Psalm found his faith going when he observed
the prosperity of the wicked.

As for me, my feet were almost gone,
* My steps had well nigh slipped.[3]*

He heard how many of God's people, led away
by the security and arrogance of sinners, doubted
if God knew, and felt as if their own righteousness were in vain.[4] From such a confession the
Psalmist himself had been saved by fears of
disloyalty to the generation of God's children.

[1] The meaning is uncertain.

[2] Ps. xvi. 8–11. As remarked above, this Psalm cannot be
fairly interpreted of the revival of the earthly Israel from disaster
and exile. It is death, Sheol, the grave, which the writer fears
either for himself or for the living generation of Israel. Of course,
it is possible to read the words of the hope by which he rises
superior to death, as if they merely meant a deliverance for a
time from impending death. But it is more natural to take them
as the assurance of immortality in spite of death. And at least
they contain the feelings by which such a survival of actual
death became sure to individual Israelites.

[3] Verse 3.   [4] Verses 4–14.

But the pressure of his doubts was too great for him until he *entered into the mysteries of God and considered the latter end of the wicked.*[1] Probably by *the mysteries*, literally, *the holy things, of God*,[2] he means the ultimate deeds of God in the full character of His holiness. The certain end of the wicked is destruction, and the conscience of the Psalmist tells him he should have known this, instead of being unreasonably embittered.[3] For himself, here and afterwards, in life as in death, the presence, the counsel, the power of God are sure. *Flesh and heart may fail : God is the strength of my heart and my portion for ever.* The Psalmist does not tell us how he shall rise, or that he shall rise at all. But the promises of all future doctrines of immortality and resurrection are here — in the faithfulness and power of the Deity, to whom His follower has committed himself. That it is the next life, to which he looks for the action of these divine attributes, is clear from the despair of his vision of this one, no less than from the terms in which his new hope is expressed.

---

[1] Verse 17.

[2] מִקְדְּשֵׁי־אֵל : some take the expression to imply esoteric doctrines of life and judgement after death which were coming into expression in Israel at the time the Psalm was written. But the above seems, from the parallelism of the verse and its context, to be the more natural rendering.

[3] Verses 18–22.

In the case of Job the hope of a personal life after death [1] is the demand of the man's conscience. He is dying unvindicated: *here* God will not appear to him nor examine his plea. Therefore he *knows* he shall see God after death. The individual consciousness for and in itself: innocence in her own strength; the ethical necessities of an unfinished cause — all demand a life to come.

Our survey has made it clear that whatever hopes of immortality arose in Israel, arose by development from the native principles of Israel's religion. The development may have been assisted by the influence of foreign faiths with which the nation came into contact, but of such we know little or nothing. Whatever were the climates which helped to ripen the germs, the germs were Israel's own. Stage by stage we discern a change of attitude on the part of Israel's faith to that view of the state of the dead which the nation received from their ancestors and their kinsfolk. The change appears to be coincident with the general ethical progress of the religion. So long as the interest of the Deity was supposed to be confined to the national interests, the future state was ignored as outside Jahweh's providence. But when the religion of Israel burst its merely national embodiment, and just in proportion as the individual realised his

[1] Job xix. 25–27.

own spiritual life and direct relation to God, Sheol had to be faced, and was faced. So fixed on the mental horizon of Israel had this gloomy prospect become, that many pious Israelites knew to pray for no more than a respite from it. These may be the earlier revolts against Sheol, and those others may be later which, as we have seen, expressed convictions of the impossibility of so dark a fate for the believer in Jahweh, and uttered hopes of his redemption from it. But the question of date is extremely difficult; and we must be content to note that the few late hopes of immortality in the Old Testament broke away, when they did, on the strength of a developed consciousness of the individual's union with Jahweh, and on those ethical principles of Jahweh's religion, which as the wrongs and tyrannies of this life accumulated, had no appeal except to a future judgement.

To follow these hopes further, to trace their essential identity through that new scenery of the next life which was developed in the apocryphal literature, and to find that what gives them their strength in the Old Testament — the permanence of individual character, the need of a future judgement, the faithfulness and omnipotence of God — is what also inspires the New Testament gospel of immortality : all this would be instructive, but it would carry us beyond our proper limits.

III. *The Use to Our Own Day.*

But you may say that all this is a matter of ancient history and its interest only scientific: ' What use is it to us preachers dealing with the religion of to-day?'

I do not forget that these lectures are primarily intended for preachers. It is because I believe in the practical value to such of the history of the Old Testament hope of immortality that I have traced this history through so much detail. Nay more: I believe that the practical value does not begin where at last the individual's assurance in his future with God breaks away from the visions of Sheol; but that as pastors and teachers you will find in every previous and inferior stage of the development something parallel to, something illustrative of, something charged with consolation for, the experience of the men and women of your own generation.

In the first place, we shall scarcely find to-day any parish or congregation of educated people, in which are not some almost as devoid of hope for the future as the most despairing Psalmist in the Psalter. In the thinking of civilised men there has been for years a steady ebb from the shores of another life. The causes of this are very discernible. There was bound to be a reaction from the excessive ' other-worldliness ' of the first half of the century : men had grown sick of its glare.

O

Their hearts easily yielded to new tendencies, drawing with irresistible force the conscience and the reverence of men upon the present and visible environment of their lives. Science claimed our wonder and expectation for the opening secrets of the material universe ; and not only the individual's future, but his present, which is the one measure and warrant of his future, shrank to nothing before the vastness of forces which rolled on their way indifferent to him and his fate. For a time the great social movements of the age seemed to come to the rescue of the individual, with a gospel of duties and hopes above the material course of nature. Yet the duties were in a present, among whose crowds he felt his littleness still; and the hopes, like those of early Israel, were for a future which his race, but not he, would share. With such tendencies religion herself largely conspired, emphasising with the absorption of a novice the wonder and sacredness of this life, and turning with the zeal of a penitent to those duties of to-day which she had too long neglected. Such influences were felt, and expressed in literature, long ago; now they have penetrated humanity. Common men and women encounter them, not upon the heights, where even the darkest mists sometimes break and roll past, but amid the never-settling dust of life, and with hearts which petty trouble has worn bare of all capacity for hope and vision. Such are the drifted souls to whom we have to preach. They are largely unconscious of their exile, but some have God, all have love. When their experience of Him falls beneath the imminence of their own death, or when their love proves her weakness in the death of others, then they are stung by the sense of their hopelessness: far out to sea, not by their own wilfulness but on the intellectual tides of the age, whose progress they had either never observed, or had only rejoiced in the stir and the motion of it. When you find such men and women, you will understand that the Psalms of Israel are not, like the fossils of our great museums, proofs of the stages which our life has passed through and left behind, but are the eternal cries of the human heart. And you will tell your people that such Psalms have been left in God's Word, for proof of how His Spirit — which is elsewhere described as *making interces- sion for us with groanings that cannot be uttered* — sympathises with those frequent, perhaps in- evitable, experiences of humanity, and presents them to God Himself ; that they are here preserved in order that all such forwandered souls may see that they have not lost the road, but that others of God's own people passed through these very shades; and lo! the end was not only a far-off sight of the Father, but the end of the agony and strife, to which they contributed their portion, was Christ Himself.

But again, the Old Testament hope of a national immortality, of a widening and ever more glorious future for the race, which absorbed the individual and gave him power to forget his own fate, has its counterpart in our day in the strong enthusiasm and unselfish service which the idea of 'a corporate immortality' has roused in numbers of the best men and women, irrespective of their own salvation. Such a belief is not incompatible — as we see both from the Old Testament forms of it and in many of its modern representatives — with a strong and even a personal faith in God. But to-day it probably attracts most of its votaries, not because it is His promise, but by the grand, confident notes of progress on the visible world, which, by the help of science, it reiterates, as well as by the unselfish and heroic tones in which the devotion of individuals to it is capable of being pitched. Not only have some of the finest poems of the century been inspired by faith in the glorious future of the race and the subordination to it of the individual, but many men and women of high character and full surrender to the service of their kind have been content to find in such a future all their aims and reward, without any expectation of a personal immortality. Life and labour in such a faith have not unplausibly been celebrated as more heroic than that of the Christian, who has worn out his strength for others, or has suffered martyrdom, in the hope of everlasting life for himself with God.

Nevertheless we cannot allow, what many assert, that the belief in a 'corporate immortality' is an advance upon that which it has recently seemed to displace. On the contrary the belief is one which has been already tried and found wanting. As our survey of the Old Testament has shown us, it is not a hope with which human hearts remained satisfied, even when it was presented to them with all the sanctions of an ethical religion, and was loyally accepted by pious men. We cannot wonder, if the moral worth and charm of 'corporate immortality' should from time to time revive their sway over the best and even the most religious of human minds. Yet wherever religion assumes its highest form in the relation of the individual man to God, his Father and Lord, there, as the experience of Israel proves to us, the assurance of personal immortality must sooner or later emerge. And there will conspire with it the strongest instincts of the love of the individual for those who are dearest to him.

Yet while this is true, it is well for us all sometimes to pitch our religious life in terms which do not include the hope of a future.

Most of the crises of religious experience may
be achieved, as some of the grandest Psalms
fulfil their music, without the echo of one of
the far-off bells of heaven. A man may pass
through the evangelical experiences of conversion, regeneration and redemption, without
thinking any more of the future than the little
child thinks, but only sure and glad that his
Father is with him. The Old Testament is
of use in reminding us that the hope of immortality is one of the secondary and inferential
elements of religious experience. Has not Christ
Himself summed up the teaching of the Ninetieth
Psalm? *Work while it is called to-day, for the
night cometh in which no man can work.*

The great thing is to be sure of our individual
relation to God. In teaching man that life is
in Him and in nothing else, and that the term
of our days here has been given us to find Him,
the Old Testament has done more for the assurance of immortality than if it had explored the
life awaiting us, or had endowed us with strong
intellectual conceptions of its reality.

LECTURE VII

THE PROPHETS AS PREACHERS TO THEIR OWN TIMES: WITH THEIR INFLUENCE ON THE SOCIAL ETHICS OF CHRISTENDOM

In the previous Lectures of this course we have had occasion to consider several elements in the teaching of the Prophets; but there are others, as relevant to our present task, which we have hardly touched. Of these the principal are the qualities of patriotism which the Prophets illustrate, their travail for their own people and their judgements upon them, their conception of national religion, with the place which they find in that for the individual, and their doctrine of social and civic duties — in a word, the ministry of the Prophets to their own times. But this cannot be adequately treated without an account of the growth in the Christian Church of the *historical* interpretation of the Prophets (as distinguished from the dogmatic and allegorical), and of what has always been the immediate consequence of that interpretation, the influence of the Prophets upon the social ethics of Christendom. In other

words, it is impossible to do justice to the preaching of the Prophets to their own time without
some appreciation of their message to all times
and of its results in Christian civilisation. I
hope to attempt this in a manner which shall be
no digression from, but a real contribution to,
our practical aim in these studies as preachers
to our own generation. But besides the civic
elements in prophecy there are others, which we
have not yet examined. We ought to realise the
conception by the Prophets of what we call Law
both in nature and in history; and their attitude
to miracle. Nor would a course of lectures upon
the preacher's use of the Old Testament be complete without some impressions of the general
style and genius of those great exemplars of
his art.

All these things I propose to take in this
Lecture; the influence of the Prophets on the
Christian Church in the first part; the qualities of
their patriotic ministry in the second part; and
in the third the other features of their preaching.

I. *The Influence of the Prophets on the Christian Church and Civilisation.*

It is pertinent to our purpose to remind ourselves once more that there is no part of the
Old Testament upon which Modern Criticism has
been so constructive as within the prophetical
writings. I do not forget that Criticism has

already removed from many of the Prophets large portions of the Books which bear their names; nor that we have entered upon a more thorough analysis of these Books,[1] which may issue in further subtractions of the same kind.[2] But whether a Book be authentic, in the technical meaning of the word, is of small interest compared with its authenticity as vision, as truth and as the revelation of God. To vindicate the authorship of this or that chapter by the man whose name it bears is but a poor service compared with the proof that it rises from real life, that it is the message of a true prophet to living men, and that it deals with the essential problems of human society.[3] In all these high respects the constructive character of Modern Criticism may be fearlessly asserted. The great principle, that a prophet, however far his visions may roam, always starts from the facts of his own day and speaks first to his contemporaries, was revived [4] by Criticism in time for the results of Archæ-

[1] See above, pp. 44 f.

[2] No doubt critical ambition has in certain directions of this analysis gone too far for certainty; and we must not anticipate the final consensus of criticism by the acceptance of the ingenious but often arbitrary adventures of individual critics.

[3] Even so uncompromising an opponent of Criticism as the late Mr. D. L. Moody came to see this. He said to me, and I believe wrote also to a friend, that 'it is not the authorship of the Books of the Bible that matters, but the contents.'

[4] The first exegete who had any real instinct of this principle was Theodore of Mopsuestia. For his teaching and other instances of the revival of this principle see below, pp. 227 ff.

ology to be used in its illustration; and nowhere has Archæology done more for the history of Israel, or Criticism more fully employed archæological evidence than throughout the prophetic period. The Hebrew Prophets were contemporaneous with the Empires of Assyria, Babylonia and Persia; and the monuments of these Empires confirm and illustrate the history which the Prophets reflect. The whole world of thought and action from which the prophetical literature springs, and upon which it reacts, is almost as clear and vivid to our eyes as the world of Shakespeare and his dramas.

The consequence of this exegetical principle and of its illustration by Archæology has been a decided revival of the use of the Prophets by the Christian pulpit. Thirty years ago in Great Britain some observers of our literature and politics alleged a considerable decrease in the influence of the Old Testament.[1] Quotations from it, and allusions to its characters and events were said to be growing less frequent in the speeches and writings of public men. In the pulpit of the same period the uses of the Old Testament were confined to the dogmatic, the apologetic, and the individually ethical. Prophecy

[1] I suppose that John Bright was at that time the one statesman of the highest rank whose style of speaking showed any influence of the Old Testament; and Mr. Gladstone and Lord Shaftesbury the only two others who seriously studied it.

was employed for the illustration of dogma, the
proof of the Divinity of Christ, and the example
of personal religion; but except for the enforcement of Sabbath observance — which, besides, was
based on the Law and not on the Prophets —
the use made of the social and civic teaching of
the Old Testament was very infrequent. The
noble examples of the preaching of social duties
which were afforded by Kingsley and Maurice [1]
bore little fruit, largely I believe because they
were not sustained upon a thorough historical
criticism of the Prophets.[2] The real recovery of
the historical preaching of the Old Testament
may be said to have started from the publication
of Dean Stanley's *Lectures on the Jewish Church*,
and Stanley, while he owed much to his own
vision of the Holy Land and to his superb gift of
historical painting, was in his views of the religious development of Israel a pupil of Ewald.
I need hardly remind you of how the combination
of a historical and a practical treatment of the

[1] See below, at the close of this section.

[2] Now that we have this we can admire still more than their
contemporaries did, the moral sympathy and intuition which
enable both these preachers, and especially Maurice (*Prophets and
Kings of the Old Testament*), to grasp so firmly the essence of the
Prophets' messages to their own day, and to apply it so powerfully
to the nineteenth century. Nor need we hesitate to give some
of the same praise to Pusey, who, although his interest as a commentator is mainly in the dogmatic and predictive value of the
Prophets (*Minor Prophets*), knew, as his University Sermons
prove, how to enforce from the pulpit, with great power, their
ethical teaching.

Old Testament has progressed in England, upon that reconstruction of Israel's history which succeeded Ewald's,[1] under the powerful leadership of the Old Testament scholars of Oxford and Cambridge; or how it has spread through the Nonconformist ministry upon the impulse of teachers who are equally loyal to the principles of historical criticism. Let me give but one instance of the combination of the methods of modern criticism with fervid and practical preaching from the Prophets — one proof of how false it is to suppose that the adoption of critical results impairs a preacher's power in applying the Old Testament to his own generation. Dr. Farrar accepts the legitimacy of the critical methods, he accepts not a few of their results;[2] yet his preaching has always been warmly ethical and directly applied to the social problems and vices of our day.

In my own country and Church the similar revival of ethical preaching from the Old Testament was due in the first place to the teaching of Professor A. B. Davidson, in its powerful union of spiritual insight with fidelity to the historical situations of Israel, and sympathy with them; and in the second place to the long trial of his pupil, Professor William Robertson Smith,

---

[1] See above, Lecture II., Section I.

[2] *Lives and Times of the Minor Prophets*, pp. 19, 20; *The Second Book of Kings* and *Daniel* (Expositor's Bible), *passim*.

for the critical opinions which he published in the *Encyclopædia Britannica*.[1]

The official result was Professor Smith's removal from his chair, by what many of us still think to have been an arbitrary use of ecclesiastical power on the part of a majority of the Free Church General Assembly of 1881. But the critical principles for which he fought were never condemned, and his trial — carried from one Church Court to another and debated in almost every Free Church Presbytery in the country — turned out to have been the education of large numbers of men in the meaning of criticism and its effects upon Scripture. Professor Smith appealed from the Church Courts to the people in two series of lectures : one of which, upon *The Prophets of Israel*, was published at a time auspicious to its subject for another reason. In Scottish preaching the broad influence of Thomas Chalmers had almost disappeared;[2] social subjects were infrequently treated by the pulpit, and the Gospel was preached with but little

[1] Ninth ed., articles ' Angels,' ' Bible,' ' Chronicles,' ' Deuteronomy,' etc.

[2] There were of course several notable services to social ethics rendered by Scottish ministers : Dr. Begg's, on behalf of farm-servants ; Dr. Guthrie's, for city children ; and Dr. Blaikie's work, *Better Days for Working People*. But these and other social efforts were for the most part pursued outside the pulpit. One still useful series of sermons on the Old Testament are those of William Arnot on the Book of Proverbs, *Laws from Heaven for Life on Earth*.

reference to the social and economic duties of
Christians. Then came Socialism upon us, with
all its trumpets sounding; and although this
movement has converted but few to its dogmas,
it has assisted to rouse the civic conscience in
the Church, and to awaken everywhere a new
interest in social questions. Coincident with the
beginnings of this interest was the publication
of *The Prophets of Israel ;* and from the coincidence we may venture to date a revival of
the Prophets in the Scottish pulpit. Every
department of religious activity felt its effects.
Sermons became more ethical; the studies of
Bible-classes in the Old Testament, instead of
being confined to the historical Books, were
extended to the prophetical; and a considerable
body of popular literature has appeared, which
expounds the teaching of the Prophets and in
many cases applies it to modern life.[1]   The
effect, then, in Britain of the modern criticism of
the Prophets may be reckoned as constructive
and practical in the highest degree.

[1] I am unaware how far this latter phenomenon has appeared
in other lands. But in Holland there was the work of J. J. P.
Valeton, jun., *Amos en Hosea*, 1894, which contains this passage :
' These prophecies have a word of God, as for all times, so
especially for our own. Before all it is relevant to " the social
question " of our day, to the relation of religion and morality. . . .
Often it has been hard for me to refrain from expressly pointing
out the agreement between Then and To-day.' And in Germany
there was Cornill's Frankfort lectures to educated laymen, *Der
Israelitische Prophetismus* (1894). Both of these are by advanced
critics of the first rank.

I have thus begun with our own times, because they are naturally of most religious interest to us. But I now ask you to go back with me upon that survey which I promised of the influence of the Old Testament, and in particular of the Prophets, upon the social ethics of Christendom from the earliest times to the age before our own. We shall see how strangely diverse the character of that influence has been. The candid student, who carefully traces its effects upon European civilisation, is still left to question whether the cruelties and superstitions which were sanctioned by an appeal to Hebrew example, or the legislation and struggles for reform which were inspired by the Law and the Prophets, have been the more conspicuous and influential. Yet of this there can be no doubt, that where a historical criticism of the Old Testament, however imperfect, was cultivated, there the immediate effect upon Christian preaching from the Old Testament was sound and practical to a very high degree.

Even before the establishment of Christianity as the religion of the Roman Empire the political influence of the Old Testament began to be pervasive and conspicuous. No one can examine early Christian inscriptions without being struck by the fact that the quotations from Scripture which they contain are almost all drawn from the Books of the Old Testament, but are often modi-

fied so as to give them a Christian significance.[1]
The application of the Old Testament to domestic
life must have been nearly universal in early
Christianity. The sense of the Divine protec-
tion of the home, and the influence of those
examples of family virtue which the Hebrew
Scriptures record, are frequently expressed; nor
can such teaching as that of Deuteronomy and
the Proverbs have failed to permeate the private
life of the Church. Besides these there were the
more formal and public results. Excluded from
the society of the world in which she existed,
the primitive Church had to legislate not only
for the worship, but for the social life and discipline of her members. In her circumstances,
she could organise only upon a theocratic basis,
and such was found already developed and detailed within her Old Testament Canon. It is
easy to perceive how, in the government of the
Church — especially in her hierarchy and in her
judgement of heretics — there came to be sanctioned, by appeal to the letter of the Hebrew
Scriptures,[2] principles and tempers which were

[1] I was very much impressed by this when reading the early
Christian inscriptions still extant on the hard basalt of Hauran
and other regions east of the Jordan ; and the impression was
confirmed by a study of Le Bas and Waddington's collection of
Greek inscriptions. On lintels of houses and tombstones the LXX.
version is frequently quoted, with the substitution of Χριστός for
Κύριος or Θεός (cf. *Historical Geography of the Holy Land*, p. 634).

[2] Especially in the *Apostolic Constitutions*, and by Cyprian.
Cf. Diestel, *Gesch. des Alten Testaments in der Christlichen*

hostile to Christ's teaching, and which in their subsequent development have engendered the rankest tyranny and superstition. On this I dwelt sufficiently in the first Lecture.

While these evils were aggravated through the adoption of Christianity by the Imperial power, we perceive from this event onwards another effect of the Old Testament of a more wholesome quality. The influence of the Jewish codes upon the legislation and public morals of the Empire from Constantine to Justinian has never been critically treated; but this is certain, that 'the laws of Moses were received as the divine original of justice';[1] and that it was their example which braced Roman legislators to put down the bestial sins, and to treat all sexual vice with more severity than the Imperial authorities had previously attempted.[2]

Following the example of the Apostles, the preachers of the early Church, whether in argument or homily, made continual use of the Old Testament. The prevailing method of inter-

---

Kirche, pp. 141 ff.; Gibbon, *Decline and Fall*, ch. xxviii., end of first paragraph.

[1] Gibbon, ch. xliv.: vol. v. p. 322 in Smith's edition.

[2] *Ibid.* 322 ff. Diestel (*Gesch. des A. T.*, 151 f.) mentions the *Lex Dei: sive Mosaicarum et Romanarum legum collatio*, by Licinius Rufinus, towards the end of the fifth century. It is a list of parallels between the Mosaic and Roman Laws: it is important in so far as it proves the high value which was accorded to the Mosaic Law in that period, but it 'does not prove a direct influence' of that law on the Imperial legislation.

pretation was the allegorical. This arbitrary
and dangerous habit arose very naturally in the
ordinary employment of the Bible for purposes
of edification; and it was confirmed, partly by
the Church's efforts to explain away the moral
and other difficulties of Old Testament history,
and partly by the exigencies of her polemic
against the Jews. In hostility to the application of Prophecy to Christ, Jewish writers insisted
upon the literal sense of the prophetic word, and
confined its significance to the history of Israel.
The Church replied by allegorising as much of
the Word as it could. Individual morals were,
of course, directly enforced from Hebrew examples;[1] but the early fathers were interested
in the Old Testament mainly for its types and
predictions of Christ. The allegorical became
the orthodox exegesis, and was at last reduced
to a theory by Origen,[2] and elaborated into
a system by the school which he founded.
The effort to distinguish the primary sense
of the text was indeed not wholly abandoned;
but the healthy instinct which led to it was
too bare of knowledge and of insight to render the result consistent or fertile. When the
heretics began to outdo the orthodox in allegorical exposition, the latter awoke to the dangers of the habit they had fostered and loudly

[1] *E.g.* by Clement of Rome, *Epistle to the Corinthians.*
[2] 185–254 A. D.

proclaimed the need of sobriety and reason in the pursuit of it. But the historical sense of the age was small, and till the close of the fourth century no exegete succeeded in finding his feet upon a sound historical basis. Thus allegory, prompted now by dogmatic audacity and now by apologetic fearfulness, exercised, with almost no restraint, its confusing and evaporating influence upon the preaching of the Christian pulpit.

To the school of Antioch belongs the fame of training the Church in sounder principles of exegesis, and, as their immediate consequence, in a more practical application of the Old Testament to the life of the day. Theodore, afterwards of Mopsuestia, was the greatest representative of the former; John, surnamed Chrysostom, the most illustrious example of the latter.[1] Both were pupils of Diodorus of Tarsus, who, though his works have perished and his fame has disappeared behind that of his successors, must have been — by the characteristics these possessed in common and probably derived from him, as well as by the few reports of his principles which have reached us — a teacher of unusual originality and impressiveness.[2] Theodore of Mopsuestia has been justly styled, ' Veteris Testamenti sobrie

---

[1] Theodore, *c.* 350–429: Chrysostom, 347–407.

[2] *Caten. Niceph.* i. 524, according to which he declared that he much preferred the historical, to the allegorical, exegesis.

interpretandi vindex';[1] he may even be hailed as the father of historical exegesis. He did not use the Hebrew original, and had to work with the Greek versions; but he was the first to break with any power from the speculative methods which the school of Origen had fastened upon the Church's interpretation of Scripture; and the first to follow with some consistency the lines of a historical interpretation. To Theodore the prophecies and types of the Old Testament had, besides their references to the future, a prior value in themselves and for the age to which they were delivered. Considering the traditions which encumbered his generation and the knowledge of ancient history at his disposal, Theodore's vision of the intrinsic worth and contemporary reference of the prophetical writings was only less wonderful than the courage with which he asserted the consequences of this principle in his criticism of the Psalms and other Scriptures.[2]

---

[1] By Sieffert in the title of his work *Theodorus Mopsuestenus*, 1827. See also, *Theod. v. Mops. u. Junilius Africanus*, by Kihn, 1880.

[2] The only Old Testament work of Theodore's which is extant is that on *The Twelve Prophets*: A. Mai, *Nova Patr. Bibl.* vii. 1854; Migne, *Patrologia Græca*, vol. lxvi. His historical explanations of the Old Testament do not of course preclude typical references to the New. Old and New are part of the same economy of Divine grace. We hear from others that he denied value to the titles of the Psalms; that he referred the Messianic Psalms to Hezekiah and Zerubbabel, leaving only three with a reference to Jesus Christ; that he denied prophetic inspiration to Job and the Solomonic literature; and rejected Chronicles with Ezra and Nehemiah.

His pupils, especially Theodoret, afterwards Bishop of Kyros,[1] carried on the example of their master.

Chrysostom began to write probably as early as Theodore. His first work on the Old Testament was, like that of the latter, exegetical: a 'Hermeneia' or 'Interpretation' of the Prophet Isaiah,[2] but he never finished it. Drawn by his superb gifts to the pulpit, he delivered to the Church the rest of his Old Testament studies in the form of Homilies, of which six, still extant, expand and apply his views — already given in the 'Interpretation' — of the first verse of Isaiah's vision and of the Seraphs.[3]

[1] Theodoret, d. 457. His works were edited in four folio volumes in 1642 by Sirmond. The first two volumes contain those on the Old Testament: vol. i. Ἐρωτήσεις or *Quæstiones* to the Octateuch, Kings and Chronicles, with a Ἑρμηνεία or Interpretation of the Psalms and Canticles; vol. ii. Interpretations of Jeremiah, Ezekiel, Daniel and the Twelve Prophets, and an epitome of his Interpretation of Isaiah. An adequate sketch of his teaching on the Old Testament is given by Diestel, *Gesch. des A. T. in der Christl. Kirche*, pp. 133 ff.: 'Dass Typus und "Wahrheit" oft noch neben einander, nicht in einander stehen, und dem ἡ μὲν ἱστόρια ἐδίδαξεν ein ἡμεῖς δὲ μανθάνομεν gegenübertritt; dass die Schrift des A. T.'s so zu verstehen ist wie sie den Juden selbst hat nützen können (cf. interrog. 52 in Genesim).'

[2] Vol. vi. of the standard edition of his works by de Montfaucon (Paris 1835). The editor quotes with approval Tillemont's opinion that this unfinished work was not later than 377 A.D.

[3] *Ibid.*: besides there are Homilies and Sermons from Chrysostom on Genesis and on David and Saul (vol. iv.); on the Psalms (vol. v.), on several Old Testament texts, and two on 'the Obscurity of the Prophetic Writings,' with others, and a 'Hermeneia' of Daniel (all of these in vol. vi.), and on the Books of the Maccabees (vol. ii.).

The introduction to his 'Hermeneia' of Isaiah
defines the principles of the new exegesis. The
ministry of the Prophets to their own generation
has never been more finely described — as a
ministry not only of judgement but of love and
fellow-suffering. 'Now of all the prophets and
saints this was the spirit: in disposition towards
them over whom they were set they excelled
the tender affection of fathers, and by a long
way outdid the sovereignty of nature . . . for
there is no qualification for office so important
as a soul that loves wisdom and knows how to
suffer with others.'[1] It is the picture of the
Prophets by one who was himself a prophet; we
will not marvel that the man who so intuitively
understood his great forerunners was impelled to
leave his study for the imitation of them among
his own people. Chrysostom's homilies on the
Old Testament are not a little engaged with
argument against the Jews, and in defence of
predictions of Christ; to that extent they are
less direct than his magnificent preaching on
the Gospels and Epistles. But from the first he
endeavours to keep allegorising in a secondary
place. He reckons historical explanation to be

---

[1] Καὶ πάντων δὲ τῶν προφητῶν καὶ τῶν ἁγίων τοιοῦτον τὸ ἔθος ·
πατέρων φιλοστοργίαν τῇ περὶ τοὺς ἀρχομένους ἀπέκρυψαν διαθέσει,
καὶ τὴν τῆς φύσεως τυραννίδα ἐκ πολλοῦ τοῦ περίοντος ὑπερηκόν-
τισαν . . . καὶ γὰρ οὐδὲν οὕτως ἐπιτήδειον εἰς ἀρχῆς αἵρεσιν
ὡς ψυχὴ φιλόσοφος καὶ συναλγεῖν ἐπισταμένη (vi. 2, ed. Montfaucon).

'the more true'; [1] and, thus discerning the ethical essence of the Prophets, he scourges the vices and consoles the sufferings of Antioch with the words of Isaiah to Jerusalem. The school of Antioch is another proof of the principle we have found instanced in our own time, that the revival of a true historical criticism means a revival of the practical use of the Old Testament in the Christian pulpit. Recognise that the fundamental meaning of the prophecies must be that which they bore to the living generation to whom they were first addressed; [2] and you are at once inspired by their message to the men of your own time.

In the Western Church the influence of Origen continued to prevail; and the interpretation of the Bible was not enfranchised from the allegorising methods of the Alexandrian school. Ambrose and Augustine [3] appear to have confined their exegetical work upon the Old Testament to the Pentateuch, some of the historical Books, the Psalms, Job, and scattered passages; upon the Prophets we have from them nothing elaborate. Properly, therefore, they fall outside the intention of this review; yet a few sentences

---

[1] *Ibid.* p. 17 on Isa. i. 22, Ἐγὼ δὲ οὔτε ταύτην ἀτιμάζω τὴν ἐξήγησιν, *i.e.* the allegorical, καὶ τὴν ἑτέραν ἀληθεστέραν εἶναί φημι.

[2] See the extract from Theodoret above, p. 229, n. 1.

[3] Besides these Hilary of Poitiers wrote on the Psalms and Canticles. See Diestel, *Geschichte des A. T. in d. Christl. Kirche*, p. 78.

may be devoted to the general style of Augustine's exegesis.[1] As an interpreter, Augustine was above all the mystic and allegorist. It is true that the restlessness and ingenuity of his mind were constantly dissatisfied with a method of exposition so cheap and so easily abused, and that his inherited inclination to allegory was besides frequently arrested by difficulties in the text and history of Scripture which this method was unable to solve. He aimed to write a commentary on Genesis *ad litteram:* 'that is to say, not according to allegorical significations but according to the inherent quality of the transactions as they happened';[2] and he expressly affirmed that the spiritual sense of a passage ought to be drawn from it 'only provided that the historical truth has first been conserved';[3] and

---

[1] Augustine's works on the Old Testament are these (given along with the volume of the Benedictine edition of his works in which each occurs) : — vol. i. *De Genesi contra Manichaeos libri II.;* vol. iii. *De Genesi ad Litteram imperfectus Liber* (only some fifteen pages); *De Genesi ad Litteram Libri xii.* (he explains the title in his *Retract.* ii. 24, thus: id est non secundum allegoricas significationes sed secundum rerum gestarum proprietatem; the work extends only to the expulsion from Eden); *Locutionum libri vii.* Genesis to Judges: *Questionum in Heptateuchum lib. vii.; Annotationum in Job lib. i.;* vol. iv. *Enarrationes in Psalmos;* vol. v. many sermons on Old Testament passages; and vol. viii. the sections of the *De Civitate Dei*, discussed below, p. 252. The *Enarrationes in Psalmos* are translated in six volumes of the Oxford Library of the Fathers (1847–57).

[2] *Retract.* ii. 24 : see previous note.

[3] *De Civitate Dei*, xvii. 3: 'audeant sensum intelligentiae spiritalis exsculpere, servata primitus duntaxat historiae veritate.'

again, 'if any Scripture is to be investigated, let us inquire in what manner a thing has been said, apart from the allegorical signification.'[1] These are sound directions, but Augustine had neither the knowledge nor the temperament to carry them out. He was ignorant of Hebrew;[2] therefore incapable of a grammatical exegesis, and dependent on the philological fancies of others. The difficulties, which his subtle mind detected in the allegorising of his predecessors, the same mind solved with fresh and more plausible imaginations. It is true that he did not always go astray — though the credit of this was his own rather than that of his methods. In so elastic a system of exegesis, so magnificent a genius for religion could not fail frequently to reach the truth: so fruitful a spirit was certain nearly always to be edifying. In a misty atmosphere like that of allegory the small man is lost altogether, while the large man often looms the larger and moves majestically. Therefore, however dim be his light, the motions of Augustine are generally worth following. Especially in his exposition of the Psalms, amid not a little to amuse and much to weary, we find almost more that is suggestive and practical. Again

[1] *De Genesi ad Litteram*, i. 2: 'quaeramus quomodo dictum est, praeter allegoricam significationem.'

[2] *Confess*. xi. 5: *De Sermone in Monte*, i. 23. The version which Augustine used was the old Latin version known to us as the *Itala: De Doctr. Christiana*, ii. 14.

and again Augustine discovers the essence of
a Psalm; or if this be missed, he leaves us
with scattered sentences of glorious insight and
inspiration. Jerome,[1] who adorns a rank as high
as Origen's in the history of the textual criticism
of the Old Testament, did not, in spite of his
occasional use of better methods, escape from
the orthodox routine of a subjective and allegorical exegesis. His principal service was to
recall the Church to the original of the greater
half of her Scriptures, and to present her with
a Latin version of the Old Testament based on
the Hebrew text. Jerome does not himself fall
within a review of the Church's preaching from
the Prophets; but for the next thousand years
he guided with Augustine the influence, for good
and evil, of the Old Testament upon the Christian
pulpit.

It was not, however, in preaching that during
this millennium the influence of the Old Testament was most effective; but on ecclesiastical
constitutions and in the defence of dogma. Of
the first of these the growth of the Canon Law
and of the claims of the Papacy are the most striking instances; of the second, the writings of the
scholastic theologians. The Canon Law almost
everywhere borrows from the Hebrew theocracy:
the Papal throne and its defenders appeal to the
rights of the Levitical hierarchy, and to the High

[1] Died 420.

Priest's assumption of the temporal power. The commentaries of Thomas Aquinas [1] on some of the Prophets,[2] while often clearly, though coldly, suggestive of truth,[3] attempt to discover predictions of the great facts of the Evangel and of all the chief dogmas of the Church in the most irrelevant passages.[4] Bernard of Clairvaux's eighty-six sermons on the Song of Solomon are representative of the *furor typologicus* of the time. Yet as Diestel rightly reminds us,[5] a great deal of the practical preaching of the Middle Ages reflects directly the examples of Hebrew history, and the plain ethical sense of the prophetic writings. And we must not forget how the Psalms, in the musical Latin to which the Vulgate had set them, were as a stream of living water through all those thousand years, refreshing personal piety and the public worship of the Church. But apart from such exceptions, the principal purposes to which the Christian Church put the Old Testament, between the disappearance of the great theologians of the fifth century and the eve of the Reformation,

[1] Died 1274.

[2] See vol. i. of the second Venetian edition (1775) of his works, comprising commentaries to Job, the first fifty-one Psalms and the Song of Songs; and vol ii. commentaries to Isaiah, Jeremiah and Lamentations.

[3] *E.g.* on Jer. vii. and xxxi.

[4] *E.g.* on Isaiah liii. the phrase, *a root out of a dry ground*, which he takes as a prediction of the virgin birth of Christ.

[5] Page 225.

were purposes typological, ecclesiastical and dogmatic. For her ethics during the greater part of that period the Church deserted the Prophets for the moralists of Greece and Rome.[1]

From the twelfth to the fifteenth century better means of understanding the Hebrew text were gradually acquired by the Church, and for the most part from the works of Jews or Jewish proselytes. With the increase of such instruments for criticism, there arose bolder attempts at sound methods of exegesis; and by necessary consequence the practical use of the Old Testament exhibited many signs of improvement.[2] It is now that we meet with the first real successor of Chrysostom in the homiletic exposition of the Prophets. Savonarola,[3] besides reviving a pure Gospel, was a preacher of civic righteousness, and he became so by his sermons upon Micah and other Prophetical Books.[4] Of twenty-

[1] For a practical instance of this see below, p. 254, on Dante's *De Monarchia*.

[2] The two names of this period which stand forth before a crowd of others in the respects above mentioned are that of the celebrated Nikolaus of Lyra (d. 1340) whose influence was very great on exegesis both before and after the Reformation: *cf.* the saying : ' Si Lyra non lyrasset, Lutherus non saltasset '; and that of Reuchlin, whose *Rudimenta Linguae Hebraeae* was not published till the beginning of the sixteenth century : 1506.

[3] 1452–1498.

[4] *Works*, in six volumes, 1633-40; *Prediche di F. Girolamo Savonarola: edizione integra . . . per cura di* Giuseppe Baccini : Florence 1889. These are the sermons preached in 1496. A short life of Savonarola and appendices are given.

nine sermons preached by him at Florence between Easter and Advent 1496, and taken down by Ser Lorenzo Violi, only two are from New Testament texts, and one of these, on the Ascension, is largely occupied by an exposition of the story of Balaam. Five expound the Book of Ruth, and thirteen the prophecies of Micah. The others are from texts in 2 Chronicles, in five Psalms, in Isaiah vi., and in Ecclesiastes vii. In all of these sermons the current politics of that year are dealt with ; and the teaching of the Old Testament is applied to the dangers and vices of the citizens of Florence.

After the Reformation the linguistic aids to the interpretation of the Old Testament rapidly multiplied, and with them the practice of a grammatical and historical exegesis became predominant. Many of the leading Reformers were as fully acquainted with Hebrew as the improved culture of their time permitted, and though still hampered by the traditional allegorising, they boldly stated, and frequently exemplified, the duty of holding to the simple sense of Scripture. 'I have grounded my preaching,' said Luther, ' on the literal word.' [1] To him, as to Melanchthon

---

[1] *Table Talk*, ch. i. His frequently expressed opinions in this regard are summed up in ch. lix. : ' Allegories and Spiritual Significations, when they are directed upon Faith and seldom used, then they are good and laudable, but when they are drawn upon the life and conversation, then they are dangerous and I am an enemy unto them. . . . St. Jerome and Origen (God forgive it

and Zwingli, allegory was permissible only as 'rhetoric' and 'ornament,' the means of attracting common and uneducated minds. As his career advanced he more fully dispensed with it: 'I have shaken it off, and my best art is to render Scripture in the simple sense.' There are also real flashes of historical insight in his critical pronouncements, that it does not matter much 'if Moses did not himself write the Pentateuch'; that many of the Prophetical Books, for example Isaiah, Jeremiah and Hosea, contain additions, and have received their present forms from later writers; and that the Book of Job is not history but a poem or drama. Apart from the value of these particular utterances the Church owes to Luther the greatest example yet offered to her of the Christian liberty of a discriminating judgement on the Old Testament.[1] Yet through-

---

them) holp thereunto that Allegories were held in such esteem. . . . Now I have shaken it off and my best art is *Tradere Scripturam simplici sensu*, that is to deliver the Scripture in the simple sense: the same doth the deed: therein is life, strength, doctrine and Art; in the other is nothing but foolishness, let it lustre and shine how it will. St. Austin gave a rule: *Quod Figura et Allegoria nihil probet sed Historia, Verba et Grammatica*, *i.e.* that Figure and Allegories prove nothing at all, but Historie, Words and Grammar ' (Capt. Henrie Bell's translation). Besides his Translation (1534) Luther's work on the Old Testament consisted of sermons and expositions in Latin and German on Genesis, Exodus and Deuteronomy; Isaiah, Ezekiel, Hosea, Joel, Amos, Obadiah, Micah, Jonah, Nahum, Habakkuk, Zechariah, Malachi, Daniel, many Psalms, Canticles and Ecclesiastes (all apparently between 1523 and 1546).

[1] See Lecture 1.

out Luther was the preacher rather than the interpreter. His exposition, like his criticism, of Scripture, if not dominated, was constantly interrupted, by his personality with its rude human vigour and its marvellous experience of Divine grace. Sometimes it is the native Luther who thus breaks out, as in the almost truculent sentences upon the Prophets, the Epistle of James and the Apocalypse; but far oftener it is the 'new Luther,' the man who has passed through the struggles in the Erfurt cloister, and has been saved by faith. Thus, though he violates 'the simple sense' of many passages, and overlooks small but not insignificant points in others, he carries our hearts with him to lofty and far-reaching views of God's purposes of salvation as they lie spread out across both Testaments. Köstlin, his principal biographer in our time, has thus justly characterised Luther's exposition: 'The whole delivery of Luther's teaching preserves that quality of fresh life which we have pointed out in connection with his first writings. . . . The fundamental doctrine of salvation, as it always moved himself, so in his utterances it constantly presses into the foreground and the centre; this is an essential peculiarity of his exposition of Scripture and of his sermons. In the former he knows how to soar on every occasion to the highest points of view, and to spread spirit and life across apparently barren sections of his course. In the treatment of such scriptures as have no immediate original connection with those fundamental doctrines, as also in the definition within a text of those details, which, in contrast to its leading thoughts, have only a subordinate importance, the claims of historical and linguistic accuracy do not always come to their rights.'[1]

The soundest exegete of the time was John Calvin: considering his means and opportunities, we may call him the greatest expositor of all time. 'To real exegetic skill he unites the full freedom of a Theodore of Mopsuestia with the profundity of a Luther.'[2] Calvin's knowledge of Hebrew;[3] his command not only of the historic circumstance but of the mental atmosphere[4] of the different periods, from which the Old Testa-

---

[1] Herzog's *Real-Encyclopädie*, second ed. ix. 72.

[2] Diestel, *op. cit.* p. 269.

[3] Calvin himself makes no assertion of his knowledge of Hebrew; and Simon, the early critic of the Pentateuch (see above, p. 33), denied that he knew enough for practical purposes. But the fact has been admitted even by his enemies — he at least is a Reformer to whom Roman controversialists allow an adequate acquaintance with the original languages of Scripture. Compare too the tributes of Diestel and Tholuck to his linguistic endowments. But indeed his mastery of Hebrew, though never displayed, is felt throughout all his commentaries on the Old Testament. Beza, his biographer, after saying that Calvin was a friend of Grynæus and Capito, adds ' seseque Hebraicis literis dedit.' See for the details *Calvin Hébraisant*, by Professor Antoine J. Baumgartner of Geneva (Paris 1889), a very interesting inquiry as to where and how Calvin learned his Hebrew.

[4] Cf. his admission of the exilic atmosphere of Isaiah lv.

ment arose; his fairness even to the confession of errors in Scripture, combined with his healthy indifference as to their presence;[1] his single-hearted aim to give the original meaning of the sacred authors; his appreciation of the essence of prophecy, not as prediction, but 'as the message of God to men,' 'the interpreting and administering of revelation';[2] his contempt for allegory;[3] his independence of tradition, and stout refusal to find proofs for doctrine in irrelevant texts;[4] his sobriety and sense of proportion — all these sincere qualities are at the command of a profound religious insight, and of a spirit desirous to know only what God has

[1] On Matthew xxvii. 9: 'Quo modo Hieremiae nomen obrepserit, me nescire fateor, nec anxie laboro; certe Hieremiae nomen errore positum esse pro Zacharia, res ipsa ostendit.' 'In what way the name of Jeremiah has stolen in here, I confess I do not know, nor do I trouble myself about it; *that the name of Jeremiah has been by error substituted for that of Zechariah, the thing itself clearly shows.*' On Acts vii. 16 — Stephen's statement that Jacob's and other patriarchs' bodies were carried to Shechem to be buried in a sepulchre which Abraham bought of the sons of Emmor (father or son?) of Sychem—Calvin remarks, 'in nomine Abrahae erratum palam esse. Quare hic locus corrigendus est.' 'As every one can see, an error has been made in the name of Abraham. Wherefore this passage has to be corrected.'

[2] So he defines it on 1 Cor. xii. 9; xiv. 6.

[3] On 1 Cor. ix. 8: 'Some hairbrained spirits take occasion from this to turn everything into allegories. Thus they change dogs into men, trees into angels, and all Scripture into a laughing-stock.'

[4] See above, p. 146, his criticism of alleged Messianic prophecies. Calvin's exegesis is curiously independent of his somewhat rigorous doctrine of Scripture.

willed to say.[1] Among Calvin's expositions
many moderns give preference to those on the
Psalms; to me it seems as if his interpretations
of the Prophets were still greater: in so far as
with the latter he finds more solid ground in
date and circumstance for his original gifts of
historical exegesis. But on every Book of the
Old Testament Calvin is a commentator whom
neither the modern exegete nor the modern
preacher can afford to neglect.

May I remind you in a sentence that I am
not now giving the full doctrine of Scripture
which the Reformers held, but that my purpose
is only to show how far founded upon grammar
and history and how far true to ' the simple
sense' their exegesis was.[2] Once more we
see the practical effect of such methods. The
great exegetes of the Reformation, and their im-

---

[1] Calvin's claim for himself is not exaggerated (Epistle Dedi-
catory to his Commentary on *The Twelve Prophets*) : ' If God
has endued me with any aptness for the interpretation of Scripture, I am fully persuaded that I have faithfully and carefully
endeavoured to exclude from it all barren refinements — however
plausible and fitted to please the ear — and to preserve genuine
simplicity, adapted solidly to edify the children of God, who
being not content with the shell wish to penetrate to the kernel'
(Owen's translation, Edin. 1846).

[2] For a statement of the Reformers' doctrine of Scripture, and
a discrimination between it on the one hand and the views of
mediæval theologians and modern evangelicals and certain Broad
churchmen on the other, see an article by Professor T. M. Lindsay
in the *Expositor*, fourth series, vol. x. (July–December 1894)
pp. 241 ff. on 'Professor W. Robertson Smith's Doctrine of
Scripture.'

mediate followers,[1] guided a Church for whose use
translations of the Bible were being made into
the various vernaculars and everywhere multiplied by the art of printing. The more scientific
exegesis had given the Bible to the people; and
the result was the practical influence of the Old
Testament upon the pulpit, the school and the
state to an extent beyond what was reached
by any previous age. Luther had unfortunately
described the political activity of the Prophets
as 'so much hay, straw and wood among the
genuine silver and gold' of their work — as if
thier political messages could be separated from
their religion ! Partly because of the sounder
example of Calvin in the historical exegesis
which he illustrated, and partly because of a
wider use of the Bible in public worship, the
influence of the Old Testament in Switzerland
and other regions of the Reformed Church, as
distinguished from the Lutheran, was more
ethical than it came to be among the Luther-
ans themselves. Yet almost everywhere the
Prophets began to speak to the new generations.
From the time of the Reformation to our own
there never has been a city of Protestant
Europe which has been stirred to higher ideals
of justice and purity, without the rewaking of
those ancient voices which declared to Jacob his
sin and to Israel his transgression. Once more

---

[1] For a full list of these see Diestel, *op. cit.* 269 ff.

the revival of a sounder criticism was followed
by the revival of a more practical preaching. The
fidelity which sought to discover what the Prophets actually meant to the men of their own
time was rewarded by the inspiration of their
message to the men of all times.

It is unnecessary to give full illustration of this
within the English-speaking Churches. Suffice
it to remember the earlier Puritans like Henry
Smith with his 'Scriptures for Magistrates' from
the eighty-second Psalm, and his 'Memento for
Magistrates' from the forty-fifth;[1] and the later
Puritans, like Goodwin, whose sermons to the
House of Commons on public occasions were
nearly always upon Old Testament texts; or
like Cromwell, whose addresses to his parliaments
so often started, or were enforced, from the same
sources.[2]

---

[1] *The Sermons of Mr. Henry Smith gathered into one volume*,
with an introduction by Thomas Fuller, and dedicated to William
Cicill, Lord Burleigh, Treasurer of England, 1657. Smith was
'commonly called *the silver-tongued preacher*, and that was but
one metall below St. Chrysostom himself' (Fuller). How practical his preaching from the Old Testament was (and the same
might be illustrated from other Puritan preachers) may be seen
from the 'one instance of many of the great prevalency he had
with his auditory' which Fuller gives. 'He preached a sermon
on *Sarah's* nursing of *Isaac*, and thereupon grounded the general
doctrine, *that it was the duty of all mothers to nurse their own
children*, allowing dispensation to such who were unsufficienced
by weakness, want of milk, or any avouchable impediment. He
prest the application without respect of persons high or low,
rich or poor, one with another.'

[2] Carlyle, *Cromwell's Letters and Speeches*, vol. iv.

The rise and elaboration of the Federal idea
of Revelation,[1] led in Great Britain to a detailed extension of the political uses of the
Old Testament in preaching which lasted even
into the nineteenth century. In Scotland especially this was inspired, not only by the institutions of the Law, but by the patriotism,
national romance and passion of the historical
and prophetical Books. To-day the proudest
memories of the Scottish people are associated
with the struggles and heroisms of Old Testament
history. It was not merely that for two centuries
the prevailing theology in Scotland conceived of
God's relation to man under the form of a covenant; but as in Israel's case the covenant was understood as national and it comprised every public
interest. The Scottish preachers, who in times
of persecution taught their suffering nation to see
herself in the Trampled Vine, the Desolate City
and the Remnant of God's pity and promise, in
times of peace enforced upon every department
of her life the whole righteousness of ancient
Israel. Nor did they always preach that legalism,
which being falsely imputed to Scotland has
moved some[2] to call her in scorn 'the Judæa
of the West.' It is true that they were some-

---

[1] Originating with the fathers of the Reformation, but reduced to a system by Coccejus — *Summa doctrina de foedere Dei
et testamento explicata*, J. Coccejo, 1648 — and other seventeenth-
century theologians.

[2] *E.g.* Heine.

times dogmatically national. Even the greatest
theologians of the seventeenth century were apt
to confine the covenant to the visible Church, and
in the spirit of Deuteronomy to include within
its obligations none that extended beyond the
limits of their own nation. The late Dr. Walker,
in his admirable work on *The Theology and
Theologians of Scotland*,[1] says that ' the seventeenth century divines were greatly hampered by
what I may call their Judaic theory of the
world's conversion. Our modern idea of the
visible Church, as a kingdom of faith pushing out
in bold aggressions on every side . . . aiming at
nothing less than the spiritual subjugation of the
world to the faith and obedience of the gospel,
was very faintly realised in that earlier period of
our history. What our fathers rather thought of
was a sort of expansion of nationalism after the
Jewish fashion, in which, when God has elect
ones among a people to be gathered in, He
takes the nation into external covenant with
Himself, and within the order, and under the
ordinances of a visible Church as His " office-
house of grace," — not excluding the aid extrinsic
of the sword of the magistrate. . . . " To have
the doctrine of the covenant preached to a
nation," says Rutherford, " and Christ offered to
them is to be the planted vineyard of the Lord.
The field is the field of the visible kingdom of

---

[1] First Edition, Edinburgh, 1872, p. 58 ff.

Christ because the world of all natural men is not the Lord's field, where He soweth His wheat, but the visible Church is only such a field." ' Thus in modern Scotland fervent Christian men were so infected by formal Judaism as to fall into the error, for which the prophet Jonah (as the type of Israel) is rebuked and punished in the Book which bears his name. It was Thomas Boston and the so-called ' marrow-men ' who came to the rescue of Scotland from so narrow and nationalist an interpretation of the covenant of grace. ' Boston and the marrow-men,' continues Dr. Walker, ' first of all among our divines entered freely into the missionary spirit of the Bible; were able to see that Calvinistic doctrine ' — that is especially in the covenanting principles which it borrowed from the Old Testament — ' was not inconsistent with world-conquering aspirations and efforts.'

Within the religious life of the nation, the legalism of the covenanting theology yielded to more spiritual forces. Most of the preachers of the Covenant, like the Prophets of Israel, kept before their people the Person of their King rather than the letter of His Law. It was not legal obedience they demanded, but those chivalrous affections which are as the fire to cleanse national life and to enkindle in a people the ardours of sacrifice and service — ' zeal for the glory of God,' ' love to the Lord Jesus Christ,' ' the sole King and Head of the Church ' — and

the faith that He is identified with the poor and
the oppressed. Of the Scottish people in that
heroic age the saying is true in which the heathen
seer described the people of Israel:

> *The Lord his God is with him,*
> *And the noise of a King is among them.*[1]

This period was not without its able exegetes,
independent of tradition and with a conscience to
interpret Scripture upon such scientific methods
as were at the disposal of their time.[2] But
either they were not consistent in carrying
out these methods, or they were more or less
destitute of sympathy with the religious meaning of what they treated, and sometimes subject
to intellectual tempers almost as dogmatic as
the traditional views which they abjured. The
period also produced philosophic critics, who
anticipated not only many of the principles,
but some of the conclusions of modern criticism.[3] And to this period belongs the fame
— often unjustly ignored by the more scientific
age which has eclipsed it — of solid contributions to the philology of the Old Testament,[4]

[1] Numbers xxiii. 21.

[2] One has only to recall Grotius.

[3] Like Hobbes, Collins and Spinoza. Simon too started the
analysis of the Pentateuch before the end of the seventeenth
century, and was followed by Astruc in the eighteenth (see
above Lecture II.). All through the period there were *Critica
Sacra* issued by various scholars.

[4] Like the works of Erpenius, Golius, Buxtorf, De Dieu,

and of the origins of the modern sciences of
sacred chronology and archæology.[1] The practical preaching of the period did not remain uninfluenced by such essays. The study of the
original languages of Scripture, as well as of
Syriac, was pursued by many of the ordinary
ministers of all the Protestant Churches in
Great Britain ; while a few of the better-known
names are still associated with the reputation of
high proficiency in Oriental learning. My own
countrymen, whether harassed by the persecutions of the seventeenth century or absorbed
by the reconstruction of their Church and her
theological controversies in the beginning of the
eighteenth, found time to produce works both
on the Hebrew language and on the exegesis
of the Old Testament. They used alike the
leisure of exile and the occasions of their parish
ministry to the furtherance of a scholarship
which more than once received the praise of

Schultens and others in the grammar and lexicography of the
Oriental languages.

[1] In chronology Scaliger's, Lightfoot's and Ussher's are the
foremost names: in archæology, among a crowd of works
the most famous are Samuel Bochart's *Phaleg and Canaan* 1646,
and *Hierozoicon* 1663; Reland's *Palaestina* 1714, and other
treatises ; with the Travels of Maundrell 1697, Pococke 1737, and
Hasselquist 1749 ff. Or in another department Goodwin, *Moses
and Aaron* 1610; Cunäus, *De Republica Hebraeorum*, libr. iii. ed.
Elz. 1632; Selden in *De Jure Naturali et Gentium* and *Uxor
Ebraica*, besides *De Diis Syriis* and *De Synedriis et Praefecturis
Juridicis Ebraeorum* ; J. Spencer, *De Legibus Hebraeorum, etc.*
1685; and Eisenmenger, *Neuentdeckten Judenthume* 1702–1711.

the great Continental Hebraists.[1]   To the high
zeal and industry with which men like John
Livingstone, Brown of Wamphray, Jamieson and
Thomas Boston repeated the examples of learning afforded them by the first Reformers we owe
the fact that a knowledge of both Greek and Hebrew has ever been required from candidates for
the Scottish ministry.   Nor did the Pilgrim Fathers
fail to carry across the Atlantic the scholarly
ideals of the early Puritans.   The first schools
of divinity in New England provided courses of
study in the originals of both Testaments, besides
an introduction to Syriac; [2] and a succession of
competent teachers of Hebrew appeared down to
the middle of the seventeenth century.[3]

[1] *The Theology and Theologians of Scotland, chiefly of the
Seventeenth and Eighteenth Centuries*, by James Walker, D.D.,
Carnwath, Edinburgh 1872; Lecture 1.   John Livingstone,
banished under Charles II., corrected the proofs for an edition
of the Syriac New Testament; and revised the Latin text of the
Old Testament, intending to print the Latin and Hebrew in
parallel columns.   His fellow-exile, Brown of Wamphray, had
equal scholarship.   Jamieson published *Spicilegia*, or notes on
the connections between Bible history and the history of Greek
and Latin authors.   Above all Thomas Boston, who mastered
Hebrew after he went to Ettrick, prepared a work on Hebrew
accentuation, of a specimen of which Schultens and Grenobius
said : ' On the supposition that the rest of this book is equal to
this sketch it will, on the whole, be the best book that has been
written on this subject.'   To this period also belongs the series of
commentaries edited by Dickson, including Hutchison on the
Minor Prophets, Durham on the Song of Solomon, and Dickson
himself on the Psalms.

[2] *New England's First Fruits*, London 1643.

[3] *Zeitschrift für A. T. Wissenschaft*, viii. (1888) 1 ff.; ' A. T.

In spite of the insight and erudition which distinguished the Old Testament scholarship and preaching of this period, these did not succeed in establishing the exegesis of Scripture upon sound principles, nor give to the Church a clear view of the development of revelation within Israel. We now perceive that their real value consisted in the indispensable preparation they provided for that modern criticism, which in the end of the eighteenth and throughout the nineteenth century has arranged the Old Testament upon historical lines and enabled the Church to trace the real history of Israel's religious development. The course of that criticism we have already followed in the Second Lecture, while its influence upon preaching has been appreciated in the beginning of this one.

We have been tracing the practical effects of a historical exegesis of the Old Testament on the preaching of the Christian Church. But our survey cannot be closed without a brief notice — all that our space permits — of the influence of the Old Testament upon the great succession of Christian treatises and arguments on government which forms an almost complete history of the political ideal from Constantine to the

Studien in America,' by Prof. G. Moore of Andover. Cotton Mather records that even women studied Hebrew (*Magnalia*, iii. 23). Moore mentions besides Jonathan Edwards' *History of Redemption*, a MS. work by the great theologian on the Messianic prophecies of the Old Testament.

period before the French Revolution. Augustine's *De Civitate Dei;* Dante's *De Monarchia;* the political tracts of Luther and other Reformers; the political prefaces to Calvin's Commentaries and the chapter on Civil Government in his *Institutes;* the arguings of Knox with the statesmen of Queen Mary; Buchanan's *De Jure Regni apud Scotos;* his royal pupil's *Jus Liberae Monarchiae* and other lectures from the throne to a murmuring people; the *Royal Defence* of Salmasius; Milton's answer to it in the *Defence of the People of England;* Samuel Rutherford's *Lex Rex* — the list might be greatly extended but is sufficiently representative. In only a few of these do we find any real attempt to distinguish between what was permanently valid in Old Testament laws and institutions and what was of transient authority — with such success as we shall presently observe. In all the others, on both sides of the great controversy which runs through them, the eagerness of the disputants to claim every plausible precedent and sanction for their respective opinions is too warm to allow of historical discrimination. And therefore it is that in this series of works we feel most acutely what I have already said is conspicuous through the whole history of the Old Testament in the Christian Church — namely, the strangely varied character of the influence which the Hebrew Scriptures have exerted upon Christian ethics.

In the *De Civitate Dei* [1] Augustine distinguishes between the ideal and the actual in the kingdom of Israel. In fact, he says, it was a ' civitas terrena,' only in essence a ' civitas Dei.' However imperfectly Israel carried out the principles of the theocracy revealed to them, these principles remain a political standard and inspiration for all time, a perpetual pattern to the Christian State. The distinction is sound but vague : and Augustine had not the historic insight to apply it in detail. His allegorising interpretation only increased the vagueness of the distinction; and he left it to the mediæval Church with outlines so elastic as to permit the champions of the divine authority of the Papacy and of the Empire to find within the Old Testament example and sanction for even the most arrogant of their claims. Augustine himself was in the habit of appealing to the Old Testament in defence of rigorous measures by the State against heretics. The precedent he set was consistently followed by the Roman Inquisition. [2]

---

[1] Books xv–xvii.

[2] Diestel (*Gesch. der A. T.* 152 f.) says that ' the whole conception by Charlemagne of the idea of the State shows many theocratic elements'; and refers to S. Rettberg, *Kirchengeschichte Deutschlands*. On p. 153 Diestel says : ' the Decalogue occurs in the laws of the Frisians.' It has been my duty for geographical purposes to go through the so-called *Assizes of Jerusalem*, the collection of legal works from the kingdoms of Jerusalem and Cyprus in the thirteenth century (ed. by Le Comte Beugnot in 2 vols. of the *Recueil des Historiens des Croisades*, Paris 1841 f.).

In *De Monarchia* Dante draws his proofs for
a temporal power, universal in its sway, chiefly
from the moralists of Greece and Rome. His
claim for the Empire's independence of the
Church, and for the derivation of its authority
direct from God, is based on the character and
history of the Roman people and on the providence of God in committing to them the
government of the world. But he clinches his
argument with the facts that the Son of God
consented to be born into the Empire, and, by
His submission to Pilate, as the executioner of
His death for man's salvation, 'confirmed the
jurisdiction of the Roman Empire over all mankind.' Dante quotes the Scriptures of the Old
Testament far less frequently than the Pagan
philosophies; and then chiefly by way of metaphor and parable. When he deals with them
logically, it is never to claim for his thesis any
sanction from their theocratic principles, but only
to answer the arguments which the supporters of
the supremacy of the Church have drawn from
the precedence of Levi before Judah, or from the
crowning and deposition of Saul by Samuel.[1]
In this we meet with a contrast which we shall

It is remarkable how this precipitate of feudalism in the East is
devoid of religious argument and appeal. Almost the only
imitation of legal tempers or processes, borrowed so lavishly by
the Canon Law from the Old Testament, is the rigorous treatment of heretics. — *Livre de Jean d'Ibelin*, chap. cxc.

[1] Book iii. chaps. 5 and 6.

often see exemplified: between the defenders of the secular power who find their arguments in the New Testament, and the champions of the supremacy or independence of the spiritual power who chiefly appeal to the Old.

Before we pass from the Mediæval Church we ought to note the influence of one great doctrine of the Prophets upon the political ideals of the age. In the Eleventh Chapter of the Book of Isaiah and elsewhere the gifts of the Spirit of God are predominantly the qualities of just monarchs and wise counsellors. The Spirit was the Author of the Intellect, and more especially of the governing and political intellect: *the spirit of Jahweh, a spirit of wisdom and understanding, a spirit of counsel and might, a spirit of knowledge and of the fear of Jahweh:* in other words, ripeness but also sharpness of mind; moral decision and heroic energy; piety in its two forms of knowing the will of God and feeling the constraint to perform it. We could not have a more concise summary of the strong elements of a ruling mind; [1] and there is perhaps no passage in the Old Testament, which impressed itself more on the political and intellectual symbolism of the Mediæval Church. Using it to interpret Christ's

[1] See the present writer's *Isaiah i–xxxix.* in the *Expositor's Bible*, pp. 179–188, from which the above paragraph is mainly drawn.

promise of the Paraclete as the Spirit of Truth,
the Church regarded the Holy Spirit, in the
words of Gregory of Tours, as 'the God of the
intellect more than of the heart.' On the painted
glass of many European cathedrals the Dove is
seen descending upon the heads of the doctors
and councils of the Church or hovering over the
figures of the sciences. Isaiah's description of
the Lord's Anointed was employed at the coronation of kings and the fencing of tribunals of
justice. It is evidently the model of the royal
hymn, *Veni Creator Spiritus*. In a Greek minia-
ture of the tenth century the Sacred Dove hovers
over King David, who displays the prayer: *Give
the King Thy judgements, O God, and Thy righteousness to the King's son;* while there stand on
either side of him the figures of Wisdom and
Prophecy.[1] Henry the Third's order of knight-
hood, 'Du Saint Esprit,' was restricted to political men, and particularly to magistrates.[2]

From what has been said above of the difference between the Lutheran and Reformed
Churches in their use of the Old Testament, it
will be clear that fewer political ideas were
taken from it by the former than by the
latter. Luther uttered some sound sentences on
the local and temporary authority of the Mosaic
Law. 'We must and do reject and contemn

---

[1] Didron, *Christian Iconography*, Eng. trans. i. 432.
[2] Cf. the Story of St. Dunstan related in Didron, *op. cit.* i. 426.

those, that so highly boast of the rights and proceedings in Moses' Laws (*Judicialia*) in temporal affairs, for we have our Imperial and Countrie Laws under which we live and whereto we are sworn. . . . Moses' Laws bound and obliged only the Jews in that place which God made choice of. . . . Therefore let us recommend and leave Moses to his Laws, excepting only the *Moralia*, which God hath planted in Nature, as the Ten Commandments, which concern God's true worshipping and service, and a civil life.'[1] This is sound, but when Luther proceeds to depreciate the political teaching of the Prophets[2] as so much 'straw, hay and wood,' we feel an evil example, and are grateful to the founders of the Reformed Church that they did not propagate it. In his appeal to the *Christian Nobility of the German Nation*, Luther attacks the claims of the Papacy and Roman priesthood, which, as we have seen, were largely supported on Old Testament texts and instances. He has to prove the priesthood of all believers, and he does so naturally from the New Testament. Like Dante in the *De Monarchia*, he uses the Old Testament[3] to rebut the claim of the Church that the Emperor because crowned by the Pope must be subject to the latter. The exodus of Israel from

[1] *Table Talk*, chap. xii., first paragraph, Capt. Henrie Bell's translation, 1652.   [2] See above, p. 243.

[3] For example, from the cases of Samuel and Saul, and Nathan and David: *An den Christlichen Adel Deutscher Nation.*

Egypt and her redemption from Babylon were to all the Reformers a type of the enfranchisement of the Church from the power of Rome.[1] In these cases the rights of the Church are the rights of the common people in face of their tyrants.

Calvin's *Institutes* are dedicated, with a prefatory address, to Francis King of the French; his commentary on Isaiah to Edward VI. of England; that on Jeremiah to the Elector Frederick; and that on the Minor Prophets to King Gustavus of Sweden. In these Prefaces Calvin points out that the monarch must labour for the word of God as essential to the welfare of his realm. He illustrates from the Old Testament that kings are the nursing fathers of the Church; and that the Church of the majority, as in France, is not necessarily the real Church of God: the true prophets were often opposed to the priesthood in Israel, to the kings, and to the bulk of the nation. It is the prophetical writings which are most worth the study of rulers : these should take as their example the few kings of Israel who were on the side of the prophets. Calvin treats of Civil Government in the last chapter of the *Institutes*. From both Testaments, but chiefly from the Old,

[1] Cf. Luther's tractate on *The Babylonian Captivity of the Church*, and Aurifaber's preface to the *Table Talk*, near the beginning.

he proves its lawfulness and its distinction from the spiritual kingdom of Jesus Christ. In God's providence all forms of government have been established, and it is impossible to say which is the best. Calvin himself prefers the aristocratic 'with curbs'; and notes that what God established in Israel was 'an aristocracy bordering on popular government.' To be successful a civil government must make piety and righteousness its first care : this is proved from Old Testament precepts, and principally from the Prophets. Can magistrates then shed blood ? They must restrain crime and avenge the sufferings of the righteous : in certain cases they ought to go to war; and they have the right to levy taxes. With regard to laws Calvin is with Luther : the views of those 'who deny that any commonwealth is rightly framed which neglects the law of Moses' are 'stupid and false.' The judicial and ceremonial laws of the Old Testament were of passing authority. Only the moral law of God is binding on us : wherever national laws are framed after this rule, they should not be condemned by us. That Christians may appeal to magistrates and laws is proved from Paul's example and from some of his precepts. The righteousness of going to law in certain cases is argued in a most Christian and reasonable manner, very properly from the New Testament rather than from the Old, for it was in the former that the advocates of non-resistance in Calvin's time claimed to find the sanction for their opinion. From the Old Testament [1] Calvin curiously seeks to prove that tyrants are appointed of God, and that it is a Christian duty to obey them — except when they order us to do what God has expressly forbidden.

Calvin emphasised from the Old Testament the duty of the civil magistrate to cut off the wicked. Unfortunately the Protestant Church too much imitated that of Rome in extending her vengeance to heretics and unbelievers ; and upon both sides of the Atlantic appealed to the practice of the rulers of Israel in defence of their excommunication from civil rights of persons who differed from orthodox opinions, and in defence of the murder of witches.

In Great Britain, after the Reformation, the political influence of the Old Testament chiefly appears in the constant controversies between the Divine Right of Kings and the Rights of the People. The Scottish contributions to this argument are well represented by Knox's debate with Secretary Lethington and other statesmen of Queen Mary, by Buchanan's *De Jure Regni apud Scotos*, and by Rutherford's *Lex Rex*. Knox, in his arraignment of Queen Mary, had argued on the ground that the Law of Moses was binding on Christians. Where it decreed that idolaters

[1] 1 Sam. viii. 11–17, and Jer. xxvii. 5–8, 12.

should be put to death, Christians ought to apply
it to those who institute or practise the mass.
By accepting his Scriptural premises — they were
unfortunately the common belief of the age —
Lethington gave himself into Knox's hands.
But Knox employed the Law of Moses less than
he did the history of Israel. Here he found
numerous precedents for the arraignment of
sovereigns by God's prophets and for their punishment by the people. To statements by Calvin
and others, that the Old Testament contained
proofs of the lawfulness of even tyrannical govern-
ments and of the people's duty of obedience to
them, Knox answered that Calvin had been
arguing against the anarchical Anabaptists and
he quoted instances of the overthrow of Jewish
kings by the people because of idolatry. Knox's
principal resource was thus Old Testament history; that of his opponents, on the contrary,
was found among the New Testament precepts
of obedience to an authority so tyrannical as
that of the Roman Emperors. The same contrast appears in the use of Scripture in the
dialogue *De Jure Regni apud Scotos*, between
George Buchanan and his royalist opponent.
The latter pleads Paul's commands to Christians
to honour and pray for tyrants like Tiberius,
Caligula, Claudius, Nero.[1] Buchanan has no
difficulty in answering him upon New Testament

[1] § lxii.

principles; but it is from the history of Israel that he proves that kings ought to be punished for evil-doing by the authority which created them.   In Israel that authority was God, in Scotland the people.[1]

The same contrast is again visible in the English forms of the controversy.   Take a judicious advocate for the divinity of monarchy like Hooker,[2] or some preposterous ones like that redoubtable royal lecturer James the First, and like Sir Robert Filmer in his *Patriarcha, or the Natural Power of Kings*.   The persistence, with which they all seek to explain away their opponents' reasons from the Old Testament, proves that it was upon this part of Scripture that the champions of democracy still chiefly sharpened their weapons.   In the first of his *Two Treatises of Government* John Locke has little difficulty in disposing of Filmer's ingenious arguments from Adam and the Kings of Israel; in doing so he exhibits the most reasonable treatment of Old Testament history — taking for granted its reality throughout — which the literature of Christendom had yet produced.

The contrast, which all those illustrated, might also be traced, if there were space, in the controversy between Salmasius and Milton, or in Rutherford's *Lex Rex;* and even through the divines of the Stuart and Hanoverian houses.   Everywhere

[1] § lxii.   [2] Eighth Book of the *Ecclesiastical Polity*.

the advocates of the Divine Right of Kings relied upon New Testament texts — as Pilate's words to Christ, *I have power to crucify or release thee;* Paul's, *the powers that be are ordained of God;* Peter's, *the King as supreme.* Whereas the Scriptures, which, after the fashion of the times, popular champions like Milton and Rutherford preferred against them were chiefly drawn from the Old Testament; from the elections of Saul and David, their rebukes by Samuel and Nathan, the subjection of the king to the covenant, the part played by the people in the coronation and deposition of the kings, as well as from many passages of the Prophets. When we read such arguments, and remember that the Book from which they were drawn was in the hands and hearts of the common people, we appreciate how much of the liberty, which the period secured for us, is due to the Old Testament.

It is obvious that the distinction between the Old and New Testaments which this controversy emphasised, is no artificial one. The political circumstances of the two dispensations were entirely different. Through Old Testament history we follow the growth, the opportunities, the judgement of a nation. The purpose of God is a people; religious discipline and experience, religious duty and hope, are almost entirely identified with national rights and responsibilities, and the struggle for national liberty and national righteousness. But in the New Testament we do not deal with a nation at all. It is an exceptional state of affairs; in which religion neither is associated with popular struggles, nor assumes the responsibilities of government, but the sole political duty of the believer is reverence to the powers that be: the guardians of the Providential Peace in which the Church of Christ was to spread across the world. This is a state of affairs not so sympathetic with modern history as the other was; and therefore it is that in this province of religion the Hebrew Prophets have been felt by the moderns to stand nearer to them than the Apostles do. The Apostles were sojourners and pilgrims: the Prophets were citizens and patriots. It is a heavenly country to which the former look forward: the latter, as we have seen,[1] without any promise of the life to come, labour for the establishment of the kingdom of God within the conditions of their own national history. And for the same reason is it that the Old Testament — though of course upon a plane of public life different from that on which our forefathers applied it — must always have a function to discharge supplementary to the more glorious office of the Gospels and Epistles. As Maurice puts it, we must count 'paramount the duty of vindicating the Old Testament as the

[1] Above, pp. 185 f.

great witness for liberty . . . the witness of
the sacredness of this earth.'[1]

We have already seen how the historical
interpretation of the Prophets with which Modern
Criticism provides us, renders more effective this
practical application of them to the social ethics
of our time.

II. *The Political and Social Preaching of the Prophets.*

The rapid survey, which we have just made,
of the influence of the Prophets upon the social
ethics of Christendom, has shown us that the
chief example to ourselves of their preaching
to their own times lies in what may be called
the double ethic of their patriotism: their faith in
the essential sacredness of their national history
and their conscience of their people's sins and
duties.

The Prophets' treatment of their national
history is instructive from more than one point
of view. The facts which they quote from
Israel's past are in agreement, so far as they go,
with the witness of the historical Books; only
the writers of the latter record a very great deal
more, both of individual and national experience,
than the Prophets deem necessary in order to
exhibit the Divine meaning of that history. For

[1] *Life*, ii., p. 490; cf. 4, 52, 454, etc.

instance, none of the eighth or the seventh century prophets lay stress upon the physical miracles which the historians of the early history of Israel record. They confine themselves to the political and ethical facts: the covenant between Jahweh and Israel, the redemption from Egypt, the guidance to Canaan, the overthrow of the heathen, the growth of ethical institutions and the inspiration of strong personalities.[1] I do not say that the Prophets were ignorant of what we call the miracles of the early history, or that they denied them. They had the stories of these before them,[2] and they believed the stories. But in preaching to their own generation they almost wholly confined themselves to the indubitable outlines of the early history and to its political and ethical significance. Now in such a selection by the first representatives of his office the preacher of to-day will find an example of the discrimination which he may show in the employment, for practical purposes, of the origin and the making of Israel. But what we are now concerned with is not so much the exact amount of the prophetic testimony to the early history of Israel as the fact that what the Prophets select from it for preaching to their own times, is just the kind of national memory and tradition by

---

[1] So, for instance, in Amos ii. 9–11 ; cf. Hos. ii. 8, 14 ff. (Eng.) xi. 1 ff.; Isa. v. 1 ff.; Jer. ii.

[2] *E.g.* Amos iv. 11 ; Hosea xii. 3 ff.

which every nation may prove the sacredness of
its own career. To Amos nationality is what it
was more explicitly to Cromwell and to Mazzini,
a divine fact. *Have I not brought Israel out of
the land of Egypt and the Philistines from Caphtor
and Aram from Kir?*[1] All nations are by the
calling and providence of Almighty God. What
the Prophets saw in Israel's making is what every
people with the Prophets' faith may see in their
own past. 'The Bible of every nation is its
history.'[2] 'What are all our histories but God
manifesting Himself, that He hath shaken and
tumbled down and trampled upon everything
that He had not planted? . . We are a people
that have had a stamp upon them from God . .
whose appearances and providences among us
are not to be outmatched by any story.'[3]

As with the past of a nation, so with its future.
Israel were the first of peoples to develop the
sense of a spiritual mission to the world; and they
did so not in the day of their strength, but in that
of their weakness and servitude. Their Exile
brought them into touch with many oppressed
nationalities; and like their symbol, Jonah, on
the helpless ship with the heathen sailors, they
were made to feel their common humanity with

[1] Amos ix. 7.   [2] Carlyle.
[3] Cromwell, *Letters and Speeches*, by Thomas Carlyle, Speech
IV. Cromwell called the Old Testament the 'recapitulation of
Providence,' meaning God's providence not only of Israel but
of all nations.

the Gentiles whom they had despised. It was in this fellowship of suffering that, for the first time, they conceived their full mission to the ends of the earth : *I Jahweh have called thee in righteousness, and will hold thine hand and will mould thee, and give thee for a covenant of the peoples and for a light to the nations : to open the blind eyes, to bring out the prisoners from the prison, and them that sit in darkness out of the house of bondage.*[1] The most comforting of all the promises uttered in connection with this world-wide mission is one whose tender words, though justly claimed for himself by every broken individual who turns to God, were principally intended for the weak and flickering nationalities threatened with extinction by the strong empires of antiquity.[2] *Behold my Servant . . . I have put my Spirit upon him . . . he shall bring forth justice to the nations. A bruised reed shall he not break, and the dimly burning flax shall he not quench ; he shall bring forth justice according to truth. He shall not fail nor be abashed till he have set justice on the earth ; and the isles shall wait for his teaching.*[3] To every modern people who have been conscious of their nationality as a Divine fact, and of their gifts and opportunities as a Divine call, this vision, granted first to Israel, has never failed.

[1] Isa. xlii. 6 f.

[2] See A. B. Davidson, *Expositor*, 2nd Series, viii. pp. 364 ff.

[3] *Ibid*. vv. 1–4.

Nor has it been less sure because, like the exiled Israel, a nation has grown weak and contemptible. While Italy was still divided and subject to many tyrannies, the despised of Europe and the mockery of her own past, her prophet, who almost alone believed in her restoration, dared to add to it a prophecy of her mission to the world.

National religion, then, according to the Prophets of Israel, is the recognition of God's hand in the nation's history; the acceptance of great ethical institutions and personalities as from His hand; the instinct and effort of moral progress; the sense of a mission to the world; the acknowledgment of the Divine calling of other nations; and sympathy in particular with such as are weak and oppressed. Such an ideal of religion the Prophets urged against two popular heresies: a non-ethical confidence in the national and established ritual; and a base 'other-worldliness' which sought in necromancy knowledge of the future and counsel for the present. To both of these the Prophets were inexorably hostile. For both were pagan. Both were founded on false ideas of God. And both withdrew the emphasis of religion from conduct and the national life. *I will have mercy and not sacrifice.*[1] *Though ye offer me your burnt offerings and your meat offerings I will not accept them; take thou away from me the noise of*

---

[1] Hos. vi. 6.

*thy songs, I will not hear the melody of thy viols.
But let justice roll down as waters, and righteousness as a perennial stream.*[1]   *And when they shall
say unto you: seek unto them that have familiar
spirits, that chirp and mutter; should not a people
seek unto their God?   On behalf of the living*
should they appeal *to the dead?   To the Torah
and the Testimony!*[2] — the Living Word which
concerns itself with living men.

On those curiously sympathetic tendencies the
Prophets' preaching has been justified by Christian experience. The rational and ethical elements of religion have always been imperilled
by those errors: whose affinity has been proved
not less by their similar effects than by their
not infrequent alliance in the same persons or
schools of religion.

The second quality of the Prophets' ideal of
national religion is their strong conscience of
their people's sins and civic duties. This is
the harder and the more misunderstood half
of patriotism. The ears of every people are
open to the celebration of its history as divine,
and even the baser hearts among it may be
flattered by the idea of its mission to the
world. But the true test of national religion is
sensitiveness to the national sins. This was the
test between the false and the true prophet in
Israel; it is our test as preachers to our

[1] Amos v. 22–24.   [2] Isa. viii. 19, 20.

own day. Is our office servile to the pride and material interests of our nation? Or do we feel with trembling that the ethical element in patriotism is, in the strong tumult of all the others, the most easily neglected, and therefore the most in need of emphasis by a people's prophets. For its sake and God's the true patriot must sometimes run counter to the currents of popular enthusiasm, and be willing to incur the charges of treason to the commonwealth, and of cowardice in face of the national destiny. We have nothing to dread from that fear of kings which once made so many prophets false; but we have all the more to watch that we do not become flatterers of the common people. If we are to defend their rights, we must be brave to declare their sins; the offices of the Prophet and of the Demagogue are absolutely irreconcileable. To most preachers, however, such temptations as I describe arise not from the nation as a whole, but from the religious section of it to which they belong. There is danger that a man grow silent upon social ethics out of regard either to the ecclesiastical policy of his denomination, or to its financial interests. In all these forms the temptation to become a popular or fashionable preacher — whether the fashion be one of religious temper or of political opinion — is so subtle, and so many succumb to it, that, as we value the honour of our calling and are jealous of our loyalty to God, we ought persistently to steep ourselves in the just and stern spirit of our great forerunners.

To go into detail upon the subjects of the civic preaching of the Prophets would amount to an exposition of the larger part of the Books of Amos, Hosea, Isaiah, Micah and Jeremiah. Let these four general statements suffice. *First*, the careers of the Prophets were contemporaneous with the development of Hebrew society from an agricultural to a commercial condition, and with the rise of the City. The social evils, therefore, with which the Prophets deal, are those still urgent among ourselves.[1] *Second*, the Prophets, while inculcating, from God's treatment of the nation, tenderness and pity in the nation's treatment of their poor and enslaved, dwell with still greater emphasis upon the need of justice and equity. We enjoy a legal freedom and justice far beyond those of the Oriental society which the Prophets addressed; but no man can deny the frequent want of honour and equity among us in such social relations as are outside of the laws. *Third*, the Prophets, when enforcing religious observances and institutions, do so most frequently for social ends, or with regard to the interests of the poorer classes of the community.[2]

[1] See *The Book of the Twelve Prophets*, i. ch. iii.

[2] *E.g.* The Sabbath : Amos viii. 5; Isa. lviii., cf. vv. 6 and 7 with 13 and 14.

And *fourth*, there is the emancipation of the individual from a *merely* national religion : the soul awaking to feel its solitary relation to God and its independence of the community only to discover a new duty and loyalty to the latter, that extends to the sharing of their sorrows and bearing of their sins — all the higher sense of individuality resulting in a truer altruism as we have already seen instanced in Jeremiah.[1] There could not be preaching more relevant to the conditions and temptations of our own life.[2]

All these features except the last might be illustrated from the works of almost every Prophet, and they are equally conspicuous in the codification of prophetic teaching, which we find in Deuteronomy. In this great system of national religion the domestic and the civic duties are enforced in no legal spirit ; but with the high morality and full tenderness of the prophetic temper. There are few of the rites and institutions of a nation — the Sabbath, Sacrifice, Prophecy, the

[1] Above, pp. 165 ff.
[2] There is a fine passage by the great philanthropist Lord Shaftesbury on the civic teaching of Jeremiah (*Life* by Hodder, iii. 454) : ' If for political and public purposes there can be in the Bible one book more valuable than another to throw light on the days we live, it is Jeremiah. He was not always "looking to the sun," but he was looking to the earth, entreating, preaching, warning, threatening, promising ; and he was in consequence regarded as a bore and a blunderer. Yet if he had been attended to, Jerusalem might have survived for many centuries ; and certainly she would have been spared the indescribable sufferings of soul and body that followed her destruction by Nebuchadnezzar.'

sustenance of the Priesthood, Justice, the Monarchy, War, Agriculture, Trade, and Money —
which are not defined by Deuteronomy with
special regard for *the poor among thy brethren : the
widow, the orphan, the slave and the stranger within
thy gates*. And the sum of the whole is not love
to God alone, but love to God and man. *Hear, O
Israel, thou shalt love the Lord thy God with all
thy heart and all thy soul and all thy strength,
and thy neighbour as thyself.*

III. *Other Features of the Preaching of the Prophets.*

Passing now from the civic to other features
of the Prophets' preaching to their own times, we
must not omit to notice one, which is not only
historically remarkable in the religious leaders of
a Semitic people, but of some practical interest
to ourselves. I mean the attitude of the Prophets to what we call miracles.

When St. Paul defined the contrast between
the Greek and the Jewish minds in the words:
*the Jews require a sign : and the Greeks seek after
wisdom*,[1] he struck a characteristic of the whole
race to which the Jews belong. The Semites
have always been notorious for unwillingness to
receive moral truth upon its own evidence and
without the attestation of some physical wonder —
not necessarily of a kind akin to the truth which

---

[1] 1 Cor. i. 22.

it was supposed to confirm. Wellhausen has remarked this quality in the early stories of Pagan Arabs;[1] and to this day ' miracles,' so far from being a difficulty to catechumens of the Christian religion in Damascus or Cairo, are regarded by them as indispensable concomitants of the Divine Word. We all know that it was not otherwise in Israel. The Old Testament contains a number of stories according to which the Word of God was accompanied with signs following, and these signs were not always like the beneficent miracles of our Lord, consonant in character to the message with which they were associated.[2] It was a recognised thing in Israel that when a prophet arose he should give the people a sign or wonder. And Christ Himself describes this attitude of the nation's mind in the words (not without reproach), *Except ye see signs and wonders, ye will not believe.*[3]

All the more striking, therefore, is the absence from the teaching of the Prophets of the eighth and seventh centuries of all miracles in the technical sense of the word, and of all appeal to miracle.[4] This absence is complete except for the single and very ambiguous offer by Isaiah of a sign to

---

[1] *Reste arab. Heidentumes*, p. 131.

[2] *E.g.* the signs which Moses gave on his first mission to Pharaoh in presence of the King.

[3] John iv. 48.

[4] I speak now of the discourses of the Prophets and not of the narratives appended to them.

the obdurate Ahaz.[1] Now such a silence on
‘ miracles ’ was not due to the Prophets’ disbelief.
The Prophets shared the faith of their time in
the possibility of miracles, and in the stories of
their ancient history which recorded ‘ miracles.’
The true explanation is given in the Book, which
is a summary of the prophetic doctrine on the
rites and institutions of Israel. The thirteenth
chapter of Deuteronomy takes for granted the
power *to give signs and wonders* on the part of
any *prophet or dreamer of dreams*. But it denies
that signs and wonders, however real, can attest
the prophet’s message as the word of God. This
message must be judged by its own character.
If it tempts to idolatry, its prophet is a false
prophet and must be put to death, notwithstand-
ing whatever miracles he may have worked. God
can have permitted these, only to test His
people’s loyalty. This is the explanation of the
abstinence from appeal to miracle which distinguishes the great writing prophets. They will
have their message travel in the greatness of its
own strength : prove itself Divine on the credit
of the high religion and morality which are its
substance, and be vindicated by the historical
events which it brings to pass. Does it reveal
the will of God ? *Jahweh God does nothing, but
He* first *revealeth His secret to His servants the
prophets*.[2] Does the prophet’s message of God

[1] Isaiah vii. [2] Amos iii. 7.

agree with God's revelation of Himself in history?
Two men cannot come together except by previous appointment:[1] the harmony of the prophetic word with the divine deed is the proof of
a purpose common to both. Does the word produce and mould that which it predicts? Then it
is divine: *it shall not return unto me void, but it
shall accomplish that which I please and it shall
prosper* in the thing *whereto I sent it.*[2] It is thus
never to 'miracle,' in the narrow sense of that
term, that the Prophet appeals as the proof of
his message, but to history. Political facts now
within his people's ken, or shortly to come to
pass — by these he is content to be judged.[3] He
asserts his power of prediction: he makes predictions which are fulfilled. Yet he does so not
through any magic vision of the future, but by
inference from the religious principles with which
God has inspired him, and by application of these
to the political circumstances and probabilities of
his own time. This I have elsewhere illustrated
in detail by a review of Isaiah's predictions
concerning the deliverance of Jerusalem.[4]

[1] Amos v. 3. On this whole passage see *Book of the Twelve
Prophets*, i. pp. 82, 89 f.

[2] Isaiah lv. 11.

[3] As for example, Isaiah when asserting the inviolableness of
Jerusalem: or the great Prophet of the Exile when he proves
the divine origin of earlier predictions of the end of the Exile
by their fulfilment in the victorious progress of Cyrus against
Babylon.

[4] *Isaiah i–xxxix*. ch. xxiv.

To me this independence of 'signs and wonders,' when we place it in contrast to the universal custom of Semitic soothsayers and the common expectancy of all Israel, is but another proof of the divinity of the Prophets' teaching. Miracles, as Christ Himself has shown us, may be given to attest a Divine Revelation, but they are not necessary to the highest faith; and in the case of the Prophets their absence is a stronger seal, than their presence would have been, of the Divine origin of prophecy.

We have seen [1] that, in appealing to the presence of God in the history of their people, the prophets of the eighth and seventh centuries selected as its evidences not so much the record of physical marvels which it contained, as the clear lines of religious guidance, political growth and moral inspiration. In the same fashion they treated the history of their own times; and saw the Divine not so evidently in its exceptions and catastrophes of natural order, as in its gradual development through political events and ethical issues to the manifest judgements of God. To them Jahweh is a God of law and order: and they delight, as Isaiah does, to reveal Him in the great commonplaces of experience and to illustrate the regularity of His methods in history by the regularity of His methods in nature.[2] Thus, whether in the ethical or in the physical

[1] Above, pp. 265 f. [2] See especially Isaiah xxviii. throughout.

sphere, we find their conception of Him to be that of *Mishpat;* according to Isaiah He is *El Mishpat*, the God who works by principle and law. And it is this, their instinct and conviction of seeing the Divine in process rather than in interruption, in law rather than in 'miracle,' in method rather than in catastrophe, which makes them appear so modern and which undoubtedly engages for them the intellectual as well as the moral sympathies of the present day.

But it is time to pass from the doctrines of those preachers who are our own greatest standards and examples, and to consider the living aids which they contribute to the style and the temper of preaching. Schleiermacher is the only great preacher of the century who would have nothing to do with the Old Testament, judging it to stand to Christianity in the same relation as Paganism does. 'For our ethics,' he says, 'the Old Testament is entirely superfluous.' We perceive the historical injustice of such a view; but Dr. John Ker has also remarked its evil effect upon Schleiermacher himself as a preacher. 'One cannot but see that Schleiermacher's style has suffered from his neglect of the Old Testament.' How much of force and charm, of passion and of poetry, have all other great preachers derived from the Hebrew Scriptures! An old German writer has said that 'Holy Writ should be our

grammar and our dictionary, out of which all
the moods of Christian speech should grow.'
The advice is sound, if we fulfil it not in the
pedantry of the letter[1] but in the spirit: not in
the servile and barren repetition of Bible texts
whether in preaching or praying; but in the
imitation of those tempers and affections which
mould the style of the sacred writers, and of that
labour which they put forth upon their art.
What may our preaching not learn from the
Prophets as to conciseness: as to the worth of
phrase; as to concreteness in our teaching; as to
the use of the circumstance and events of our ordinary life; as to the use of nature and history; as
to the duty of calling things by their right names;
as to the effort to bring grace and music into what
we say; as to the urgency which is upon all living
truth and the passion to win men which is the
heart of preaching. What preacher, who is a
student of the Old Testament, can fail to be
infected by the courage of the Prophets, and by
their downright realism [2] — a courage and realism

[1] As for instance Mohammedans base the sciences of Grammar, Rhetoric, Logic and Poetry wholly upon the Koran.

[2] 'Truth is what this people first require, and therefore the
revelation of the Lord will in the first instance be the revealing
of the truth. Men who will strip pretence off the reality of things;
men who will call things by their right names; honest satirists
and epigrammatists — these are the bearers of God's revelation.
For it is one of the means of Divine salvation to call things by
their right names, and even in God's revelation epigrams have
their place.' — On Isaiah xxx. : p. 226 of *Isaiah i–xxxix*. (*Expositor's Bible*).

which are frequently disguised in our English version: but the careful student of the original discovers them, and they thrill him to the heart. Do not believe that the end of an accurate study of the Hebrew language is simply familiarity with a number of grammatical forms more or less obscure. Painstaking students are otherwise rewarded. It is they who lay their hands on the prophet's heart and feel it beat; it is they who across the ages see the very features of his face as he calls; it is they into whom his style and his music pass.

But the ultimate fountain of the prophetic preaching is the passion to win men. This is the secret both of the pathos and the splendours of its style. To the Prophets preaching was no mere display, but a sore battle with the hard hearts of their contemporaries, in which the messenger of the Lord worked with the pity of his weakness upon him, at a supreme cost to himself and conscious that he must summon to his desperate task every resource of feeling and of art. *Go and tell this people: Hear ye indeed but understand not: and see ye indeed but perceive not. The harvest is past, the summer is ended, and we are not saved. Is there no balm in Gilead and no physician there? Why then is not the health of the daughter of my people recovered? Then I said, I will not make mention of Him nor speak any more in His Name. Yet it is in mine heart as a burning fire shut up in my bones, and I weary myself to hold it in but cannot stay. Comfort ye, comfort ye my people, saith your God: speak upon the heart of Jerusalem, and cry unto her that her warfare is accomplished, that her iniquity is pardoned. The Voice said, Cry; and I said, 'What shall I cry? All flesh is grass and all the goodliness thereof is as the flowers of the field.' The grass may wither, the flower fade, but the Word of our God shall stand for ever.*

LECTURE VIII

THE CHRISTIAN PREACHER AND THE BOOKS OF WISDOM

WE have now reached the last department of our survey, that group of writings which are known as the Books of Wisdom — Job, Proverbs and Ecclesiastes. Here as elsewhere in the Old Testament, the Christian preacher has questions of historical criticism to encounter. But either the answers, which modern critics offer to these questions, are now generally accepted by the common sense of Christians, — as for instance the ideal interpretation of the Book of Job and the date of Ecclesiastes. Or else the questions themselves, where still unanswered, have little relevance to the practical use of the writings — as for example the integrity of the two Books just named. In the literature of Hebrew Wisdom, the difficulties of the preacher arise rather from problems that are religious. The presence in these Scriptures of doubt and speculation, of revolt against views of Providence presented in other Scriptures; of indifference to those national aspects of Israel's religion, in

which the essence of Prophecy lies; and of an
ethical teaching which is apparently utilitarian
— such are the problems which beset a Christian's use of the Books of Wisdom. We shall
best approach the solution through a study of
the school of religious teachers out of which
the Books took their rise.

We have already seen that in the Providence
of God a large part of the development of Israel's
religion was achieved through the conflict and
mutual reaction of two religious schools or
tempers — the Prophetic and the Priestly. Now
besides these two, which between them represent
the growth of the national religion up to the
Exile, there was a third class or guild, that of
the Wise Men, definite enough, as early as
Jeremiah's time, to be named along with the
Priests and the Prophets.[1] Before the Exile
they are not mentioned so frequently as the
latter, and Jeremiah appears to speak of them
with impatience, and as if they were hostile
to the prophetic word.[2] Yet they worshipped
Jahweh, and are described as claiming to have
his Torah or *Revelation* with themselves. They
are not charged with idolatry, nor with magic
and soothsaying. The opinion is therefore probable, that they were men of influence who took
no part in the strife between the Prophets and
the rest of Israel, but who found their interests

[1] Jer. xviii. 18.   [2] *Ibid.* viii. 8; ix. 22; xviii. 18.

and activities in the sphere of practical morals.[1]
By more than one modern they have been called
the Humanists of Israel. Such men could bide
their time. Whatever their attitude to the Prophets had originally been, as the teaching of the
latter survived the conflicts of the generations
to whom it first appeared, and as its principles
became an accepted part of the national religion,
the Wise Men would assimilate from it those
elements — and they were not few — which were
most in harmony with their own religious temper:
such as the main doctrines of monotheism, the
ethical reasonableness of God's judgements, the
immutableness of His laws both in nature and
history. When the succession of the Prophets
came to an end; that is to say, when Israel
ceased to enjoy the political freedom and responsibility which were the indispensable occasion of
the Prophet, and developed into a vehicle of
religious truth through the centuries, then the
Wise Men came to their kingdom. Their
didactic temper, their instinct for handing down
the experience of the past to the rising generation, found its opportunity. But they could not
remain mere teachers and traditionalists. The
body of religious experience and doctrine, which
they accumulated, of itself raised questions, in
face especially of the defeat and suffering which
Israel's faith encountered from her Babylonian

[1] Cf. Wildeboer, *Lit. des A. T.*, p. 367.

and Persian lords. And as time went on there shot across it new lights from alien religions, with which the Jews in their great Diaspora came into contact. Breezes, not always the healthiest, blew upon Judaism from abroad. Doubt, question, research and even revolt became inevitable. The Wisdom of Israel grew speculative and even defiant, as well as didactic and traditional.

We cannot state the development of Hebrew Wisdom in a form less vague; we are without the data for an exact history. It is possible to give the stages of the growth of the Law of Israel; it is not possible to give those of the growth of Israel's Wisdom. The mass of it seems to be post-exilic. Ecclesiastes is undoubtedly late,[1] the Prologue to the Proverbs cannot be much earlier, and the Book of Job may spring from any date between the Exile and 300 B.C. Yet the last-named is at least founded on a pre-exilic tradition,[2] it is possible that several of the collections of the Book of Proverbs were complete before the Exile, and very probable that they contain sayings from the earlier life of the people.[3]

---

[1] The language appears the latest of all the Old Testament, while the political conditions which it reflects are those of the end of the Persian, or beginning of the Greek, Period. Ecclesiastes is now generally referred to the third century B.C.

[2] Ezek. xiv. 14.

[3] See A. B. Davidson, ' Proverbs ' in *Encyclopædia Britannica*,

The character of the teaching of the Wise may be more clearly defined in comparison and in contrast with that of the Prophets. I said that the Wise, whatever may have been their original attitude to the Prophets, assimilated in time the elements of the prophetic monotheism. But it is possible to say more than this, for in truth the origins of *every* tendency which Hebrew Wisdom developed after the Exile are to be found in Hebrew Prophecy before the Exile. Does the Book of Proverbs count *knowledge* as the essence of virtue? Even in Hosea the Prophets had been laying emphasis upon the duty of *knowing* God in His character and purposes for men;[1] and *knowledge* forms one of the bases of the doctrine of Deuteronomy. Do the authors of the Book of Proverbs enjoin and practise the systematic teaching of the young? The authors of Deuteronomy had already shown them the example. Moreover, some of the Prophets, as for instance Isaiah in the close of Chapter xxviii., discourse in the very style of the Wise Men; that is, by parable and epigram, with shrewd and gnomic phrases; and seek to illustrate the wisdom of Providence by the wisdom of the Divine processes in nature. In

ninth ed.; but on the other side Toy's Introduction to *Proverbs* in the *International Scientific Commentary*.

[1] This prophetic preparation for the Wise Men's theory of knowledge has been overlooked by Professor Toy; see his Introduction to *Proverbs*, p. xvi.

almost every prophet there is a sense of the unity of
the Reason which pervades all things ; it becomes
more and more articulate from Amos, through
Isaiah, though the writer who added to the Book
of Amos the famous apostrophes to the creative
power of Jahweh,[1] and through Jeremiah, to the
great Prophet of the Exile.   These, and no Greeks,
were the teachers of him who wrote the great
psalm of Wisdom in the Eighth of Proverbs.
Even for the processes of speculation and of
doubt which they carried to such daring degrees,
the Wise found precedents in the experience of
some of the most constructive of the Prophets.
Job's challenges to the Almighty are partly
anticipated by the bold questions of Jeremiah ;
and in Habakkuk we perceive the beginnings of
that scepticism of faith with its solution in patient
endurance of wrong and loyalty to God — *Watch
for the Vision for it shall come and shall not tarry,
now the just man shall live by his faithfulness* —
which we feel at the heart not only of Job, but
of Ecclesiastes.[2]   In their interests and in their
doctrines the Wise were the Prophets' heirs.

And yet though they thus inherit from the
Prophets many sympathies and even doctrines,
the Wise Men differ from the Prophets in the
style, temper and standpoint of their genius.
The gift of the Prophet is vision, but the genius

---

[1] *Book of the Twelve Prophets*, i. pp. 201 ff. ; ii. p. 8, n. 5.
[2] *Ibid.* pp. 136, 140 ff.

of the Wise Man is experience born of insight and observation. Both insist upon Law and declare what must be. But while the Prophets for the most part look forward and tell the people what shall come to pass because God has such a character and such a purpose, the Wise Men look back and tell what shall come to pass because under God it has always been. Both insist upon righteousness. But while the Prophets look forward to those ideals of justice and mercy which have never yet been fulfilled on earth, the Wise Men feel beneath them the great commonplaces of moral reward and retribution, which actually work themselves out in the experience of men. And so (as a rule) while the Prophet is passionate, the Wise Man is shrewd. While the Prophet calls to swift warfare for God, the Wise Man speaks of the slow discipline of life, with its results in wisdom, counsel and ' cunning.' There are, of course, exceptions. Many of the Prophets, as we have seen, illustrate the results of wisdom in the ordinary politics of their day, and sometimes employ the Wise Men's style of writing. Two at least of the Wise Men, the poet who composed the eighth chapter of Proverbs, and the religious genius who gave us the Book of Job, have all the Prophet's gift of vision. But in the main the two classes are distinct — as distinct as the temper of hope is from the temper of experience.

T

Again, the scope of their respective interests was not the same. The Prophets have set to them the task of winning Israel's faith for the unity of God; but for the Wise that faith is won, and they take it for granted. The Prophets have to combat idolatry; but by the Wise the idols are ignored as if they had never existed. It is an agony to the Prophets to establish the righteousness and wisdom of God; with the Wise Men these are an axiom. A great deal of this difference must have been a difference of epoch, and of the historical tasks lying respectively to their minds. The passion of the Prophets arose from their being watchmen and even martyrs for truth not yet accepted by the conscience of the people; the more quiet temper and methods of the Wise were due to the fact that the common sense of Israel acknowledged the principles from which they worked. The one class are a body of men wrestling with their contemporaries; the other a body of teachers directing their younger disciples. About the former is all the eagerness of the dawn; the latter have on them something of the placidity of the afternoon. Nay, round one at least of the Wise Men the twilight has already fallen; and Ecclesiastes gropes among deeper shadows than those from which the morning star of prophecy at first arose. Yet to this distinction also there is an exception, for Job contends with his contemporaries as valiantly as Jeremiah. With him the Spirit of prophecy beats, and breaks away from the conventional religion of Israel as powerfully as with Amos or Isaiah. It was a right instinct, therefore, which led the early Church to count Job among the Prophets.

Again, the Prophets, as we have seen,[1] were intensely national. You remember what patriots Isaiah and Jeremiah were; how in particular they loved their own Jerusalem; and how clear to us her aspect shines in many of their visions. We see her walls, her public places, her housetops. We are admitted to the intrigues of her political parties, her throne-chamber, her Temple. We can trace the march of foreign foes through the land, see the trails of fire and smoke they leave behind them, and hear them speaking across the walls of the capital with its timid defenders. And these are but instances of the particular and national temper of the Prophets. Throughout it is God's love for Israel and Israel's destiny in the world on which they delight to dwell. But all this patriotism and noise of running history are absent from the Books of Wisdom. It is probable indeed that the secular sorrows of Israel are reflected in the sufferings of Job.[2] But neither there nor in the Book of Proverbs is Israel or Judah or Jerusalem once

---

[1] Lecture VII.
[2] Davidson's Introduction to Job, *Cambridge Bible*, p. xix. f.

mentioned. The author of Ecclesiastes takes Solomon, *King in Jerusalem*, only as a type of the particular aspect of Wisdom, which he illustrates. Except in the titles of the Book of Proverbs no monarch is named, no country and no city. Politics are indeed discussed : the wilful ways of kings and the fickleness of the crowd. The Wise Man speaks everywhere from the midst of the people. There are descriptions of the life and scandals of a great city: its drunkards, its scorners, its simple youths and public temptresses : more vivid than in any prophet. But all is human and universal. Those streets so full of temptations; those corners with their scoffers and sots; those gamblers and wantons; those oppressed poor whose oppression is their poverty — they are not only Jerusalem. To-day they are Vienna, and Paris and London and New York. Into his description of Job's disease the poet may have wrung the sufferings of Israel; but what the patriarch deplores is the human commonness of his fate, and it is by the strength of a man's conscience that he throws out his challenges in the face of the Almighty. Thus the preacher may work through the Books of Wisdom, finding only the immutable elements of human experience in sin and sorrow, the brevity of life and the certainty of death, the inevitableness of doubt and the conflict of faith with stern facts.

In dealing with the separate Books and their
value to the Christian preacher, I have time only
to make a few general statements concerning Job
and Ecclesiastes, and then to give a summary of
the teaching of the Book of Proverbs.

There are three practical uses of the Book of
Job which must be remembered in connection
with the purpose of these lectures. (1) The Book
is the supreme instance of the neglected truth that
Revelation is not confined to literal history. (2) It
is an illustration of the uses of religious doubt and
revolt. And (3) it is a fine discipline for pastors
in the treatment of hearts racked by experience,
and by the inevitable conflict of faith with the
facts of life.

(1) The Book of Job is anonymous. The
name of the hero, the fame of his piety, and perhaps also the nature of his trials, are founded on
tradition; [1] but since Luther the growing and now
accepted opinion of Protestant scholars [2] is that
the Book is not literal history — 'Job spake not
in that sort as in the Book is written, for it is not
easy [? possible] in tribulation and temptation
to speak after that manner' [3] — but is the ideal

[1] Ezek. xiv. 14.

[2] See any good introduction to the Book of Job, *e.g.* Professor
Davidson's in the *Cambridge Bible for Schools*. The opinion that
Job was not an actual man but 'a parable' was held by early
Jewish scholars. See the tradition of this in the Talmud, 'Baba
Bathra,' 15.

[3] Luther, *Table Talk*, chap. xxxi., Captain Henrie Bell's
translation.

presentation, by one of the greatest poets whom
the world has ever known, of the experience
of innocent suffering, of the conflict of its conscience with orthodox religious explanations, of
the doubts and defiance which it excites, and
of their only possible solution in personal trust
and submission to God — 'he had by himself such
cogitations: it fell out and happened so indeed
as is written.'[1] There is no Book of the Old
Testament in which the 'minor authenticities'[2]
are of such little account in comparison with
the magnificent genuineness of the experience
which the Book contains. Is it silent about
its author ? It holds itself almost equally aloof
from all questions of its foundation on the facts
of any single life. It deals with the perennial
problem of Israel's faith, the suffering of the
righteous. It exposes, explodes and dissipates
the obdurate superstition (which even Christ
had to combat[3]), that suffering and adversity
always mean punishment, and that such an
explanation of them is the only means of vindicating God's righteousness. If for this the
Book provides no substitute in a positive, explicit doctrine of suffering, it at least clears the
ground for such a doctrine, as that appeared even
under the Old Testament,[4] and was consummated
in the Cross of Christ. Meanwhile it supplies

---

[1] *Ibid.* [2] Compare above, p. 172.
[3] Luke xiii. 2 ; cf. John vii. [4] Isaiah xl–lv., Prov. iii. 11, 12.

in the most divine, because the most gentle and
natural manner, new inspiration to patience,
loyalty and hope, with the constant proof that
suffering endured in these tempers lifts the mind
to a stronger and more original hold upon God
Himself. No man can deny that this is, in the
truest sense of the word, a revelation, with its
own indispensable function in the preparation
for Christ. And it is presented in the form of a
drama of religious experience, which, though in
revolt against the orthodox dogmas of the day,
is yet absolutely fair to these by drawing the
characters of their representatives so as to bring
out all the good that is in them ; and which
in itself is wonderfully vivid, sincere and real.
Before such divine doctrine and true human
experience, questions about the ' literal ' history
of the Book are felt to be impertinences ; and
we acknowledge the truth — so significant for the
interpretation of other Scriptures [1] — that Revelation is not coincident with the bare letter of
actual facts, but may be conveyed to us, in its
highest substance, through the ideal presentation
of these by an inspired artist or poet.

(2) It has been a trouble to some that processes and results, so full of the doubt and
contradiction of principles affirmed by other
Scriptures, should ever have been regarded as
of equal divinity with these, and admitted into

[1] See above, p. 74, 89, 107 f.

the Canon of the Jewish or of the Christian
Church. Let me only point out that no narrow
theories of inspiration can account for this —
men are able to hold such theories only by ig-
noring it [1] — but to an open mind it is the proof
of guidance in the growth and selection of
the Scriptures by a Spirit with standards and
sympathies very much wider than the standards
or sympathies of any single school of religious
belief. In the Old Testament Books of speculative and experimental Wisdom we see the same
condescendence on the part of God as we see in
the rudimentary stages of the history.[2]   His
Spirit sympathises with His children's rude and
painful struggles after light; with their discon-
tent with the earlier achievements of religion,
and with their revolts against ancient dogmas.
Moreover, it rewards the rebel by the gift of new
aspects of truth, and by guidance to firmer and
more original faith in God.   Therefore, so far
from these passages of argument and of doubt,
which the Scripture contains, being less evangelical than the prophecy and history, they also
are proofs of Grace: the seeking and the saving
of them that have wandered or are lost.   Let me

[1] It is too little noticed that the advocates of a verbal inspiration of Scripture (or of kindred theories) have to reckon not only
with the discrepancies of fact in the Old Testament, but with the
presence in it of opposite religious tempers ; and of the contradiction by some Books of the teaching in others.
[2] See above, p. 143 f.

quote to you the fine words of one who has done more than any other teacher of our day for the spiritual understanding of the Book of Job: —
'The revealing Spirit was in a certain sense an indwelling Spirit, uniting Himself intimately with all the highest affections and noblest aspirations of the men whose mind he illuminated. And these men were not persons, who stood as mere objective instruments to be addressed; they were of the people. Every feeling of the people, every movement of life at its lowest stratum, sent its impulse up to them; every hope or fear was reflected in their heart: and with all these movements and reflected emotions . . . the Spirit of Revelation, which was not a Spirit of knowledge merely but of life, sympathised and, if the word can be used, coalesced. The people of Israel as the Church of God lived a profound life; in its outstanding men that life was at its profoundest and broadest; and as at the first the Spirit of God moved upon the face of the waters that covered the earth, so He moved upon that unquiet sea of the Church's mind, agitated with emotions, with presentiments, with fears, with speculations, and out of them all brought more perfect forms of truth.' [1]

(3) The third lesson for the practical preacher, which I have promised to show in the Book of Job, concerns his attitude towards religious

[1] A. B. Davidson.

doubt and revolt when these shall draw to
him for counsel. The speeches of Job's friends
ought to be studied by every man who pro-
poses to make the guidance and consolation
of his fellow-men, in their religious interests,
the duty of his life. For these speeches are,
every one of them, lessons both in how, and how
not, to discharge that delicate and responsible
office. The writer of the Book of Job is thoroughly fair to the traditional views of which it
is his aim to show the insufficiency. He represents them by men of honesty, and even
at first of courtesy, who take up their task
in the sincere desire to help Job out of all
his troubles. In particular we have much
to learn from the approach of Eliphaz the
Temanite to his afflicted friend. But the
author shows how all the three comforters of
Job misunderstand the heart; how little they
have fathomed human experience; how easily
worn out are their love and patience; how
they prefer to vindicate their own views of
God to saving the soul of their brother; and
how above all they commit the sin of not per-
ceiving that God Himself may be working
directly on that brother's heart, and purposes
to teach them more than they can ever teach
him. Love was what he looked for and trust:
but they gave him argument which for a time

only drove him the further from God. You remember what he says :

> *To him that is ready to faint kindness is due*
> *from his friend,*
> *Even to him that is forsaking the fear of the*
> *Almighty.*[1]

There is doubt about the true reading ; but
none can mistake the meaning. And yet how
ignored this great verse has been! How different
were the history of religion if men had kept
it in mind! How much sweeter and swifter
would the progress of Christianity have proved!
The physicians of religious perplexity have too
often been Job's comforters ; and the souls in
doubt, who should have been gathered to the
heart of the Church with as much pity and care as
the penitent or the mourner, have been scorned
or cursed, or banished or even put to death.

But it must be evident to every reader that,
freely as the Wise Men speculated, they never
regarded speculation as an end in itself, or even
as a means by itself. They held it impossible
to separate thinking from the practice of life,
and in a remarkable degree foreshadowed the
statement of Christ : *if any man will do His*
will he shall know of the doctrine. Practical life
was not only their starting-point. It was the
return and refuge of all their thought. If they

[1] vi. 14.

were baffled in their search for knowledge that did not paralyse their wills. Duty was plain. The difference between right and wrong was plain. God Himself was past doubt in His character of Lawgiver and Judge. *Let us hear the conclusion of the whole matter: fear God and keep His commandments, for this is the* duty *of every man.*[1]

But that brings us to the Book in which the practical and didactic Wisdom of the Old Testament is most fully set forth.

The Book of Proverbs.

Mr. Ruskin tells us that in the Bible of his boyhood he preserved till old age the list of chapters which his mother gave him to commit to memory. ' With this list thus learned, she established my soul in life. And truly, though I have picked up the elements of a little further knowledge in mathematics and meteorology and the like in after life, and owe not a little to the teaching of many people, this maternal installation of my mind in that property of chapters, I count very confidently the most precious and on the whole the one essential part of all my education.'[2]

In the inventory of a property so splendidly appraised we find four chapters of the Book of Proverbs — the second, third, eighth and

21698

---

[1] Ecclesiastes xii. 13.   [2] *Praeterita*, i. 57.

twelfth. And I suppose that to the generation of Ruskin's father and to his own generation, the Book of Proverbs proved a necessary part of a religious education. That they are cast in the oldest and most simple form of tradition — for, as the Easterns say, some are born and some die, and the old tell the young what they know; that they are addressed from a serene age to youth which has not lost its faith or its absoluteness; that they say nothing of the intricacies or the qualifications of middle manhood; that they echo almost no accents and reflect few lights of any particular period of history; that their instances are drawn from the essential human experiences and their humour and wit are those of the common people — it is this which has given the Proverbs of Israel their wide popularity and caused their employment in the education of so many races.

But of late years the Book of Proverbs appears to have become neglected in the education of the young. It may be that in the more spiritual temper which religion has assumed in our time and in our quickened, because better informed, love of the historical and prophetical Scriptures — the one with its romance, the other with its lofty ideals — there has been a tendency to revolt against the alleged Utilitarianism of the Proverbs; just as there has been a revolt against the legalism of other Scriptures which used to play a greater part in education than they now do, I had believed this feeling to be more an instinct than an articulate conviction, till the other day, when the leading English weekly gave to it a very definite expression. The article I speak of described the temper of the Book of Proverbs to be one which not only does not commend itself to the mind of youth; but which it is our duty to keep away from the young, as a prudential and a sordid temper, laying stress upon the consequences of character rather than upon its essential rightness and beauty, enforcing virtue more because of the rewards she can bestow than for her own authority. This charge may be confidently met by two assertions. In the first place it is impossible to teach the folly of evil without pointing to its consequences; and secondly, the Book of Proverbs does not limit itself to this primary stage of morality but, as we shall presently see, enforces Virtue for her own sake, paints Wisdom with an essential worth and beauty, and appeals quite as much to the generous affections and enthusiasm of youth as to their prudence and common sense.

The Book consists of eight unequal parts — a Prologue on the whole subject of Wisdom: one continuous and rhythmical address occupying the first nine chapters; then from Chapters x. to xxix. four collections, great and small, of proverbs proper, popular sayings lying loose, for the most part, without arrangement as to subject or style; then in Chapter xxx. a number of enigmatic or numerical proverbs in a more or less artificial form; then the warning of a mother to her son against women and wine; and finally the incomparable eulogy of the Virtuous Woman, in which *virtuous* is to be taken in its older and nobler sense of strength and bravery; but strength and bravery exercised within the home.

Now with regard to the collections of Proverbs proper, the bulk of the Book, it has been one great drawback to their use that for the most part they were not gathered by their ancient editors into groups corresponding to their subjects. The first duty of the reader or teacher who would feel the full volume of their wisdom, and all its various shrewdness, is to make such a grouping for himself.[1] Education, Friendship, Marriage, Religion ; God the Maker of all; Morality and Religion as one ; God's interest in

[1] An admirable arrangement of the Proverbs under their proper subjects has been made by Professor Foster Kent of Brown University, Rhode Island: *The Wise Men of Ancient Israel and their Proverbs*, New York, etc., 1895 (a capital handbook); but every teacher, who wishes to grasp the Book, should first make such an arrangement for himself, and then test and correct it by Professor Kent's. Besides Professor Toy's (of Harvard) Commentary on *Proverbs* in the International Critical Commentary, the teacher or student will find useful the late Rev. W. Arnot's *Laws from Heaven for Life on Earth*, and Dr. Horton's volume in the *Expositor's Bible*. See, too, Dr. Davidson's art. 'Proverbs,' in the *Encyclopædia Britannica*, ninth ed.

the little things of conduct; God as the searcher
of hearts, and the rewarder of virtue; God and
the King; God and the Poor; Equality of all
men before God; or Sin: its deceitfulness and its
ruin of the character, of the joy and of the freedom of life; or such subjects as the giving and
taking of reproof, sins of the tongue; idleness,
anger, poverty and riches, the value of substance
in life, sorrow and comfort — gather the Proverbs
under these and other heads, and for the first
time you will appreciate the resource, the sanity,
the humour, the occasional brilliance, the frequent
grotesqueness of the popular wisdom of Israel.

If before I pass to the sublimer teaching of
the Prologue I may select for illustration one of
the more persistent lessons of this scattered
wisdom, I will choose that upon the giving
and taking of reproof. Both the Prologue and
the Proverbs themselves insist with a very em-
phatic frequency upon this difficult and painful
duty. Almost to weariness they reiterate that in
education and morality mere abstract teaching of
the truth is not enough; and that personal discipline, criticism and even sore and humbling
blame are necessary, not only for the young from
the old, but for all men and women from their
friends and contemporaries. You will find the
words *rebuke*, *reproof*, *discipline* and *correction* in
every few verses of the strenuous and unsparing
doctrine of the Wise.

Now it may be objected that criticism so persistent and articulate defeats its own ends; and that we live under the more powerful Example of One who came not to judge the world but that the world through Him might be saved. In the things to which Christ cleared our dim eyes; in the wonderful patience of our God to which we waken every morning; in His fatherly trust of our foolish and wayward souls; in the sunshine, the fresh air, the sweet love and confidence of our fellow-men His children, all that goodness of God which by a thousand gentle touches leads us to repentance; or again in the compassionate holiness of Christ's own life, the infinite obligations and ideals of our manhood which His character and service of men unfold; or again in the holy lives about us which possess themselves silently in His Patience and reflect His Purity and Unselfishness — in all these we feel a divine judgement of our souls, beside which the criticisms even of the best and wisest of men sound petty and irrelevant.

Yet on the other hand we cannot shut out the noisy facts of the world we dwell in; and while we refuse to accept them as substitutes for that silent judgement of the Divine Love, which is the only sufficient rebuke and discipline of our souls, we must see that we use them, inevitable as they are, for *its* instruments and contributories. We live in a world that will not spare any man its criticisms. Some of them may be ignorant and cruel (I will deal with these in a little), but in many others we know that our consciences will not permit us to hear anything but an honest, and often a kindly, statement of what we really are or thoroughly deserve.

Our own age has been very hungry for abstract and impersonal truth ; but by an exaggeration of the liberty and the rights of men, of which it is so proud, there has never been an age more impatient of personal criticism. And yet personal criticism, involving as it must strokes painful and humbling, is absolutely necessary for us all, not only from those whom we revere, or from those whom we love, but from those whom we dislike, or whom we know to dislike us. The only successful teaching of youth is that into which the element of personal criticism bravely enters, and is loyally accepted by its subject. Nor is there any friendship healthy which does not permit of the same strenuous duty among its obligations. In their trials and misfortunes, still more in their errors and faults, men are constantly tempted to turn to their weakest friends for a sympathy which is often insincere and generally undeserved. Happy rather is the man who is strong enough and true enough to choose his friends not for their agreeableness or their sympathy, but for their honesty and severe ideals.

Better is open rebuke than love that is masked.
He that walketh with wise men shall be wise,
But the companion of fools shall be broken
for it.[1]

Yet even when criticism is stupid, irrelevant
and cruel, it is, according to the Proverbs of
Israel, a healthy and a stimulating discipline.
Stripes that wound cleanse away evil, and strokes,
things without sense and with only pain in them,
the innermost parts of the belly.[2]

We all know how often a stinging judgement
of us totally misses the mark for which it was
intended; charging us with a fault of which we
know we are innocent. Yet it at least opens
our close and sleepy hearts; it lets in the
air; it compels us to examine. We may resent
unjust criticism, but no wise man fails to profit
by it. Did such criticism only drive us to
prayer; did it only force us in self-defence to
carry our hearts before the judgement of God:
a resort to which we are not very prone and
often require to be driven: surely it would do
us good. But unjust criticism will effect more
for us than this. Rising as it often does from
the purely conventional standards of society, or
from a formal and pragmatical conception of
religion — under which we ourselves may have
fallen — it compels us to question and explore,
and so lifts us to fresh views of morality and

[1] xxvii. 5; xiii. 20.   [2] xx. 30.

new understanding of God. In this same literature of Israel's wisdom we can see how Job
himself was, by the unjust criticism of his friends,
stung to revolt against the formulas of the
popular religion, and thereby rose to new
research, with its end in larger views of truth,
and a more original hold upon God.

So much for the Proverbs of Reproof. A
teacher or preacher who has made the classifica-
tion advised above, will find materials as sound
and various under any of the other titles
suggested.

But it is time now to turn from these scattered
couplets to the great poem with which the Book
of Proverbs opens, Chapters i. to ix. This is
remarkable not only for its very beautiful per-
sonification of Wisdom, but for the fact that it
contains in Chapter viii. almost the only metaphysic to which the poetry of the Wise attained.

And first I think you shall feel from it how
very unjust is that charge of utilitarianism of
which I spoke. For from the outset we learn
that the Wisdom which the Wise inculcate is
not the slow, prudent thrift of life, gathered by
petty experiences, more or less sordid and selfish:
but is the reverent and whole-hearted acceptance
of great principles, such as capture the heart, stir
us to enthusiasm, and lift us above ourselves.
In contrast to the prophets who won their truth
by vision, the wise men got theirs by experience.

Yet do not understand by this that they would counsel their disciples to wait for their own experience — to gather wisdom merely by trying life as it came to them. They would have them begin with wisdom from the first, get hold of her principles, submit to her discipline, and then test her in all their daily fortunes and duties. We often hear the phrase: 'Experience teaches fools': but not so often its counterpart, *the strength of the wise is their wisdom.* Addressing those who stand on the borders of manhood, wistfully looking forward to that experience of life from which in their time most men have foolishly fancied that Wisdom is to be gained, the Wise Poet passionately reiterates that there is a Wisdom which comes before experience and without which experience itself is too often only the belated and melancholy recognition of what might have been. To the young and the simple he cries: I have something to give which life by itself can never give; but of which if you take it now you will find experience to be daily the stronger proof and richer reward. *The beginning of wisdom*, he says, *is to get wisdom.*[1] Principles are absolutely necessary for all who begin the work of life: principles which we accept, according to this Poet, partly on their own authority and partly upon their illustration in the lives we love and honour the most. Before all ex-

[1] iv. 7.

perience are Conscience and the Fear of God; obedience to those who are wiser and reverence for the accumulated wisdom of the nation. The Wise Men found their principles, as Mazzini put it, in the agreement of conscience and history: the harmony of the moral sense in a man himself with the best experience of his race. Hence on reverence, on meekness, on the native instinct for truth; as on the self-evidencing character of truth and its beauty, the poem insists again and again. But this is all in a direction the very opposite of utilitarianism.

The pursuit of Wisdom is another subject of the Poem : which regards it as a mutual and responsive process — we seeking Wisdom, but Wisdom also seeking us.

By an age like our own, which has so much lost both the faculty of attention and of pro-longed meditation — and which demands from its most voluminous teachers that its mental food shall be broken up for it and given under headlines and in paragraphs — by such an age the instruc-tion of this Poem may well be taken to heart. I know no teachers who lay more stress upon the cultivation of the mental power of attention : that sure and expert grip of the mind without which both reason and faith are impossible and memory itself becomes a confused and inarticulate pain. They urge them *to lay hold on wisdom, to purchase understanding, to hearken, to listen, to*

*fasten — so that thou incline thine ear unto wisdom
and apply thine heart to understanding. Yea if
thou seek her as silver and search for her as for
hid treasures then shalt thou understand the fear of
Jahweh and find the knowledge of God.*[1] These
powers of attention and concentration the poem
allies with purity of heart, illustrating the dis-
tractions and dissipation of impure or covetous
thoughts. On the whole subject of the moral
habits and the intellect, or the connection between
purity of heart and the enthusiasm for hard work,
there is no teaching in all literature more sane
and more bracing.

But to such strenuous endeavours the Poem
tells us there is a liberal response from the very
heart of the universe. Wisdom is not conceived
after the fashion in which others have dreamt of
her, as a slumbering deity difficult to rouse ; or as
a jealous one awake only to guard her secrets from
men and to baffle them in their pursuit of her —
the path to her presence strewn with the bones
of those who have sought her in vain. She is
human and near and kind: a Woman clothed
with beauty, visible to every eye and with desire for all in whom the love of her beauty has
been wakened : pitiful, solicitous, urgent, liberal,
redemptive :

> *I love them that love me
> And they that seek me early shall find me.*[2]

[1] ii. 2–4.   [2] viii. 17.

Like the highest wisdom of all the great races, this also is represented as popular. Though the fellow of God and the artificer of the Universe, her home is in the habitable parts of the earth, and her delights with the children of men. Like Socrates and like Jesus she is a street-preacher, a frequenter of markets and the assemblies of civic life :

> *Wisdom crieth aloud in the street.*
> *She uttereth her voice in the broad places.*
> *She crieth in the chief place of concourse*
> *At the entering in of the gates.*
> *In the city she uttereth her words.*[1]

But she is popular and public only for a higher end. In the secret of the Universe beats the desire to save men, and the Wisdom of God is at the heart of it redemptive :

> *Unto you, O men, I call,*
> *And my voice is to the sons of men.*
> *O ye simple, understand wisdom,*
> *And ye fools, be of an understanding heart.*
> *For whoso findeth me findeth life,*
> *And he that misseth me wrongeth himself.*[2]

Wisdom descending from God's right hand to plead with the man on the street ; the final passion and glory of all the forces and faculties of the Universe, to win the common and the simple from sin ! It is again the Spirit of Christ that we feel.

[1] i. 20 f.   [2] viii. 4 f., 35 f.

And hence we have those alternative pictures of Wisdom and Sensuality, whose realism is so striking. Why are both thus set side by side, as women of beauty and attraction, urgent entertainers of mankind, but with the intention that the Wisdom of the higher life shall be made to appear as popular, pervasive and persistent as ever the cunning of the lower has proved itself to be; that our hearts shall be driven to feel as hunted and haunted by temptations to a life of virtue and wisdom, as they ever were by the temptations of the flesh and the world?

That is a vision, which the preacher of to-day must heartily welcome: when the opportunities to vice are on every side so open, so attractive, in many cases so apparently secure; when on the other hand our unpurged eyes feel righteousness to be so abstract and so arduous. The vision of Wisdom would show us that this is not true. Righteousness is not abstract nor unreal; not hard to find in the crowd about us, nor in her beginnings beyond the reach of any, however thronged or trampled by the world. Everywhere her gates are open, her presence manifest, her joys obvious and solid. She dwells with men. There is not an arena on which we are called to live, but is brilliant with the incarnate examples of righteousness and purity. She dwells with God, and was with Him when the world was made. The forces of the Universe are

on the side of the will that chooses virtue : and
to the ignorant and the wandered, if they have
but one spark of desire for what is pure and
honest and lovely, the heart of God Himself
comes forth with the desire to teach, to lift,
to restore.

This is the Spirit of Christ in Hebrew Wisdom,
and with it we may suitably close our study of
Wisdom's Books.

INDEX

INDEX OF SCRIPTURE REFERENCES

21698

By GEORGE ADAM SMITH, D.D., LL.D.

The
Historical Geography
of the Holy Land

Seventh Edition. With Scripture Index and Six Colored
Maps, specially prepared. 8vo, cloth, 730 pages, $4.50

. . . No one work has ever before embodied all this variety of material
to illustrate the whole subject. His geographical statements are pen-pictures.
We are made to see the scene. No important problem is untouched. Without question it will take its place at once as a standard work, indispensable to
the thoroughgoing student of the Bible. — *Sunday-School Times.*

. . . An exhaustive collection of material lay outside the plan of the author.
His intention is rather to show how the history of the land is conditioned by
its physical structure. It is thus the idea of Karl Ritter which rules the treatment and presentation. Very comprehensive sections are concerned, not with
the history, but with the nature of the land. . . . The author pays special
attention to the military operations. One could sometimes imagine that an
officer is writing, who, above all, regards the land from the point of view of the
military strategist. In this connection especially the history of Israel in its
chief crises in Old Testament times receives striking illumination. Large passages are frequently quoted from the Old Testament in order to explain them
by the exhibition of their geographical background. In addition the author
has a special gift of vivid representation. He makes the history transact itself
before the eye of the reader in dramatic form. One sees, everywhere, that the
landscapes which he describes stand before his own eyes. Thus the book is
an extremely valuable means of aid to the understanding of the history, especially of the Old Testament. — Prof. SCHÜRER, of Kiel, in the *Theol. Litera-
tur-Zeitung.*

The book is too rich to summarize. . . . The language is particularly well
chosen. Few pages are without some telling phrase happily constructed to
attract attention and hold the memory, and we often feel that the wealth of
imagery would be excessive for prose were it not that it is chosen with such
appropriateness and scientific truth. . . . To the reader much of the pleasure
of perusing the volume comes from its luxurious typography, and the exquisite
series of orographical maps prepared by Mr. Bartholomew from the work of
the Survey. These maps alone are more suggestive and enlightening than
many treatises, and they are destined, we trust, to enliven many a sermon, and
turn the monotony of the records of Israelitish wars into a thrilling romance. —
Speaker.

A. C. ARMSTRONG & SON
3 and 5 W. 18th Street, New York

By GEORGE ADAM SMITH, D.D., LL.D.

THE BOOK OF ISAIAH

In Two Volumes. Crown 8vo, cloth, $1.50 each.

VOLUME I. CHAPTERS I.—XXXIX.
VOLUME II. CHAPTERS XL.—LXVI.

This is a noble volume of a noble series. Isaiah will ever be the cream of the Old Testament evangelistic prophecy, and as the ages go on will supply seed-thought of the Holy Ghost which grow into flowers and fruits, vines and trees, of divine truth for the refreshment and nourishment of the intellect, heart, character, and life. *How can any pastor or instructor of the public, young or old, afford to be without such aids?* — *Baltimore Methodist.*

Prof. George Adam Smith has such a mastery of the scholarship of his subject that it would be a sheer impertinence for most scholars, even though tolerable Hebraists, to criticise his translations : and certainly it is not the intention of the present reviewer to attempt anything of the kind, to do which he is absolutely incompetent. All we desire is to let English readers know how very lucid, impressive — and, indeed, how vivid — a study of Isaiah is within their reach ; the fault of the book, if it has a fault, being rather that it finds too many points of connection between Isaiah and our modern world, than that it finds too few. In other words, no one can say that the book is not full of life. — *Spectator.*

It would be difficult to say how highly we appreciate the work, or how useful we believe it will be. — *Church Bells.*

He writes with great rhetorical power, and brings out into vivid reality the historical position of his author. — *Saturday Review.*

Mr. Smith gives us models of expositions ; expositions for cultivated congregations, no doubt, but still expositions which may have been largely preached in church. They are full of matter, and show careful scholarship throughout. We can think of no commentary on Isaiah from which the preacher will obtain scholarly and trustworthy suggestions for his sermons so rapidly and so pleasantly as from this. — *Record.*

The Book of the Twelve Prophets
COMMONLY CALLED THE MINOR

In Two Volumes. Crown 8vo, cloth, $1.50 each.

VOL. I.— AMOS, HOSEA AND MICAH. Seventh Edition.
VOL. II.— ZEPHANIAH, NAHUM, HABAKKUK, OBADIAH, HAGGAI, ZECHARIAH I. — VIII., "MALACHI," JOEL, "ZECHARIAH" IX.—XIV., AND JONAH. Fourth Edition.

In Dr. Smith's volumes we have much more than a popular exposition of the minor Prophets. We have that which will satisfy the scholar and the student quite as much as the person who reads for pleasure and for edification. . . . If the minor Prophets do not become popular reading it is not because anything more can be done to make them attractive. Dr. Smith's volumes present this part of Scripture in what is at once the most attractive and the most profitable form. — DR. MARCUS DODS, in the *British Weekly.*

Few interpreters of the Old Testament to-day rank higher than George Adam Smith. He is at home in criticism, in geographical and archæological questions, and in philology. . . . Hardly any commentator of the present day is more successful than he in putting the student at once into the heart of an Old Testament problem. — *S. S. Times.*

The above four volumes are contained in "The Expositor's Bible," and are subject to special subscription rates in connection with that series. Descriptive circular on application.

A. C. ARMSTRONG & SON
3 and 5 W. 18th Street, New York